ENGLISH ROYAL FREE CHAPELS

1100–1300

a constitutional study

ENGLISH ROYAL FREE CHAPELS

1100-1300

A CONSTITUTIONAL STUDY

J. H. DENTON

MANCHESTER UNIVERSITY PRESS

Published by the University of Manchester at
THE UNIVERSITY PRESS
316–324 Oxford Road, Manchester M13 9NR

ISBN: 0 7190 0405 5

Printed and Bound by Butler & Tanner Ltd
Frome & London

1622980
CONTENTS

To my mother and father

PREFACE

During the twelfth and thirteenth centuries there were well over a hundred English secular colleges. Many were disintegrating during the early years of the period; others were founded in the thirteenth century. Some were large and influential churches, while others were small and relatively insignificant. Among these colleges the secular cathedrals stand out. Second to the secular cathedrals are the churches in episcopal patronage, especially the great minsters of Ripon, Beverley and Southwell in the diocese of York. A third group is formed by the royal secular colleges, known by the thirteenth century as royal free chapels. The royal secular colleges are of importance because they showed the possibility of royal supremacy and independence from Rome in an age when the control and discipline of churches were usually matters of episcopal or papal jurisdiction. Interdependence was a major factor in the co-existence of *regnum* and *sacerdotium*; but the royal secular colleges serving extensive parishes and free from episcopal or papal control provide concrete examples of a cleavage in both principle and practice. My task has been to discover which secular colleges possessed a privileged status and to examine the nature of the privileges they enjoyed. I have placed the status of royal colleges under review. To this extent the book is a constitutional study. The material for a comparative study of the internal organisation of the royal colleges does not exist, but evidence from many sources sheds light upon their legal standing—that is, upon their spiritual liberties and immunities. The subject itself suggests concentration upon the twelfth and thirteenth centuries, but the years 1100 and 1300 are terminal dates only in a very general sense. Material from the fourteenth century has been used freely, and I have thought it necessary in the final chapter to examine briefly some of the evidence concerning the pre-Conquest status of the royal colleges.

I am profoundly indebted to Professor C. R. Cheney, who has given most generously of his time during the final preparation of the book for the press. My thanks are due also to Mrs A. K. B. Evans, of the University of Leicester, Dr I. D. Bent, of King's College, London, and to my colleague, Mr Eric John, all of whom kindly read the first draft of the book and offered corrections and helpful criticism. The documents in the appendices are drawn from a number of record collections, and I wish to thank the owners, especially the deans and chapters of Lichfield, St Paul's and Westminster, for permission to print them. I am grateful, too, to the custodians of these and other manuscript collections for their ready assistance. Transcripts of Crown copyright records in the Public Record Office appear by permission of the Controller of H.M. Stationery Office.

J. H. D.

October 1969

ABBREVIATIONS AND SELECT
BIBLIOGRAPHY

Barlow 1950: F. Barlow, *Durham Jurisdictional Peculiars* (London, 1950).
Barlow 1963: idem, *The English Church, 1000–1066* (London, 1963).
BEAR: Bibliothèque des Écoles françaises d'Athènes et de Rome.
BIHR: Bulletin of the Institute of Historical Research.
B.M.: British Museum.
Cal. Charter Rolls: Calendar of the Charter Rolls (6 vols., HMSO, 1903–27).
CCR: Calendar of the Close Rolls (HMSO, 1902–).
Cheney 1931: C. R. Cheney, *Episcopal Visitation of Monasteries in the Thirteenth Century* (Manchester, 1931).
Cheney 1956: idem, *From Becket to Langton* (Manchester, 1956).
Chichester Chartulary: The Chartulary of the High Church of Chichester, ed. W. D. Peckham (*Sussex Record Society*, xlvi, 1942–3).
Councils and Synods ii: *Councils and Synods*, ii (1205–1313), ed. F. M. Powicke and C. R. Cheney (2 parts, Oxford, 1964).
CPR: Calendar of Patent Rolls (HMSO, 1901–).
CYS: Canterbury and York Society.
DB: Domesday Book (2 vols., Record Commission, 1783).
Dickinson 1950: J. C. Dickinson, *The Origins of the Austin Canons* (London, 1950).
EHR: English Historical Review.
Foedera: Foedera, Conventiones, Litterae . . . , ed. T. Rymer (3 vols. in 6, Record Commission, 1816–30).
Hamilton Thompson 1917: A. Hamilton Thompson, 'Notes on secular colleges of canons in England', *Archaeological Journal*, lxxiv (1917), 139–99.
Hamilton Thompson 1921: idem, 'The jurisdiction of the archbishops of York in Gloucestershire', *Bristol and Gloucestershire Archaeological Society*, xliii (1921), 85–180.
Hamilton Thompson 1927: idem, 'The college of Bridgnorth', *Archaeological Journal*, lxxxiv (1927), 1–87.
Hamilton Thompson 1947: idem, *The English Clergy and their Organisation in the later Middle Ages* (Oxford, 1947).
HMC: Historical Manuscripts Commission.
HMSO: Her/His Majesty's Stationery Office.

Kempe 1825: A. J. Kempe, *Historical Notices of the Collegiate Church of St Martin-le-Grand* (London, 1825).

Knowles 1932: M. D. Knowles, 'Essays in monastic history, IV and V: The growth of exemption', *Downside Review*, l (1932), 201–31, 396–436.

Lemarignier 1937: J. F. Lemarignier, *Étude sur les Privilèges d'Exemption et de Juridiction Ecclésiastique des Abbayes Normandes des Origines à 1140* (*Archives de la France Monastique*, xliv, 1937).

Magnum Registrum Album: The Great Register of Lichfield Cathedral, Magnum Registrum Album, ed. H. E. Savage (*SHC*, 1924).

Mollat 1951: G. Mollat, *Le Roi de France et la Collation Plénière des Bénéfices Ecclésiastiques* (Paris, 1951).

Monasticon: W. Dugdale, *Monasticon Anglicanum*, ed. J. Caley, H. Ellis and B Bandinel (6 vols. in 8, 1817–30).

Owen and Blakeway 1825: H. Owen and J. B. Blakeway, *A History of Shrewsbury* (2 vols., London, 1825).

Papsturkunden: W. Holtzmann, *Papsturkunden in England* (3 vols., Berlin, 1930–1952).

Potthast: *Regesta Pontificum Romanorum*, ed. A. Potthast (2 vols., Berlin, 1873–5).

P.R.O.: Public Record Office.

PRS: Pipe Roll Society.

Prynne i, ii and iii: W. Prynne, *An Exact Chronological Vindication and Historical Demonstration of our British, Roman, Saxon, Danish, Norman, English Kings' Supreme Ecclesiastical Jurisdiction* (3 vols., London, 1665–8).

Regesta i, ii and iii: *Regesta Regum Anglo-Normannorum, 1066–1154*, i, ed. H. W. C. Davis, ii, ed. C. Johnson and H. A. Cronne, iii, ed. H. A. Cronne and R. H. C. Davis (Oxford, 1913, 1956, 1968).

Rot. Chartarum: Rotuli Chartarum, 1199–1216, ed. T. D. Hardy (Record Commission, 1837).

Rot. Lit. Claus.: Rotuli Litterarum Clausarum, 1204–27, ed. T. D. Hardy (Record Commission, 1833–4).

Rot. Lit. Pat.: Rotuli Litterarum Patentium, 1201–16, ed. T. D. Hardy (Record Commission, 1835).

RS: Rolls Series (HMSO, 1858–1911).

SHC: Staffordshire Historical Collections (Staffordshire Record Society, until 1936 *William Salt Archaeological Society*).

Styles 1936: D. Styles, 'The early history of the king's chapels in Staffordshire', *Transactions of the Birmingham Archaeological Society*, lx (1936), 56–95.

Styles 1950–1: eadem, 'The early history of Penkridge church', *SHC*, 1950–1, pp. 3–52.

Taxatio: Taxatio Ecclesiastica Angliae et Walliae Auctoritate P. Nicholai IV c. 1291, ed. T. Astle, S. Ayscough and J. Caley (Record Commission, 1802).

VCH: Victoria County History.

W.A.M.: Westminster Abbey Muniments.

Wood 1955: S. Wood, *English Monasteries and their Patrons in the Thirteenth Century* (London, 1955).

Wood-Legh 1934: K. L. Wood-Legh, *Studies in Church Life under Edward III* (Cambridge, 1934).

CHAPTER I

INTRODUCTION

In a set of clerical petitions which have been assigned to 1295, the English prelates inquired among other things about the king's chapels. 'Since there are at least fourteen chapels of the king of England—namely his portable chapel, Waltham, Wolverhampton, Tettenhall, Penkridge, Stafford, Bridgnorth, Derby, Shrewsbury, Wimborne Minster, Bosham, St George's in the castle of Oxford, and also, so it is said, the chapel of Dover, where there is now a priory, and the church of St Martin-le-Grand London, which is not by ancient standing one of these chapels but was granted by prelates to William Rufus, son of the Conqueror—the clergy petition that the truth should be inquired about these chapels and that justice should be done to the prelates concerning their jurisdiction in them.'[1] The king apparently made no reply to the clergy's request, and the desired inquisition has been long delayed. The present study takes as its starting point the clergy's desire for clarification of their rights in the royal chapels. The thirteen churches named by the prelates—ignoring for the moment the king's portable chapel—include most, but not all, of the royal churches which form a particular category of royal chapel. The theme of this inquiry is the survival of spiritual liberties in some of these royal churches through the centuries of papal reform. It is a theme which William Prynne illustrated fully enough, but none has traced it since. Despite the Church's assertions of exclusive jurisdiction over spiritual matters, English kings retained prerogative spiritual rights. The rights were not mere claims: they amounted to the actual, if deputed, control of the cure of souls within many of the parishes of the royal chapels.

---

[1] *Councils and Synods* ii, 1146.

This introduction concentrates upon terminology. Almost all the royal chapels with which I am concerned can be shown to have been royal secular colleges. To use the term 'secular college' is to describe a particular kind of church which was a community of canons. There was a wide divergence in the constitution of the English secular colleges at any given time. In addition, the concept of collegiate life itself changed radically during the central middle ages.[1] It is possible to make a general distinction between the Anglo-Saxon minster, a community of canons partaking of the common revenues of the church, and the post-Conquest college in which each canon had his separate prebend. Yet there is very little evidence to shed light upon the internal organisation of many of the secular colleges. Some of the royal secular colleges emerge during the later middle ages as fully corporate institutions with 'capitular meetings . . . common seal . . . [and] common fund',[2] but obscurity surrounds most of them in earlier centuries. To use the term 'secular college' whenever there is evidence of prebends is necessarily to use the term loosely, but this does not rob the term of its significance, for the distinction between the parish churches served by a rector or a vicar and the churches which were communities of canons is a distinction of fundamental importance. The ecclesiastical area within which the royal college enjoyed parochial responsibilities was described as its 'parochia' or 'decanatus'. By the thirteenth century 'decanatus' had become the more common. The word 'capellaria', used to describe Bosham, St Oswald's Gloucester, Blyth and Pevensey, appears to refer to both the church and its area of jurisdiction. In using the words 'parish', 'deanery' or 'chapelry' I shall be guided by the documents under discussion.

The terms 'capella regis' and 'libera capella' require close investigation. Some initial clarification is essential because of the confusion which can arise, and has arisen, about the use of these phrases. Both were combined in the description of the royal secular colleges, for during the thirteenth century a royal college

---

[1] See Hamilton Thompson 1947, esp. pp. 85–7, and K. Edwards, *The English Secular Cathedrals in the Middle Ages* (Manchester, 2nd ed., 1967), esp. pp. 4–7.

[2] Hamilton Thompson 1947, p. 86.

was described with increasing frequency as a 'libera capella regis'. During the twelfth century a royal church was styled sometimes 'capella regia' or, as in royal charters, 'mea dominica capella' or 'mea dominica capellaria'. It will be seen that the phrase 'sicut mea dominica capella' was applied to at least three religious houses, the Benedictine abbeys of Westminster and Battle and the Augustinian priory of St Bartholomew Smithfield. These are unusual cases which will require separate explanation; and there is in fact every reason to believe that when the terms 'mea dominica capella *or* capellaria', 'capella regia' and 'libera capella regis' were used they described the same kind of church. They referred to royal secular colleges. But this conclusion leads immediately to two very important exceptions. In the first place, it is clear that a 'capella regis' or even a 'libera capella regis' was very often an oratory or a private chapel of much less status than a secular college. To this point I shall return. In the second place, as the above-mentioned clerical petition of '1295' indicates by its reference to the king's portable chapel, there was a royal chapel permanently associated with the king. This royal chapel must be studied in isolation from all others, and merits a brief examination here.

For the sake of clarity when the term 'capella regis' is used to describe the chapel of the king's household it is best translated as the 'Chapel Royal'.[1] The constitution and powers of the English Chapel Royal are not at all clear during the centuries preceding 1448–9, when the Liber Regie Capelle was compiled; but in recent years light has been shed on some of the problems associated with it.[2] The personnel of the Chapel Royal was never large. In Edward I's reign its full complement was probably six chaplains, six clerks and at least four sumpterers. By the middle of the

[1] For the Chapel Royal see *Liber Regie Capelle*, ed. W. Ullmann (Henry Bradshaw Soc., xcii, 1959), esp. pp. 1–8.

[2] See the unpublished theses of B. L. Trowell, 'Music Under the Later Plantagenets' (Cambridge Ph.D., 1960), and I. D. Bent, 'English Chapel Royal, 1066–1327' (Cambridge Ph.D., 1969), and idem, 'The English Chapel Royal before 1300', *Proceedings of the Royal Musical Assoc.*, xc (1963–4), 77–95; and see A. B. Cobban, *The King's Hall within the University of Cambridge in the Later Middle Ages* (Cambridge, 1969), esp. pp. 20–1.

fifteenth century the Chapel numbered forty-nine, including a
yeoman, a sergeant, ten choirboys and two servants.[1] The Chapel
was responsible above all for the daily service and the major
ceremonies of the king and his court; its concern was therefore
primarily with liturgy and ritual. It was distinct in a few particulars
from other major Chapels Royal outside England. As part of the
household it was necessarily ambulatory. The Chapel Royal in
England was not a place. And as a department of state it was
separate from other departments of state. The whole royal
household cannot be regarded as constituting the Chapel Royal.
But by the fifteenth century the dean of the Chapel had assumed
extensive powers over the whole household, estimated to number
some twelve hundred.[2] In some matters he exercised the authority
of a bishop, taking full cognisance of criminal cases and proving
wills, and he recognised no superior in spiritual matters except the
archbishop of Canterbury. It is for these reasons that Professor
Walter Ullmann has described the Chapel as 'a perambulatory
bishopric in constant and personal attendance on the king and his
entourage'.[3]

Yet both the office of dean of the Chapel Royal and the wide
spiritual rights which the dean exercised were, so it seems, relatively novel in the fifteenth century. The office of keeper of the
king's chapel and relics was specified in the Constitutio Domus
Regis of 1136,[4] but we learn from William FitzStephen's life of
Thomas Becket that it was the king's chancellor, and not the
keeper, who had exercised oversight ('dispositio et cura') of the
Chapel Royal.[5] In 1313 the chancellor is described as the 'chef de
la chapele nostre seignur le Roi'.[6] The first stage in the creation of
the office of dean can be traced back to the early fourteenth
century; one member of the Chapel's personnel was being singled
out, for we learn of a 'capitalis capellanus' in 1312 and a 'chief

---

[1] I. D. Bent, *ubi supra* (1963–4), 90–1, and *Liber Regie Capelle*, pp. 15–16.
[2] Ibid., p. 56.   [3] Ibid., p. vii, and see A. B. Cobban, op. cit., p. 104.
[4] *Dialogus de Scaccario and Constitutio Domus Regis*, ed. C. Johnson (London
1950), p. 129, and see Barlow 1963, pp. 122–5.
[5] *Materials for Becket*, ed. J. C. Robertson (RS, 1875–85), iii, 18.
[6] *Foedera*, II, i, 193.

chapellein' in 1318. Just how far the king's household was exempt from the normal procedures of ecclesiastical control during the middle ages is a wide question; undoubtedly the king's clerks customarily enjoyed privileges associated with their service of the king. A clause in the Articuli Cleri of 1316 implies, for example, that when the Exchequer was in session the barons of the Exchequer and their clerks were a law unto themselves, and the king stressed, in line with earlier royal policy, that no royal clerks when engaged on royal service should be required to reside in their benefices. Yet, at the same time, Edward II reiterated his father's reply to one of the clerical complaints of 1280 by professing respect for the rights of correction which belonged to the ecclesiastical ordinaries: 'Placet domino regi ut clerici suis obsequiis intendentes, si delinquant, per ordinarios ut ceteri corrigantur.'[1] If the king's chief chaplain or dean is to be likened nonetheless to a bishop, it must be stressed that he was a bishop without a see. If, by the fifteenth century, he had parishioners, he had no diocese and no cathedral church. The king's other chapels were distinct from the Chapel Royal. And the deans of some of these other royal chapels, whose powers can be traced back to the twelfth century and beyond, are very much more comparable with the episcopate. They certainly had their parishes, if not their dioceses, and their secular colleges were not unlike cathedral chapters. My concern is with these 'capellae regis' and not with the Chapel Royal.

Only the most important of the royal chapels were secular colleges. The king's private oratories and the king's hospitals were often described as his chapels. We must begin by examining the royal chapels as a whole. A comparison of the English royal chapels with the French royal chapels is illuminating. The royal chapels of France during the last four centuries of the middle ages have been examined in detail by G. Mollat, and he has listed more than a hundred (royal colleges, castle-chapels, royal hospitals) over which the king of France exercised the right of collation.[2]

---

[1] *Statutes of the Realm*, i (Record Commission, 1810), 172, and *Councils and Synods* ii, 879–80.

[2] Mollat 1951, pp. 48–62. This is not a complete list of French royal chapels:

Without interference from bishop, archbishop or pope, the king appointed to the ecclesiastical offices in the college, hospital or private chapel. This called for a winking at canon law, by the king as also by the pope. The right of collation to prebends and chapels carried with it rights of deprivation and reservation. The king himself issued to his chaplains dispensations for non-residence. And we find the saintly Louis IX insisting on the prevention of plurality. For these benefices the controlling court was the *parlement* itself. On the king's behalf it maintained the correct ecclesiastical procedures of appointment, and the king's confessor played a part in the execution of the royal right.[1] Despite the obvious clash with canon law which all this implied, the spirit of co-operation between Crown and Church is apparent at many points. Perhaps co-operation is especially apparent because it is not altogether meaningful here to speak of exceptional rights. Over a king's court or a king's chapels the pope might plead overall spiritual control, but the control could not operate in practice. And this was no privilege of kings alone: other lords also possessed the *collation plénière*.[2]

But it is important to look carefully at the nature of these royal chapels of France. Mollat stresses one essential feature of the benefices over which the king of France exercised complete rights: not one of them possessed the cure of souls. They were isolated from

---

for the royal chapel of Châteauneuf-sur-Loire see below, p. 19; and for the privileged royal chapel at Fontainebleau (founded by St Louis: *Abbayes et Prieurés*, ed. Beaunier and Besse, vi (*Archives de la France Monastique*, xv), 19) see *Privilèges Accordés à la Couronne de France par le Saint-Siège*, ed. A. Tardif (Paris, 1855), no. 228. And for additional royal hospitals, see J. Imbert in *Revue d'Histoire Ecclés.*, xlix (1954), 203, n. 1, citing idem, *Hôpitaux en Droit Canonique* (Paris, 1947), pp. 229–30.

[1] Mollat 1951, pp. 98, 108, 171.

[2] Ibid., pp. 138–9. In England no set rule seems to apply to the colleges of lay lords other than the king (see below, pp. 126–9); but it appears that in these secular colleges bishops usually suffered no significant damage to their jurisdiction. For the dispute first with the bishop, then with the archdeacon, of Worcester, concerning the rights of the college of St Mary Warwick which belonged to the earl of Warwick, see R. M. Haines, *The Administration of the Diocese of Worcester in the First Half of the Fourteenth Century* (London, 1965), pp. 27–8.

parochial responsibility. They were in a real sense private canonries or chaplaincies. Their predecessors, the demesne churches or *Fiskalkapellen* of the Carolingians, can hardly have existed apart from service to the occupants of the demesne.[1] And the problem of the protection of episcopal jurisdiction in the parishes annexed to canonries of privileged colleges was not peculiar to England.[2] But after the twelfth century the exercise of cure of souls (except for the royal family and the royal court) never appears to have belonged to the privileged chapels of France or Germany. Mollat has no doubt that the French royal prebends and chaplaincies were offices *non curata*. The king, he tells us, enjoyed complete independence from bishop and from pope 'sauf quant à la cure d'âmes'. There were distinct similarities between the benefices over which the king possessed the full right of collation and the benefices over which other lay lords exercised the same control: 'Aucun n'avait charge d'âmes et tous consistaient en prébendes ou chapelenies sises les premières dans des églises ou les secondes dans des châteaux'.[3] And it was not only the French royal chapels which possessed no cure of souls. A recent short survey of the royal chapels of the west, which in fact concerns the chapels of France, Bohemia and Hungary, with a passing glance at Aragon, mentions cure of souls only to demonstrate its irrelevance in a study of these institutions.[4] Many of these royal chapels were constituted as colleges during the later middle ages, and from the beginning they were quite independent of the parochial structure of the dioceses within which they were formed.

The English royal colleges, with prebends which were benefices with cure of souls, will appear all the more distinct by comparison with the French royal chapels. But many royal chapels without cure of souls existed in England as elsewhere. In a chapter

[1] J. Fleckenstein, *Die Hofkapelle der deutschen Könige* (Stuttgart, 1959-66), i, 99 (and see P. Gorissen's review of this first volume: 'La chapelle palatine des souverains carolingiens', *Revue d'Histoire Ecclés.*, lvi (1961), 465-70).

[2] For the duke of Burgundy's chapel at Dijon, see below, p. 20.

[3] Mollat 1951, pp. 4, 139-40.

[4] N. Grass, 'Zur Rechtsgeschichte der abendländischen Königskirche', *Festschrift K. S. Bader* (Zürich, 1965), pp. 159-84. And for the German royal colleges or chapels see J. Fleckenstein, op. cit., ii, 272-6.

entitled 'Royal visitations of hospitals and free chapels' Dr K. L. Wood-Legh pointed the way in 1934,[1] to a study of the king of England's control over all his chapels, a study comparable with that of Mollat. The challenge was not taken up. The present study is in some measure concerned with the border-line between those royal chapels with parochial responsibilities and those without, but it concentrates upon the former. Royal castle-chapels figure prominently, but royal hospitals not at all, for parochial obligations were only rarely associated with hospitals.[2] While royal hospitals—occasionally referred to as royal chapels—never impinge upon the present theme, this does not mean that their freedom from episcopal interference is in any doubt.[3] Chapels without cure of souls constituted a very wide group during the middle ages; a glance must be taken at some of those in England which were in the king's hands.

The word 'cappella' or 'capella' is thought to derive from the description of the repository in which the early kings of France housed the cape ('cappella', a diminutive of 'cappa') of St Martin.[4] It came to refer to a small oratory, or to the subordinate or outlying church of a parish. The 'capella' was often dependent upon the mother church. Now, chapels, royal or otherwise, were often described as free chapels, especially during the later middle ages. What was a 'libera capella'? The case of a new manorial chapel at Noseley in Leicestershire helps us to define a 'libera capella'.[5]

[1] Wood-Legh 1934, pp. 38–59.

[2] R. M. Clay, *The Medieval Hospitals of England* (London, 1909), p. 203.

[3] See, for example, *CCR 1302–7*, p. 225, concerning the hospital of St John Oxford. St Nicholas Carlisle is given as the example of a royal hospital (in which the king's chancellor not the bishop had the right to visit) in *Registrum Omnium Brevium* (London, 1531), p. 40b. Both are among the royal hospitals noted in Wood-Legh 1934. For the 'king's free chapel' of St Mary Magdalene Bamburgh, which was a hospital, see *Calendar of Inquisitions Miscellaneous* (HMSO, 1916–), vi, no. 30; and for a file of documents, dated from the time of Edward I, concerning the visitation of royal hospitals, see P.R.O. C47 (Chancery Miscellanea) 20/1.

[4] See Du Cange s.v. capella.

[5] A. Hamilton Thompson, 'The manor of Noseley, with some account of the free chapel of St Mary', *Transactions of the Leicestershire Archaeological Soc.*, xii (1921–2), 233–64 (esp. 236), and see Hamilton Thompson 1947, pp. 124–5.

Founded during the latter part of the thirteenth century, this new chapel was established under episcopal supervision; it was extra-parochial but certainly not exempt from the bishop. It is described as a free chapel because it was not dependent upon the parish church of Noseley. This had become the most common use of the term 'libera capella': the freedom was freedom from the parish, not freedom from the bishop.[1] A free chapel of this sort had no parochial responsibilities, and all the rights of the local parish church were themselves safeguarded.[2] There are many reasons for believing that the Crown would not suffer episcopal interference in its private chapels wherever they were constituted, but use of the term 'libera capella' is not in itself an indication of freedom from episcopal jurisdiction. Non-parochial chapels like Noseley appear to have been common. Chapels apparently of this kind on the king's manors were described as free chapels, like the king's free chapel of his manor of Nayland,[3] the free chapel of St Mary in the king's manor of Faxfleet,[4] and the free chapel in the royal manor of Windsor park.[5] Every royal castle had its free chapel, and many had more than one. Examples of small royal chapels, served by chaplains appointed by the king, can be multiplied—for example, the royal 'hermitage' of Cripplegate London,[6] the free chapel of St John Colney in the diocese of Lincoln[7] and the free chapel of Aber in the diocese of Bangor.[8]

With chapels, as with many aspects of ecclesiastical administration, the legislation of the Church in the twelfth century echoed the decrees of early church councils.[9] Even over private chapels the Church sought to exercise some supervision. For example, in 1138 it was set down at the Council of Westminster that oratories

[1] E.g. *Registrum S. de Gandavo*, ed. C. T. Flower and M. C. B. Dawes (CYS, 1934), pp. 643, 655.

[2] See *Councils and Synods* ii, 766, 1002–3, and J. R. H. Moorman, *Church Life in England in the Thirteenth Century* (Cambridge, 1955), pp. 15–16.

[3] *CCR 1302–7*, p. 75.   [4] *CPR 1324–7*, p. 277.

[5] A. K. B. Roberts, *St George's Chapel, Windsor Castle, 1348–1416* (Windsor, 1947), p. 5, and *The Registers of Roger Martival*, iii, ed. S. Reynolds (CYS, 1965), p. 214.   [6] *VCH London*, i, 586, and Prynne iii, 1250.

[7] *CPR 1307–13*, pp. 98, 148.   [8] Ibid., 110, 195, 198, etc.

[9] P. Thomas, *Le Droit de Propriété des Laïques* (Paris, 1906), pp. 34, 39.

should be established only with the bishop's consent.[1] New decrees could be applied perhaps to newly established chapels or chaplaincies, but only with difficulty to the ancient ones.[2] Where special rights were claimed for chapels, they were usually claimed as ancient rights. A small private oratory which was not endowed and therefore not a benefice could easily remain beyond the control of the bishop or his official or his archdeacon. But some private chapels were quite elaborately constituted and quite lavishly endowed. If such a chapel in lay hands were already well established in the thirteenth century, it might be defended against the interference of the bishop. For example, when by reason of wardship the manor of Nympsfield with its free chapel of Kinley came into the custody of Edward I, the king protected this free chapel, along with its chaplains, clerks and ministers, from the jurisdiction of the bishop of Worcester.[3] He did not

[1] Cheney 1956, p. 166.

[2] See *Councils and Synods* ii, 429.

[3] Prynne iii, 247 (*CCR 1279-88*, p. 14), and *Calendar of Inquisitions Misc.*, i, no. 1160. Two entries in episcopal registers suggest a more organised religious house. *A Calendar of the Reg. of Wolstan de Bransford*, ed. R. M. Haines (HMSO, 1966), p. 29: 'chapel of house of Kinley'; and *Register of Bishop Godfrey Giffard*, ed. J. W. Willis Bund (Worcestershire Historical Soc., 1902), p. 115: 'Induction of brother William, canon of the priory of Kinleya, to the rule of the same priory. And the same William took the oath of obedience before Master Will. Pykerel. 8 Kal. Oct. 1279' (calendared from Worcs. Record Office, Register Godfrey Giffard, fo. 97r (p. 185)). This latter entry is evidence of the episcopal interference against which the king complained. I have been unable to verify the tradition (from R. Atkyns, *Gloucestershire* (London, 1712), p. 581) that this house was 'seized by William I and restored by William II', as noted in D. Knowles and R. N. Hadcock, *Medieval Religious Houses* (London, 1953), p. 332.

The list of secular colleges printed in ibid. (pp. 325-46), useful though it is, must not be relied upon to give accurate information. For example, 'Ferring' (p. 330) 'appears to have become collegiate as there was a free chapel or peculiar jurisdiction here *temp.* Edward III'. The evidence *temp.* Edward III is *CPR 1334-8*, p. 228, which concerns a free chapel at Feering, Essex, not Ferring, Sussex; the free chapel (neither a college nor a peculiar jurisdiction, on this evidence) perhaps belonged, as did the manor and church of Feering, to Westminster Abbey: R. Newcourt, *Repertorium Ecclesiasticum Parochiale Londinense* (London, 1708-10), ii, 258-9.

claim it as a royal chapel, but he nevertheless supported its freedom from the bishop. It is not clear on what grounds the king claimed this freedom for a chapel which was in his hands only by reason of wardship, but he may have been extending to this chapel the privileges associated with all the royal chapels. It is difficult to believe that the Crown's intervention bore any long-term effects. Indeed, in 1340 Bishop Bransford visited the chapel of Kinley.[1] Some customary rights may have been retained in some non-royal chapels, but freedom from the bishop's jurisdiction became a principle which applied only to royal chapels.

Confusion arises because, even in the thirteenth century, the terms 'capella' and 'ecclesia' were often used interchangeably.[2] There may often have been some reason behind the use of two distinct terms. It is interesting, for example, that the prior of Thetford had held a free chapel in the church of Hockham: '. . . concedit quod habeat cappellam suam liberam in curia sua quam prius habuit in eadem ecclesia de Ocham . . .'[3] It is difficult to say whether there is any reason for the use of both terms to describe the church on the king's manor of Stonesfield.[4] But it is important to note that this church was a parish church and, although described by the bishop of Lincoln and by Henry III as both 'ecclesia' and 'capella',[5] it never appears to have been called a 'capella regis' or a 'dominica capella'. In one context the king refers to this church of Stonesfield as a chapel possessing ancient customs.[6] But whatever proprietary rights the king may at some time have exercised over this church and others like it, it is clear that in the thirteenth century the bishops of Lincoln had fully established their right to institute the chaplain whom the king presented.[7] Episcopal jurisdiction was not being by-passed in this

---

[1] *A Calendar of the Reg. of W. de Bransford*, loc. cit.

[2] E.g. R. V. Lennard, *Rural England, 1086–1135* (Oxford, 1959), p. 399n., and *Curia Regis Rolls* (HMSO, 1922–), x, 223, 320.

[3] *Curia Regis Rolls*, xiii, no. 695.

[4] See *Rot. Lit. Claus.*, i, 593.   [5] *CPR 1247–58*, pp. 11, 193.

[6] Prynne ii, 497: '. . . legata defunctorum et quaedam alia ad capellam nostram de Stinefeld secundum antiquam et approbatam consuetudinem pertinentia . . .'

[7] *Rotuli Hugonis de Welles*, ed. W. P. W. Phillimore, F. N. Davis and H. E.

royal church. And there is no reason to believe that a parish church in the king's patronage—as distinct from a collegiate church—would under normal circumstances gain freedom from ordinary ecclesiastical jurisdiction, even if it retained for some time a designation 'capella'.

It is clear from an examination of royal chapels in general that, excluding the Chapel Royal, the royal chapels can be divided into two groups. A large number of royal chapels were private oratories of one sort or another; others were collegiate churches. The first group, like the French royal chapels, possessed no cure of souls. They were not churches with parishes. And there is no evidence to suggest that any single parish church was regarded as a royal chapel. The royal collegiate churches were distinct both from the parish churches and from the non-parochial oratories.

In the midst of the different usages of the term 'capella' it is important to distinguish a particular association of the word with royal demesne churches. The chapel of Dalwood, in the diocese of Salisbury, is an example of a chapel which was the outlying church of a parish. It had come to depend upon the church of Stockland. Dalwood had been given by King John to Robert Chantemerle as a quarter of a knight's fee,[1] and in a dispute in 1217 with the patron of Stockland (the abbot of Milton) Robert claimed the advowson of the chapel of Dalwood. Accurate or not, his claim sheds light upon the position of the king's chapels: 'Robertus dicit quod terra ubi capella sita est fuit aliquando de dominico domini regis et usagium fuit quod omnes ecclesie de dominicis domini regis vocabantur capelle et ideo vocat eam capellam, set dicit quod libera est, et non pertinet ad aliquam matricem ecclesiam.'[2] What had been, it is claimed, a chapel in one sense of the word (a royal church) was being called a chapel in a different sense (a dependent church). It would be unwise to lend full credence to Robert Chantemerle's contention that all the 'ecclesie'

Salter, ii (CYS, 1907), 13. And see *Rotuli Roberti Grosseteste*, ed. F. N. Davis (CYS, 1913), p. 494, and *Rotuli Ricardi Gravesend*, ed. F. N. Davis (CYS, 1925), p. 221.

[1] *The Book of Fees* (HMSO, 1920–31), i, 88.

[2] *Bracton's Note Book*, ed. F. W. Maitland (London, 1887), iii, 313–14.

on royal demesne had been called 'capelle'. The situation in the twelfth century was not as clear-cut as that. But Robert's claim may well reflect, however palely, a situation which had existed before the Conquest, perhaps before the growth of the parochial system of single manorial churches. Certainly the royal demesne churches to which the term 'royal chapel' was applied were not parish churches as such but were rather secular colleges usually of ancient standing.

Bracton confirms the two quite distinct meanings of the term 'capella'. One kind of 'capella' is beneath the parish church in status, but the reverse is true of a second kind of 'capella'. He tells us that there are privileged royal chapels, and that in this context the term 'capella' signifies, not subjection to a mother church, but rather complete lack of subjection. It is possible, indeed, for a church actually to belong to this second kind of chapel. A chapel, he wrote, might well enjoy some special privilege 'ut si sit capella domini regis quae nulli subiecta est ecclesiae nec ad aliquam pertinet, sed ecclesia poterit esse pertinens ad capellam talem'.[1] Here is the distinction between a chapel which was subordinate to the parish church and a particular kind of royal chapel. Of the royal chapels Bracton makes no attempt to distinguish between those which were non-parochial and those which had churches or parishes belonging to them, but it appears that only the most important royal chapels—the royal secular colleges—could in fact possess parishes. Bracton provides us with a definition of the royal secular colleges: they were privileged chapels of the king which were subject to no church and could have parishes belonging to them. They were referred to more and more consistently during the thirteenth century as the 'royal free chapels'. I shall use the term 'royal free chapel' only to refer to the royal chapels with parochial responsibilities, but this is not to imply that 'libera capella regis' was used so exclusively in the middle ages.[2] That the royal free chapel can be treated as a distinct kind of church is plain, for no other 'capella', unless the term was being used very

---

[1] G. E. Woodbine, *Bracton, De Legibus et Consuetudinibus Anglie* (New Haven, 1915–42), iii, 215.

[2] See above, p. 8, n. 3.

loosely to signify 'ecclesia', actually possessed its own parishes. These royal chapels with churches dependent upon them could not be described as 'free' in the sense which had become common. Their freedom must be other than a freedom from the local parish church, and indeed the royal free chapels claimed a freedom very much wider than this. They claimed to be free from all ordinary ecclesiastical jurisdiction.

In this study of the royal free chapels I have made no attempt to write the history of each collegiate church. My concern is with the spiritual liberties of these churches, and I have examined a given church only if there is evidence concerning its relationship with the ecclesiastical ordinaries. I have tried, nonetheless, to keep them all in mind and to draw each one into the general picture. The nature and extent of their freedom from the Church's jurisdiction can only be measured when set against both the normal processes of ecclesiastical control and the canonical teaching of the Church. It is important therefore to discuss, in chapter II, the official attitude of the Church towards the English royal free chapels. The first extant papal bull concerning the liberties of English royal chapels was issued in 1236. From this date I shall look back, in chapter III, to the evidence concerning royal free chapels in the twelfth century, and forward, in chapter IV, to the position during the reigns of Henry III and Edward I. The castle-chapels will then require some brief and separate treatment. In the final chapter I shall examine the question of continuity between the Anglo-Saxon royal minster and the post-Conquest royal college, and draw together the evidence concerning the spiritual liberties enjoyed by the royal free chapels.

CHAPTER II

THE CLAIM OF EXEMPTION

During the thirteenth century and later the kings of England persistently claimed that their royal free chapels were completely free from all ordinary ecclesiastical jurisdiction. They would have them isolated, as much as possible, from the dioceses within which they were constituted. To substantiate their assertions they claimed, as we shall see, that the royal chapels had obtained papal grants of exemption. If such grants existed, then the royal colleges and their parishes amounted to areas of peculiar jurisdiction recognised by the Church. If the grants did not exist and freedom from episcopal jurisdiction was nevertheless insisted upon, then the royal colleges were maintaining what was in canon law an illegal and irregular position. Many bishops and archdeacons disputed the spiritual liberties of the royal free chapels. By the very claim to possess papal support for the exemption of the chapels, the kings of England acquiesced in the view that the exercise of episcopal jurisdiction was under the sole control of the Church. The crucial question is: how much support did the papacy actually give to the royal free chapels?

During the twelfth century episcopal rights were re-defined. Bishops became increasingly Argus-eyed. As a result, freedom from diocesan control was something to be fought for, something to be watched over. This freedom can be studied in two ways. In the first place, it can be studied by concentrating upon the papal grants of exemption to monasteries. It is the privileged religious houses which provide a precise definition of the word 'exemption'. Freedom from the diocesan depended, according to the Church's ruling, upon canonical exemption, that is, upon the possession (by a religious house not belonging to an exempt order) of a papal bull specifying both the house and the privilege. A grant of exemption meant the making of an exception. It implied an established pattern of episcopal jurisdiction. It conceded freedom from the bishop's jurisdiction and the immediate subjection of the house to the pope's jurisdiction. At a glance the history of exemption for English religious houses seems to be solely concerned with the exempt orders (the Cluniacs, the Cistercians, the Premonstratensians and the Military Orders), the six exempt Benedictine houses (Bury, St Albans, Malmesbury, Evesham, St Augustine's Canterbury and Westminster),[1] and the one exempt abbey of Augustinian canons (Waltham Holy Cross).[2] But the history of the exemption of religious houses will not be written within limits so easily defined.[3] Further orders and much smaller houses were to gain exemption. 'The development of papal power favoured the exemption of monasteries from diocesan visitation.'[4] Where a religious house was a house obeying a rule (was not, that is, a secular college) its exemption came during the twelfth century to depend, with only a few exceptions,[5] upon written papal sanction. Sometimes it is not clear whether a grant amounted to exemption. The liberty granted to Tavistock Abbey by Celestine III in 1193 has been interpreted as exemption, and the abbey paid census 'ad indicium libertatis', but the bull is not at all explicit and the abbey was not thought of as exempt in the thirteenth century.[6] Celestine's bull of 1192 for Tonbridge priory is much more explicit. This is a very interesting example of a relatively insignificant house obtaining one of the most important of privileges.[7] The early bulls for the houses of the order

[1] See Knowles 1932 and *The Monastic Order in England* (Cambridge, 1950), pp. 575–91. Battle Abbey is discussed by Knowles but does not fully merit inclusion among the canonically exempt: see below, pp. 86–8.

[2] See below, pp. 66–9. For St Botolph's Colchester, which claimed exemption by the use of a forged bull, see below, p. 81.

[3] See Cheney 1931, pp. 36–48.   [4] Ibid., p. 44.

[5] For the exempt priories (which were first secular colleges) of Bromfield, St Oswald's Gloucester and St Martin's Dover, see below, pp. 47–66.

[6] H. P. R. Finberg, *Tavistock Abbey* (Cambridge, 1951), p. 235, and W. E. Lunt, *Financial Relations of the Papacy with England, 1327–1534* (Cambridge, Mass., 1962), pp. 55–6. The bull is printed in *Monasticon*, ii, 498–9, and G. Oliver, *Monasticon Dioecesis Exoniensis* (London and Exeter, 1846), pp. 95–6.

[7] See below, p. 82.

of Sempringham confirmed liberties and immunities but reserved the canonical jurisdiction of the diocesan; the houses were to be free from all unlawful ('indebitas et inconsuetas') exactions of archbishop, bishops, archdeacons and deans, but not from 'synodalia' or 'episcopalia'.[1] Yet full exemption was eventually gained for this order in 1345.[2]

But to concentrate upon papal grants of exemption is in a sense to study only the tip of the iceberg. There is a more hidden but extremely important side to the history of freedom from episcopal jurisdiction. The work of Professor Barlow on the peculiars of the monastery of Durham[3] amply illustrates that the whole development of the proprietary churches, the *Eigenkirchen*, must be kept well in mind. To establish episcopal control over churches had been to proscribe the rights of the owner, but this process of asserting a new kind of control over churches was not entirely successful. It is important from the outset to stress the distinction between the freedom of religious houses from the diocesan and the freedom of churches.[4] While some exempt abbeys exercised complete control over an area immediately surrounding their houses, an area which often included one church (as at Westminster, Battle and Bury St Edmunds),[5] only St Albans and Evesham among the Benedictine abbeys retained during the struggles of the twelfth century the full exercise of spiritual jurisdiction in their churches. St Albans secured special privileges for fifteen of its churches; and in the ecclesiastical deanery of the Vale of Evesham, which coincided with the hundred of Blackenhurst, the abbey of Evesham acted as its own bishop.[6] This complete

[1] *Monasticon*, vi, 960, and C. R. Cheney, 'Some papal privileges for Gilbertine houses', *BIHR*, xxi (1946–8), 54–8.

[2] W. E. Lunt, op. cit., p. 59.   [3] Barlow 1950, passim.

[4] See Lemarignier 1937, passim but esp. p. 12 and n. 69.

[5] M. D. Knowles, 'Essays in Monastic History, VI: Parish Organisation', *Downside Review*, li (1933), 502–5, 515, idem, *The Monastic Order in England* pp. 592–606, M. D. Lobel, 'Ecclesiastical banleuca in England' in *Oxford Essays for H. E. Salter* (Oxford, 1934), pp. 122–40, and N. D. Hurnard, 'The Anglo-Norman franchises', *EHR*, lxiv (1949), 318–19.

[6] M. D. Knowles, *ubi supra* (1933), 517–22, and W. Page, 'Some remarks on the churches of the Domesday Survey', *Archaeologia*, lxvi (1914–15), 63.

exemption for both a monastery and its churches was unusual. But it must be remembered that papal bulls usually confirmed established rights which had been obtained by custom or perhaps by royal grant. And full jurisdiction 'in spiritualibus', whether exercised over one church or a number of churches, was not a privilege enjoyed exclusively by some exempt Benedictine abbeys.[1] It could depend more upon the retention of customary rights by agreement with the bishop than upon the acquisition of a papal bull. Cathedral monasteries or churches possessed peculiar jurisdictions. Dr Kathleen Edwards has written of the secular cathedrals, 'By the thirteenth century all the chapters had established their right to the ordinary jurisdiction in the churches appropriated to their common fund; while in those appropriated to prebends, the individual prebendaries had their own courts, with proof of wills and powers of correction.'[2] Some bishops, too, notably the archbishop of Canterbury[3]—like the bishops in

[1] Cf. M. D. Knowles, *ubi supra* (1933), 512; and see Dom Berlière, 'Les archidiaconés ou exemptions privilégiées de monastères', *Revue Bénédictine*, xl (1928), 116–22.

[2] K. Edwards, *The English Secular Cathedrals in the Middle Ages* (2nd ed., 1967), p. 125, and Hamilton Thompson 1947, pp. 73–5.

[3] Barlow 1963, p. 251. But the peculiar jurisdictions of bishops clearly became exceptional. On this score the unusual exemption from all jurisdiction except the pope's which John of Pontoise, bishop of Winchester, obtained from Boniface VIII in 1297 is of interest. For the full text of the bull, see *The Register of John Grandisson*, ed. F. C. Hingeston-Randolph (London, 1894–9), pp. 91–2; it is calendared in *Les Registres de Boniface VIII*, ed. G. Digard *et al.* (BEAR, 1907–39), no. 1680, and *Calendar of Papal Letters*, ed. W. H. Bliss and J. A. Twemlow (HMSO, 1894–), i, 569, and abridged by Pontoise himself in *Registrum J. de Pontissara*, ed. C. Deedes (CYS, 1915–24), p. 544. The exemption applied to his whole diocese, and to all his subjects, and to all his possessions and the possessions of his church throughout the province of Canterbury. With additional support from the pope, the bishop claimed that those of his churches which were outside his diocese (as Wyke Regis in the diocese of Salisbury and Witney in the diocese of Lincoln) were now free from the well-established jurisdiction of the diocesan. But adjustment to new procedures because of an unusual and temporary immunity was not at all easy. See *Registrum S. de Gandavo*, ed. C. T. Flower and M. C. B. Dawes, pp. 569–70, 599, *Registrum Pontissara*, pp. 544–5, 796–7, and *Les Registres de Boniface VIII*, no. 2614.

Normandy[1]—possessed and controlled churches in the dioceses of other bishops. Professor Barlow has stressed that 'rights which become obnoxious to reformers when in lay hands may yet be owned by ecclesiastical persons and corporations without offence'.[2] In the twelfth century the laity had been, or rather were being, successfully excluded from the possession of *episcopalia*. But the king was no mere layman. He was *sui generis*. And the royal free chapels were his ancient proprietary churches. They possessed no papal confirmation of their rights until the thirteenth century, and even then the papacy never in fact gave its consent to the spiritual liberties which some of them secured. The general bulls of the thirteenth and early fourteenth century serve indeed to illustrate just how remote papal authority was in these colleges of canons which the king could claim belonged to the Crown.

The earliest known papal bull concerning the English royal chapels as a group was issued by Pope Gregory IX on 27 April 1236.[3] Earlier bulls of protection of 1214 and 1228 had been concerned with the king's own chapel in the singular,[4] and a bull of 1231 had protected the chapel where the king was ('capella ubicunque fueris').[5] Pope Gregory was also responsible, in 1234, 1236 and 1237, for the first of a long series of bulls which granted to the king of France the freedom from interdict (except with papal licence) of his chapels.[6] The grant for the French royal chapels was drafted in very similar terms to later papal grants for English royal chapels. These bulls of Gregory IX reflect the growing concern for the protection of the royal chapels from the incursions of the local bishops, and they were in the nature of confirmations. Innocent III, in an interesting letter of 29 January 1213, had already relaxed an interdict upon the royal chapel of Châteauneuf-sur-Loire in the diocese of Orléans as prejudicial to

[1] Lemarignier 1937, p. 13, n. 72.

[2] Barlow 1950, p. xi.

[3] See Appendix IV.

[4] *Foedera*, I, i, 119 (for further editions see *Letters of Innocent III*, ed. C. R. and Mary G. Cheney (Oxford, 1967), no. 960), and *Foedera*, I, i, 189.

[5] *Foedera*, I, i, 199.

[6] See Luc d'Achery, *Spicilegium* (Paris, 1723), iii, 606, and *Privilèges Accordés à la Couronne*, ed. A. Tardif, passim.

royal rights.[1] In a similar spirit, Gregory IX's bull concerning the English chapels was a confirmation of the 'liberties and immunities bestowed out of piety upon the royal chapels by your ancestors the kings of England'.

This papal concern for the protection of royal chapels must not be misrepresented. Innocent III's policy towards royal or ducal chapels is set down in a letter of 1207 to the duke of Burgundy. This letter joined the decretal collection of Gregory IX and was incorporated into canon law.[2] Alexander III had already placed the newly founded private chapel of Dijon under papal protection ('in ius et proprietatem nostram et ecclesiae Romanae') and given it freedom from any bishop or other ecclesiastic: 'auctoritate apostolica prohibentes ne cui episcopo vel aliae ecclesiasticae personae liceat quidquam iuris sibi in eadem ecclesia, vel clericis eidem ecclesiae servientibus, vendicare.'[3] But the dean and other canons who held parish churches took advantage of the privileged status of the college and claimed that their parish churches were exempt from the bishop. Innocent III assured the diocesan that jurisdiction over these churches belonged entirely to him. He declared that the bishop must respect the exemption of the chapel; but when it was a question of parish churches or of other matters belonging to episcopal jurisdiction, then the bishop of Langres must fulfil the duties of his office. Here is a precise and unambiguous statement of policy by the pope. The freedom of the dean and canons must not result in usurpation of episcopal rights.

Quocirca fraternitati tuae presentium auctoritate mandamus quatenus in quantum exempti sunt eiusdem ratione capellae apostolicis privilegiis deferas reverenter, sed in quantum ratione parochialium ecclesiarum vel alia iurisdictionem tuam respicere dignoscuntur officii tui debitum in eosdem libere prosequaris.

We must interpret Gregory IX's grant to the English royal chapels in the same way that Innocent III interpreted the grant of

---

[1] *Patrologia Latina*, ed. J. P. Migne, 214–7 (*Innocentii Papae III Opera Omnia*), lib. xv, 227.

[2] Ibid., lib. ix, 265, and Decretals, V, xxxiii, 16 (E. Friedberg, *Corpus Iuris Canonici* (Leipzig, 1879–81), ii, 862).

[3] P. Thomas, *Le Droit de Propriété des Laïques*, pp. 174–5.

freedom to the chapel at Dijon. There is no suggestion that Gregory IX's confirmation of the liberties and immunities of the English royal chapels was intended as an attack upon episcopal rights. The bull has the flavour of a routine grant, and it is difficult to believe that the extent of the existing 'liberties and immunities' of the royal chapels was taken into account at the papal curia. The bull extended to all the royal chapels a grant which had already been made to the royal free chapel of St Martin-le-Grand. A papal letter of 1176 confirmed St Martin-le-Grand in all its possessions and added this striking clause: 'Preterea libertates et immunitates necnon antiquas et rationabiles consuetudines ipsius ecclesie ratas habemus et firmas easque perpetuis temporibus illibatas manere sancimus.'[1] The wording of later papal grants to St Martin-le-Grand, dated 1223 and 1229, corresponds even more closely to the grant to all the royal chapels: 'necnon libertates et immunitates a clare memorie Willelmo et Henrico regibus Anglie pia ecclesie vestre liberalitate concessas.'[2]

Gregory IX did not make the grant of 1236 without a precedent, nor without some prior consideration, for at the request of the king he had ordered an inquiry into the position of the royal chapels. A papal letter dated 20 July 1231[3] reveals that Henry III had sought the pope's assistance, since local bishops were usurping the rights of his chapels, which were, so the pope declared, in respect of their temporalities subject only to the king and in respect of their spiritualities only to the pope. The bishop

---

[1] *Papsturkunden*, i, no. 140.

[2] For the two bulls (of Honorius III dated 19 January 1223 and of Gregory IX dated 2 April 1229) see W.A.M., Book 5, fos 12r–13v and W.A.M., MS 13167, m. 4v. The original of the bull of Gregory IX is W.A.M., MS 8115.

[3] This bull was one of 24 found among the memoranda of John Francis (a keeper of the Great Seal in 1310: T. F. Tout, *Chapters in Administrative Hist.* (Manchester, 1920–33), vi, 7), and lodged with the Exchequer in 1315 (*Red Book of the Exchequer*, ed. H. Hall (RS, 1896), iii, 1046). It was in the king's treasury of the Exchequer when the calendar of bulls was made by Walter Stapledon in 1323 (F. Palgrave, *The Antient Kalendars and Inventories* (London, 1836), i, 10), and transcripts of it survive among the Chancery Miscellanea of the P.R.O. and in W.A.M. See Appendix III.

of Ely was commissioned to inquire into the truth of the king's allegations so that the pope, instructed by his findings, could take necessary action. Perhaps the bull of 1236 was in some way the outcome of that inquiry. The papacy was apparently willing to confirm the freedom of the royal chapels. But the exact extent of this freedom is not defined. It is significant that for Innocent III the freedom of the royal chapel of Châteauneuf-sur-Loire had meant the freedom of the 'locus' but not the freedom of the chaplains, who as members of the clergy were subject to the ecclesiastical jurisdiction of the diocesan,[1] and certainly not the freedom of any parish churches. And, above all, we must keep in mind what Bonaguida of Arezzo was to write in his Consuetudines Curiae Romanae (c. 1245–46) about papal grants of 'all liberties, approved immunities and reasonable customs'. Such grants should not be taken very seriously: 'Item leviter habetur tale privilegium. Confirmamus tibi omnes libertates, immunitates approbatas et rationabiles consuetudines a Romano pontifice vel regibus vel aliis Christi fidelibus concessas.'[2] Gregory IX was making few concessions. And he had taken for granted the direct dependence of the English chapels in spiritual matters upon the pope; just how empty this claim was only becomes clear in the course of the thirteenth century.

The first bull confirming the liberties of English royal chapels itself demands an examination of the material at hand concerning royal free chapels before 1236. As secular colleges following no very distinct pattern of organisation, they developed, on the whole, little community tradition; in only a few cases have their records survived. For this reason, and also because there was apparently little conflict between them and the local bishops until the thirteenth century, the references to them are brief and scattered. But we are not entirely ignorant of the early status and privileges of quite a large number. To these we must now turn.

---

[1] *Patrologia Latina*, ed. J. P. Migne, loc. cit.: 'cum si forsan capellanus memoratae capellae deliquerit, ut suum poena teneret auctorem, non locus in regis praejudicium, sed ille debuerit interdici.'

[2] L. Wahrmund, 'Die "Consuetudines curiae Romanae"', *Archiv für Katholisches Kirchenrecht*, lxxix (1899), 19.

Chapter III

THE ROYAL FREE CHAPELS OF THE TWELFTH CENTURY

Before looking in detail at the history of particular royal free chapels it will be instructive to note some of the changes which were taking place during the twelfth century and to examine some of the problems of interpreting the available evidence. Most of the royal free chapels had been Anglo-Saxon minsters; there is a strong probability that this is true in some cases where the evidence is not conclusive, as at Gnosall and Pevensey. But the system of minsters—mother churches which were communities of priests serving quite large areas—was declining long before the Conquest. The situation as it existed after the Conquest was essentially residual. To study the royal minsters in the twelfth century is to see the process of disintegration continuing yet slowing down. The royal 'capellaria' at Pevensey with its dependent churches completely disintegrated during the twelfth century. Changes taking place elsewhere were not so complete. The cases of St Oswald's Gloucester and, to a lesser extent, Bosham illustrate how the secular colleges had been losing their landed wealth. In the one case Domesday Book shows the land which had belonged to the college forming the temporal barony of Churchdown; similarly the manor of Bosham became quite distinct from the college of Bosham. In neither case does the parochial extent of the college appear to have been much depleted. The trend was a common one: from the twelfth century onwards we are dealing in essence with churches whose main possessions and rights were 'spiritual' possessions and rights.

Further important changes were taking place in the twelfth century. First, a number of the royal colleges were converted into monasteries. Two became Augustinian houses, St Oswald's

Gloucester and Waltham; two others became Benedictine priories, Bromfield and Dover. Links were retained with their early status as royal chapels, but to a different extent in each case. Second, there was a marked tendency for the Crown to give away its royal chapels in perpetuity. This was not, of course, the appointment of a clerk to the office of dean, but rather the permanent granting away of the college, usually to a bishop or an abbot, to be held *ex officio*. In some cases, as at Bosham and Derby, the prelate to whom the chapel had been given was himself regarded as dean. The king was disposing of his patronage rights. Of those royal chapels to be examined in this section, Bosham was given to the bishop of Exeter, Bromfield to the abbey of Gloucester, St Oswald's Gloucester to the archbishop of York, St Martin's Dover to the archbishop of Canterbury, Steyning to the abbey of Fécamp, and Gnosall to the bishop of Coventry. While this change of ownership might well have very important effects upon the history of a royal chapel, once again the privileged status of the college was not necessarily affected. The king had no direct control of many of his own chapels, but this did not mean that he would necessarily regard the privileges of such chapels as unworthy of support.

Although the royal secular colleges were for the most part neither very large nor very wealthy, they provided livings for some of the most important civil servants. The lists of the deans of St Martin-le-Grand, of Bridgnorth and of Wimborne Minster provide immediate evidence of that.[1] Only for those colleges which remained under the king's direct control are lists of deans relatively easy to compile, and lists of prebendaries for any of the colleges must at the best be very piecemeal.[2] A more extended study of each college would be necessary before any satisfactory

[1] See *VCH London*, i, 564–5, Hamilton Thompson 1927, pp. 50–2, and *VCH Dorset*, ii, 113.

[2] Bridgnorth is the only exception, for here the king, rather than the dean, collated to the prebends. For the lists of prebendaries, see Hamilton Thompson 1927, pp. 52–62. The prebendaries individually and independently exercised full spiritual and temporal jurisdiction within their prebends; each prebend constituted a separate peculiar (ibid., p. 7).

lists could materialise, and upon them a study of the men who obtained the deanships and prebends would depend. The importance of these men must be borne in mind, for it would often be the royal clerks themselves who were fighting for the privileges of the royal chapels. Although it may be fair to portray the kings of England as constantly striving to protect their rights in the royal chapels—and it is certainly fair in regard to Henry III and Edward I—yet the official records rarely allow us to distinguish between the king himself and his administrative staff. Occasionally the distinction can be made, but usually my reference to the action of the king in this matter or that must be understood as a reference to the action of the king's government.

In many cases the material concerning royal free chapels does not refer to dependent 'churches' or to 'vicars' because both are orthodox terms implying institutions or offices over which the ecclesiastical hierarchy exercised its normal procedures of control. The local churches of the vills within the deanery of a royal free chapel might be described as 'chapels anciently prebendal' annexed to the college or church[1] or as 'portions' of the college or church;[2] and the clerk serving in the 'prebendal chapel' or 'portion' might be described as a chaplain, not as a vicar.[3] Yet, while we may be reluctant, like some of our documents, to speak of parish churches served by the vicars of prebendaries, we have no choice but to speak of parishioners:[4] the cure of souls and the exercise of spiritual jurisdiction could not be excluded from the deaneries. The deanery was the parish of the college, and within the deanery the prebendal chapels were like parish churches and the chaplains were like vicars. When a deanery itself was described as a 'beneficium non curatum' this can hardly have implied that the dean refrained at the very least from supervising the exercise of cure of souls in the deanery;[5] it was rather an attempt

[1] *The Register of Wm. Greenfield*, ed. A. Hamilton Thompson (*Surtees Soc.*, 145, 149, 151–3), i, 184.   [2] *Taxatio*, p. 243b.   [3] Below, p. 39, n. 2.

[4] See, for example, the king's letter to the parishioners of Penkridge: Prynne ii, 996 (as *CPR 1258–66*, p. 40).

[5] For the association of cure of souls with the office of dean, see Hamilton Thompson 1945, pp. 63n, 76.

to prevent the deans from being regarded as pluralists. After all, if the Crown itself could determine that a church was free from ecclesiastical control, then the Crown could also determine that a church could be held as an additional benefice without any infringement of ecclesiastical law: the deanery of Wolverhampton was to be described as a 'beneficium secundum consuetudinem et regiam libertatem non curatum'[1] and the deanery of St Martin-le-Grand as a 'beneficium secundum consuetudinem dicte capelle cum alio beneficio curato compassibile'.[2] With the ecclesiastical reorganisation of the twelfth and thirteenth centuries, the royal free chapels became distinctly anomalous. In measuring their position within the *societas Christiana* we must beware of using orthodox yardsticks.

It is clear that there is a sense in which the Church, or more precisely the papacy, was perfectly willing to regard royal colleges as exempt from episcopal jurisdiction and control. The problem is not the college itself but rather its parish. The question is: were the prebendal churches of the colleges regarded as free from the bishop's interference? Yet the question is not a very pertinent one. These royal chapels existed to serve a community. It can hardly have seemed possible to separate the college from its deanery; the difficulties involved when a separation of jurisdiction was attempted will be illustrated by the case of Bosham. My concern is a chapel's whole relationship with its bishop. How far did the freedom claimed for royal free chapels in the thirteenth century exist in the twelfth century? By the thirteenth century the bishop's control over his diocese included the right to institute to a church, the right to visit and the right to correct. Before the thirteenth century his powers are not so easily defined. In the twelfth century the bishop's rights were often referred to as *episcopales consuetudines*; these were the payments customarily due to the bishop and they were associated with the functions which he exercised, whether in providing chrism or conducting synods. It is not possible to be precise about the nature and extent of episcopal customs, and practices may have varied significantly

[1] *Registrum S. de Langham*, ed. A. C. Wood (CYS, 1956), p. 62.
[2] *Registrum S. de Sudbiria*, ed. R. C. Fowler (CYS, 1927–38), ii, 178.

from diocese to diocese. No doubt variations also existed concerning freedom from episcopal customs. We must examine
separately the evidence which each case produces.

This examination of royal free chapels in the twelfth century is
not an attempt to deal with every known royal college. Many will
be overlooked because of paucity of evidence. Of the important
group of royal colleges in the diocese of Coventry and Lichfield,
I shall examine only the churches of Wolverhampton and Gnosall,
omitting any mention at this stage of Bridgnorth, St Mary
Shrewsbury, Penkridge, Tettenhall, Stafford or Derby.[1] Together,
the parishes of these churches formed an extensive area of jurisdiction, and there are indications that the Crown thought of them
as a group, as when Henry III ordered the deans and canons and
chaplains of six of them (excluding Gnosall and Derby) to assist
Berard of Ninfa in the collection of the arrears of legacies and
obventions due to Richard of Cornwall for his Crusade.[2] In
addition to these royal free chapels, Wimborne Minster in the
diocese of Salisbury will also be excluded, for no evidence
appears to have survived to shed light on its status. There are few
signs of any dispute about the exercise of jurisdiction in this church.
This is unusual, but it should not be assumed that the situation
here was completely peaceful throughout the middle ages. In 1290
the archdeacon of Dorset was attempting to further his claims to
jurisdiction over the church against the findings of a recent inquisition which had declared in favour of the dean and canons.[3]
But the rights of this college appear nevertheless to have been
very largely unchallenged. Wimborne Minster had been founded
as a nunnery early in the eighth century, and at some unknown
date before the Conquest was constituted as a secular college.[4]

[1] For the Staffordshire chapels (Wolverhampton, Penkridge, Tettenhall and
Stafford), see the work of Mrs Dorothy Styles: Styles 1936 and Styles 1950–1.
For St Mary Shrewsbury, see Owen and Blakeway 1825, ii, esp. 304–10, and
for the small royal free chapel of St Juliana Shrewsbury, which may have been
collegiate at an early stage in its history, see below, pp. 122–4. For Derby and
Bridgnorth, see below, pp. 110–12, 119.

[2] *CPR 1247–58*, p. 371.

[3] *Rotuli Parliamentorum* (Record Commission, 1783), i, 52a.

[4] *VCH Dorset*, ii, 107–13.

The small college, with its dean and four prebendaries, appears on all the surviving lists of royal free chapels at the turn of the thirteenth century;[1] the claim that this church and its deanery were free from all ordinary ecclesiastical jurisdiction was apparently secure. In other royal free chapels there is much more evidence of conflict with the ecclesiastical ordinaries.

St Martin-le-Grand London

From one point of view it may seem strange to begin with St Martin-le-Grand.[2] The clerical petition of '1295' stated that St Martin-le-Grand was not one of the royal chapels by ancient standing, but had been granted by prelates to William Rufus.[3] The statement, if inaccurate in detail, was not without foundation. This college appears to have developed out of a church founded by a priest, Ingelric, and his brother before 1068, and it acquired many of its endowments during the century following the Conquest. Many of its churches in the diocese of London were obtained piecemeal and they formed no compact parochial area. This was a new royal free chapel, distinct from the chapels of ancient standing. But it became a most important royal free chapel; and because it was appropriated to Westminster Abbey in 1503 some of its archives have been preserved, especially a cartulary roll and a cartulary book.[4] It is the only royal free chapel of the twelfth and thirteenth centuries for which internal archival evidence has survived, and this evidence enables us to trace the growth of a privileged college.

It was assumed in the papal bull of July 1231 that St Martin-le-

---

[1] Above, p. 1, *The Register of Walter de Stapeldon*, ed. F. C. Hingeston-Randolph (London, 1892), p. 99, and *CCR 1313-8*, pp. 172-3, 596.

[2] For the site and boundaries of St Martin-le-Grand, see E. A. Webb, *The Records of St Bartholomew's Smithfield* (Oxford, 1921), i, plate II, and M. D. Honeybourne, 'The sanctuary boundaries and environs of Westminster Abbey and the college of St Martin-le-Grand', *Journal of the British Archaeological Assoc.*, xxxviii (1932), pp. 324-32, and plates II and III. And for the college as a place of sanctuary during the later middle ages, see I. D. Thornley, 'Sanctuary in medieval London', ibid., pp. 308-15.

[3] Above, p. 1.   [4] W.A.M., MS 13167 and Book 5.

Grand was an ancient church. The bull, ordering the bishop of Ely to inquire about the king's complaint of attacks by certain bishops upon the royal chapels, had mentioned only one royal chapel: '. . . certain chapels on the king's demesne which were founded and endowed in ancient times and are called royal chapels, one of which is the deanery of St Martin . . .'[1] While the status of other chapels, as for example Dover,[2] was under discussion at about the same time, the papal inquiry into the rights of royal chapels may have particularly concerned the college of St Martin-le-Grand. The papal confirmations of the church's liberties and immunities in 1223 and 1229[3] were not in any sense bulls of exemption. They could not prevent disputes about the exercise of spiritual jurisdiction. The dean and chapter of St Martin-le-Grand were claiming that the church of Maldon in Essex belonged to them *pleno iure*, and they appealed to Rome after the archdeacon of Essex had suspended a clerk who was serving at Maldon and had put an interdict on the church. The actions of the archdeacon were regarded as two distinct attacks upon the rights of St Martin-le-Grand, for in May 1233 Pope Gregory appointed separate judges delegate to hear each case.[4] The king and the dean and chapter accepted that the liberties and immunities confirmed by the pope included the complete freedom of the church from the jurisdiction of the diocesan and his archdeacons. In effect, an exempt deanery, with parochial rights in the hands of the dean and the prebendaries of the college, was already in existence here. How had this deanery been created?

A charter of William the Conqueror is the first impressive piece of evidence concerning St Martin-le-Grand.[5] The charter,

[1] Appendix III.

[2] See *Monasticon*, iv, 536b, and below, p. 61.

[3] Above, p. 21.

[4] See the two original bulls dated 11 and 20 May 1233: W.A.M., MSS 8116, 8117.

[5] See W. H. Stevenson, 'An Old English charter of William the Conqueror', *EHR*, xi (1896), 739–44, *Regesta* i, no. 22, and W.A.M., Book 5, fos 9r–10r. Concerning the charter's authenticity, see also J. H. Round and W. H. Stevenson in *EHR*, xii (1897), 105–10. The earliest extant copy is an *inspeximus* of June 1309: *Cal. Charter Rolls*, iii, 129.

executed ('Peracta vero est hec donacio . . .') Christmas Day 1067, and confirmed on the occasion of Queen Matilda's coronation, Whitsuntide 1068, concerned the grant by the priest Ingelric[1] of land in Essex to the canons of St Martin-le-Grand, a church which had been built by Ingelric and his brother within the walls of London. The charter confirmed St Martin's in its possessions and granted to it all the liberties and customs enjoyed by any other church in the kingdom.[2] Churches were noted among its possessions, but only the church of Maldon by name. The charter was ratified by the cardinals, Peter and John, when they visited England in 1070. Thus far faith can be put in the terms of the document. W. H. Stevenson saw no reason to question its authenticity, in the Old English or the Latin form. But one clause has aroused some suspicion; the college was given complete freedom from the exactions and interference of bishops, archdeacons, deans and their ministers: 'Sit vero ipsa prenominata Beati Martini ecclesia, et eiusdem ecclesie canonici episcoporum, archidiaconorum, decanorum, ministrorumve suorum universali exactione et inquietudine quieta et omnino sequestrata.' Because of this clause L. C. Loyd concluded that in its present form the charter is a compilation of a later date.[3] His conclusion was supported by the opinion of F. M. Stenton, whom he cites: 'So far as I know there is nothing of this date comparable to the privileges given to this not very distinguished church. The mention of freedom from the exaction of archdeacons is highly incongruous at the beginning of William's reign.' While the clause is unusual and could be thought to read like a later gloss upon the statement in the charter of freedom from all liberties and customs, yet we may question the belittling of the status of the new and well-endowed church and also wonder at the validity of regarding the

[1] For whom see J. H. Round, *The Commune of London* (Westminster, 1899), pp. 28–36, and J. Le Neve, *Fasti Ecclesiae Anglicanae 1066–1300*, i (London, 1968), compiled by D. E. Greenway, p. 89.

[2] '. . . et si quas alias libertates vel consuetudines [que] aliqua ecclesiarum regni mei Angl[ie] meliores habet.'

[3] L. C. Loyd, 'The date of the creation of the earldom of Shrewsbury' in G. E. Cokayne, *Complete Peerage* (1910–59), xi, 156–7 (App. K).

reference to archdeacons as incongruous.[1] Contemporary French charters granted freedom from interference in very similar terms, as, for example, in a gift of 1070 of two altars to the abbey of St Germain-des-Prés: '. . . nulli aut episcopo vel archydiacono aliqua occasione sint dedita aut ullius consuetudinis redibitione sint obnoxia . . .'.[2] And in a dispute in 1092 the monks of Worcester were claiming freedom from the exactions of archdeacons and rural deans: '. . . quod nullus diaconus nullus archdiaconus de monachorum ecclesiis seu clericis se intromittat . . .'.[3] It may well be that William I's charter is a completely authentic confirmation of the freedom of the church of St Martin-le-Grand from episcopal and archidiaconal exactions.

On the death of Ingelric, before the time of the Domesday survey, Eustace, count of Boulogne, took over his lands, including the college of St Martin-le-Grand. Despite the fact that Eustace at first impropriated some of the possessions of the canons (including the church of Maldon),[4] the rights of the college were probably little affected by the transfer of patronage to the counts of Boulogne; and contact with the English Crown, though perhaps less direct, was certainly not lost. Eustace re-granted the church of Maldon to St Martin-le-Grand along with all the church's 'liberties', and the possessions of the college steadily increased. Henry I confirmed the priest Turstin's gift of St Botolph, Aldersgate, a church 'in the royal demesne', to the canons of

---

[1] For Edward, archdeacon of London, who became a monk of Christ Church Canterbury in 1070 x 1089, see J. Le Neve, op. cit., p. 8.

[2] M. Prou, *Receuil des Actes de Philippe Ier* (Paris, 1908), nos. 48–9, cited in J. Vendeuvre, 'La *libertas* royale des communautés religieuses au XIe siècle: la *libertas* viz-à-viz des évêques', *Nouvelle Revue Hist. de Droit Franç. et Étranger* xxxiv (1910), 339, n. 2.

[3] *Hemingi Chartularium*, ed. T. Hearne (Oxford, 1723), ii, 530.

[4] See the charter of Count Eustace, printed in Kempe 1825, pp. 34–5, 179–80 from B.M., Lansdowne 170, fos. 61r–v, and see W.A.M., Book 5 (Cartulary of St Martin-le-Grand), fo. 18v. B.M., Lansdowne 170 contains (fos. 52r–118v) a sixteenth-century version of the fifteenth-century cartulary W.A.M., Book 5 (for the intermediate MS from which the B.M. MS was apparently copied, see I. D. Thornley, loc. cit., p. 309, n. 6); Kempe worked exclusively (but not by choice) from B.M., Lansdowne 170, but all references here will be to W.A.M., Book 5.

St Martin-le-Grand, and confirmed them too in the possession of the church of Newport, Essex, which was also on royal demesne.[1] Both these grants (dated ?1115 and 1108 × 1122) are of great significance, for the terms of the royal letters suggest that the canons took over all rights in these churches. Henry instructed the bishop of London that the dean (Roger, bishop of Salisbury) and the canons were to hold the church of St Botolph, Aldersgate, 'of parochial rights and lands and customs' and 'as freely as Turstin and his predecessors ever held it',[2] and that they were to hold the church of Newport with its lands and chapels and tithes and all other appurtenances 'freely for ever'. Just how free the churches were from the bishop's jurisdiction in all its aspects is nonetheless a matter for debate: the question seems to hinge on the interpretation of the clause describing St Botolph's as held 'in . . . consuetudine'. Perhaps the free customs enjoyed by these churches included those episcopal customs which were largely financial rights and which did not concern the bishop's order.[3] It is difficult to avoid the conclusion that already, if not before, what can only be described as an exempt church controlling exempt parishes was being created. Queen Matilda (crowned 1136, died 1152) was countess of Boulogne in her own right, and she gave to the college, as provision for a tenth canon, the churches of Chrishall and Witham. The grant of the church of St Mary Chrishall included all the customary rights and services belonging to the 'liberty' of the church.[4] The church of Witham was the mother church of the queen's manor of Witham and it was given to the canons along

---

[1] *Cal. Charter Rolls*, v, 16–17, and *Regesta* ii, nos. 1106–7, 1362. The grants were confirmed by King Stephen: *Regesta* iii, nos. 521, 535, 538. The church of St Botolph was described as 'sita in dominio meo', and the grant of the church of Newport included 'plenariam decimam et de dominio meo et de omnibus rebus de quibus decima rationabiliter dari debet' (and see *CPR 1225–32*, p. 406, and *DB*, ii, 7a).

[2] '. . . bene et in pace et honorifice et libere teneant ecclesiam supradictam et ei pertinentia in parochia et terra et consuetudine . . .'; and '. . . in pace illam teneant et libere sicut idem Turstinus et antecessores eius umquam melius tenuerunt.'

[3] See below, pp. 91, 137–9 and Barlow 1950, p. xv.

[4] *Regesta* iii, nos. 553, 555.

with churches, chapels, lands and tithes belonging to it, to be held just as freely as the canons held their other churches.[1] After the death of Count William of Boulogne in 1159 it seems clear that Henry II took into his own hands those estates of the honour of Boulogne which were in his dominions.[2] From this date St Martin-le-Grand, with its prebends already constituted,[3] was under the direct control of the king.

There is little evidence during the twelfth century of disputes concerning the exercise of spiritual jurisdiction. The situation was no doubt influenced by the fact that the deans were often prominent churchmen, as for example Roger, bishop of Salisbury, and Henry of Blois, bishop of Winchester.[4] The lack of animosity appears to have fostered a lack of precision, at least about the extent of the freedom of churches belonging to the college. But by the middle years of the century there was a 'new spirit' which 'inspired the ordinaries to scrutinise and define'.[5] An undated letter, probably from Archbishop Theobald, shows that there was already room for dispute.[6] The interpretation which Theobald placed upon the privileges of St Martin-le-Grand is of particular interest. The archdeacon and deans of Essex had attempted to exact dues from the church of St Mary Maldon which belonged to St Martin's and, having failed, had laid an interdict upon the church and suspended a priest. The archbishop intervened on behalf of the canons, declaring that the archdeacon and deans had acted unlawfully. But they had acted unlawfully, in Theobald's opinion, because they had exceeded episcopal rights; the exactions and services they had demanded from the church were temporal, not spiritual. The archbishop was acting in the belief that the

---

[1] *Regesta* iii, nos. 541–2, and see no. 539.

[2] See J. H. Round, *Studies in Peerage and Family History* (Westminster, 1901), p. 172.

[3] See L. Voss, *Heinrich von Blois* (Berlin, 1935), pp. 151–2 (from W.A.M., MS 13247), Kempe 1825, pp. 65–7, and W.A.M., Book 5, fos. 18v–19r.

[4] *VCH London*, i, 564.

[5] Barlow 1950, p. 62.

[6] A. Saltman, *Theobald, Archbishop of Canterbury* (London, 1956) pp. 393–4; thought to be a letter from Thomas Becket by L. Voss, op. cit., p. 154, who follows W.A.M., Book 5, fo. 25r (and see Kempe 1825, p. 68).

church of Maldon was in no way exempt from episcopal jurisdiction ('episcopalia iura'); and in another letter, concerning the
chapel of Bonhunt attached to the church of Newport, the archbishop raised no objection to the archdeacon bringing a case
against the canons except that the dean himself was not able to be
present.[1] Two papal bulls, of 1144 and 1176,[2] protected the
college and confirmed its possessions, but made no specific mention of exemption. The second of the bulls did confirm the
college's established rights, 'its liberties and immunities and its
ancient and reasonable customs'. The problem turns upon the
interpretation of the phrase 'reasonable customs'; but, however
loose the wording of the bull and however lightly the papacy
regarded such grants, it could be taken by the canons of St
Martin-le-Grand as a general confirmation of the church's freedom, especially in the absence of a clause saving the authority of
the diocesan. But the actual extent of the freedom of its annexed
churches remained a problem in need of clarification.

There is certainly no evidence to suggest that the bishop of
London had any control over the appointments to the deanship
itself of St Martin-le-Grand. Without reference to the bishop,
King Richard in 1189 and King John in 1199 collated the deanship
with all its liberties and free customs upon William of Sainte-
Mère-Église in the first instance, and Richard Briger' (?Briwerre)
in the second, both royal clerks, who were to hold the office 'with
the gift of prebends and of churches and with the free administration of all things belonging to the church of St Martin'.[3] In 1225
the status and privileges of the college were set down in the
clearest possible terms.[4] Despite warnings from the king, the
archdeacon of Colchester had persistently attempted to obtain
procurations from the church of Newport; failing in his efforts, he
had appealed to Rome and the case was delegated to the archdeacon, the chancellor and the dean of Oxford. Henry III forbade

---

[1] A. Saltman, op. cit., p. 391, and L. Voss, op. cit., p. 152.

[2] *Papsturkunden*, i, nos. 30, 140.

[3] P.R.O. C47 (Chancery Miscellanea), 12/5 no. 16; and *Cartae Antiquae*,
ed. L. Landon (*PRS*, new ser. xvii), no. 233, and W.A.M., MS 13155.

[4] Prynne iii, 62–3, and *Rot. Lit. Claus.*, ii, 80a.

the papal delegates to hear the case. He claimed the deanery of St Martin as a demesne chapel completely exempt from the jurisdiction of the diocesan and his subordinates: the dean received his stall in the choir and his place in the chapter by the royal hand alone; and the church of Newport formed a very large and important part of the deanery, for the dean himself possessed the prebend of Newport. It is clear that the king now regarded an attack upon the privileges of this chapel as an attack upon the royal dignity. When a new dean was appointed in September 1225 it was the constable of the Tower of London who was ordered to assign to him a stall in the choir and a place in the chapter.[1] Earlier grants had followed a common charter form: 'Sciatis nos dedisse et concessisse et presenti carta nostra confirmasse . . .' In 1225 the form had changed. At first the clerk making the Chancery enrolment used this phrase: 'Noveritis nos concessisse et quantum ad patronum pertinet dedisse . . .' But this was altered to 'Noveritis nos contulisse . . .' In making the appointment the king was exercising both the right of patronage and the, otherwise episcopal, right of institution. He collated. Whatever the position had been during the twelfth century, there is no question at all that an exempt deanery was now a reality. Lest his inhibition to the papal delegates should go unheeded, the king himself appealed to the pope against the action that was being taken against the dean of St Martin-le-Grand by the archdeacon of Colchester. There is no mistaking the king's attitude towards his chapel. Once again, in 1231, the privileges of St Martin were affirmed.[2] 1622980

Yet in at least one of the churches in the possession of the college of St Martin-le-Grand it is clear that the bishop of London was establishing some spiritual control. In the case of the church of Witham with its chapel of Cressing the bishop was able to intervene because of a dispute between the dean of St Martin-le-Grand and the canons. The church had belonged to the community of canons, but the dean had apparently attempted to usurp their rights. The dean resigned whatever right he had in the church to

---

[1] CPR 1216–1225, p. 550.
[2] Cal. Charter Rolls, i. 129, and CCR 1227–1231, p. 478.

the bishop of London, Eustace of Fauconberg, and both the dean
and the canons committed the church to the ordination of the
bishop. An agreement drawn up in 1223[1] was an act of appropriation with the ordination of a vicarage. Although the church was
appropriated to the canons, it is clear that quite a wealthy vicarage was created out of it, and the ordination and collation of the
vicarage were to belong, for ever and without disturbance, to the
bishops of London. The canons were to receive a pension of seven
marks annually from the vicarage—a reduction in the payment
from the church to which they had been accustomed, for only
two years before this agreement Pope Honorius III had confirmed the canons in their possession of an annual twenty marks
in the church of Witham.[2] Whoever the bishop collated was
to swear fealty to the canons in their chapter. The agreement
may have appeared as a reasonable compromise, but from
the point of view of ecclesiastical jurisdiction the bishop had
established control. He himself had the right to collate to the
church. Any doubts there may have been about the exercise of
episcopal jurisdiction at Witham were now dispelled.

There are signs that the bishop was also establishing some rights
in the churches within the city of London. The dean and chapter
of St Martin-le-Grand were proposing to build a free chapel of
St Leonard within the boundaries of the churchyard ('atrium') of
the church of St Martin-le-Grand for those parishioners who had
been in the habit of attending divine service and receiving the
sacraments at the altar of St Leonard inside the church of
St Martin-le-Grand itself. The bishop of London and the dean
and chapter of St Paul's intervened to prevent a chapel from
being established outside the jurisdiction of the diocese; an
agreement was drawn up between 1229 and 1241 whereby
the building of the new church was to proceed, but the whole
parish of St Leonard (to be known as St Leonard in St Vedast's
Lane or, later, as St Leonard Fosterlane) was to worship within

---

[1] See Appendix I. The church of Witham is noted as appropriated to the
chapter of St Martin-le-Grand in *Taxatio*, p. 22.

[2] W.A.M., MS 13248: original bull addressed to the dean and chapter (incipit:
'Solet annuere sedes apostolica'), dated Lateran 5 March 1221.

the chapel as in a parish church, the rector was to be instituted by the bishop, and along with the ministers and parishioners he was to be entirely subject to the jurisdiction of the bishop and the archdeacon of London. This subjection was specifically stated as bringing in its tow annual visitations due to the cathedral church, the payments of *cathedraticum* and synodals, and all the payments which other parochial churches of London were bound to make.[1] There can thus be no doubt about the intended status of the newly established church of St Leonard. The bishop had given his consent to the construction of a new church only on the understanding that episcopal rights were unimpaired.

But the position of the London churches is not at all straightforward. As soon as the bishops' registers supply us with information it is clear that the bishop of London exercised the right of institution to all seven London churches. The bull of 1144 had noted as possessions of St Martin-le-Grand the church of St Botolph, the church of St Alphege and two churches of St Nicholas.[2] In all four churches—that is, St Botolph without Aldersgate, St Alphege, St Nicholas Coleabbey and St Nicholas at the Shambles—the rectors were in later times presented by the dean of the college to the bishop of London for institution, as the registers show.[3] Likewise, the diocesan possessed the right of institution to the church of St Katherine Coleman.[4] As noted in the *taxatio* of 1291, a part of the spiritual income of these churches was classed as a pension belonging to the canons of St Martin-le-Grand. In most cases the rector's portion was very small. Another church in the city of London, the church of St Anne (or St Agnes) Aldersgate, was also in the patronage of the dean and chapter, at least from the time of Bishop Ralph Baldock,[5] and the bishop also exercised the right of institution here.

[1] *Early Charters of the Cathedral Church of St Paul London*, ed. M. Gibbs (Camden, 3rd ser. lviii, 1939), no. 290, and *Registrum Radulphi Baldock*, ed. R. C. Fowler (CYS, 1911), p. 316.   [2] *Papsturkunden*, i, no. 30.

[3] G. Hennessy, *Novum Repertorium Ecclesiasticum Parochiale Londinense* (London, 1898), pp. 86, 105, 345, 352.

[4] Kempe 1825, p. 201 (and *Taxatio*, p. 19), and G. Hennessy, op. cit., p. 116; and see W. E. Lunt, *The Valuation of Norwich* (Oxford, 1926), pp. 326–7, 331–2.   [5] G. Hennessy, op. cit., pp. 94–5.

Yet despite this control over the appointment of rectors serving the London churches of St Martin-le-Grand, it appears that the bishop failed to exercise full spiritual jurisdiction even in the new church of St Leonard. Together the London churches amounted to a spiritual peculiar of a sort. In 1314 the dean of St Martin-le-Grand excommunicated the 'vicar' of St Botolph without Aldersgate and notified the king in the usual way; the king in his mandate to the sheriff of London referred to the church of St Botolph as immediately subject to the jurisdiction of the royal chapel of St Martin-le-Grand.[1] Later in the fourteenth century a parishioner, Robert de Pleseley, who lived in St Martin-le-Grand's Lane died and the dean claimed probate of his will; the dean's right was only superseded by the archbishop of Canterbury's claim to prerogative jurisdiction on the grounds that Robert had goods in several dioceses of the province.[2] Particularly instructive is a letter, most probably of Edward III, and if so dated at Woodstock 27 May 1336.[3] In this letter the king informed the mayor and sheriff of London of the immunity of St Martin-le-Grand from all ordinary jurisdiction, and he listed the churches which must be free from outside interference: no one must exercise the right of visitation or in any way exercise ordinary jurisdiction by citing, suspending, interdicting or excommunicating the 'canons, vicars, servitors, or parishioners' of St Martin's itself or of any of the seven London churches. Despite the bishop's right of institution to these churches and despite the agreement concerning the new church of St Leonard, their immunity was being defended.

The bishops of London had not failed to exert some authority, both in London and in the church of Witham. But there were other churches attached to the college in which the bishop had established no rights of superior jurisdiction. The church of Witham and the churches in London were all apparently held in

---

[1] Kempe 1825, p. 92 (wrongly dated) and W.A.M., Book 5, fo. 21v.

[2] *Registrum Simonis de Langham*, ed. A. C. Wood (CYS, 1956), pp. 355–9.

[3] W.A.M., Book 5, fo. 16v. The letter begins: 'Cum capella nostra S. Martini Magni Lond' una cum prebendis et capellis eidem annexis et in privilegiis specialiter contentis libera sit et ab omni iurisdictione ordinaria exempta penitus et immunis et iurisdictioni ministrorum nostrorum subiecta. . . .'

common by the canons. But the churches of Newport, Chrishall
and St Mary Maldon (all in Essex) had been prebendal churches
from the time of the constitution of the prebends in 1158.[1] The
church of Newport was part of one prebend (held by the dean);[2]
the church of Chrishall part of another; and the land and tithes of
the church of Maldon formed another (held by two canons,[3] and
later known as the prebend of Keten in Maldon).[4] In addition,
four prebends (which appear to have become five by 1291) had
been established in the parish of Good Easter.[5] Perhaps one of
these four was regarded as a prebend with cure of souls;[6] in any
case, it seems clear that all ecclesiastical jurisdiction in the church
of Good Easter remained in the hands of St Martin-le-Grand.[7] As
later evidence confirms time and again, the churches of Newport,
Chrishall and St Mary Maldon remained outside the jurisdiction

[1] L. Voss, op. cit., pp. 151–2, and Kempe 1825, pp. 65–7.

[2] Although the assessment of 1254 assigns a vicarage of five marks to Newport, it was not a perpetual vicarage ordained by the diocesan: 'sed non est
constituta ab episcopo, et ideo nullus vicarius, sed capellanus serviens pro
predictis v marcis' (W. E. Lunt, *The Valuation of Norwich*, p. 351).

[3] And see *Taxatio*, p. 21.

[4] *Registrum S. de Sudbiria*, ed. R. C. Fowler, i, 32 and ii, 159.

[5] L. Voss, op. cit., p. 151, Kempe 1825, p. 66, W. E. Lunt, *The Valuation
of Norwich*, p. 362, and *Taxatio*, p. 16.

[6] One of the prebends, called 'Imbert' in Good Easter, was a 'beneficium
non curatum' (*Registrum S. de Sudbiria*, ii, 173). Another of the prebends was
held in 1291 by 'Bertham de Gors' (*Taxatio*, p. 16), probably the future Pope
Clement V; and another was held by John of Caen in 1291 and this prebend
was later called 'Faucons' (*Reg. Sudbiria*, ii, 149) or 'Fawkeners' (P. Morant,
The History and Antiquities of Essex (London, 1768), ii, 458).

[7] R. Newcourt, *Repertorium Ecclesiasticum*, ii, 233, is explicit on this score,
but the evidence which he cites (St Paul's Cathedral, W.D.9 ('Statuta Majora'),
fo. 88r) is not quite so explicit. This section of Register W.D.9 is the 'Registrum Fulconis Basset Quondam London Episcopi' which consists of a list of
the churches of the diocese. The item for Good Easter refers to the four canons
having prebends in this parish and retaining their tithes 'ad fabricam ecclesie
beati Martini'. It is noted, however, that here, as also in the church of St
Mary Maldon (fo. 63v) and in the church of Newport (fo. 75r), there was no
vicar as such. A certain Thomas (no doubt the chaplain) paid two and a half
marks to the four canons from the fruits of the church, which was valued at
ten marks.

of the ecclesiastical ordinaries. Later disputes concerning the freedom of St Martin-le-Grand were infrequent, but they resulted in
forceful statements of the royal claim that the college and its
prebendal churches were completely exempt from ordinary jurisdiction.[1] It is a striking fact that so many of St Martin's churches
had been on royal demesne; but this condition alone was no safe-
guard against the exercising of episcopal rights, for as the Domesday survey shows there was a royal manor not only at Maldon
and at Newport[2] but also at Witham, where Edward the Elder
had founded a burgh.[3] The churches of Maldon, Newport,
Chrishall and most probably Good Easter remained free because
of their association with a royal chapel. But this college, which
was in a real sense the creation of the Anglo-Normans, was not
a typical royal free chapel. Although we know little of its early
history, it had gained its lands and its churches in much the same
way as the newly established monasteries. The fact that it was in
London singled it out. It was developing a peculiarly close attach-
ment to the royal household, becoming a place of administrative
and judicial business and 'a corporation of officials rather than a
religious house'.[4] A royal letter of protection was to describe it, in
1255, as 'freer than his other chapels in England'.[5] Was, then,
St Martin-le-Grand the only royal chapel that had secured the
exemption not merely of its college but also of its prebendal
churches? The question can only be answered by looking at the
early history of other royal free chapels.

[1] See Prynne iii, 223, 1288, *Select Cases Exchequer of Pleas*, ed. H. Jenkinson
and B. E. R. Formoy (Selden Soc., 48), pp. 133-4, *CCR 1288-96*, pp. 304-5,
CCR 1302-7, pp. 72-3, 530, *Register of Wm. Ginsborough*, ed. J. W. Willis-Bund
(Worcestershire Historical Soc., 1907), pp. 203-4, and *VCH* London,
i, 558-9.

[2] *DB*, ii, 5b, 7a.

[3] *DB*, ii, 1b, and R. H. Britnell, 'The making of Witham', *History Studies*,
i (1968), 13.

[4] T. F. Tout, *Chapters*, ii, 15 (and see vi, 318-9), F. M. Powicke, *Henry III
and the Lord Edward* (Oxford, 1947), p. 713, n. 3, and G. A. Williams, *Medieval
London* (London, 1963), p. 26.

[5] *CPR 1247-58*, p. 400, Kempe 1825, p. 39, and W.A.M., Book 5, fo. 15r.

Wolverhampton

While the chapels of the diocese of Coventry and Lichfield need to be studied as a group, for all of them except Wolverhampton there is very little accessible evidence to shed light upon their early privileges and status. It was not until the second half of the thirteenth century that there was an insistent and unmistakable claim that each one of these colleges, with the exception of Gnosall, was completely exempt from the jurisdiction of the ordinary. That these claims were largely defensive and not wholly novel can hardly be doubted; but for the twelfth century the college of Wolverhampton must, at present, be taken as the one test case.

The minster of Wolverhampton had been well endowed in 994 by lady Wulfrun,[1] but little is known of its pre-Conquest history, especially since the charter of Edward the Confessor granting freedom to the priests there is spurious.[2] Between 1074 and 1085 William the Conqueror gave the church of Wolverhampton to his chaplain, Samson,[3] 'cum terra et omnibus aliis rebus et con-suetudinibus sicut melius predicta ecclesia habuit tempore regis Edwardi'.[4] The canons held most of their land in alms directly from the Crown, and they were to claim in a letter to Pope Eugenius III (1145–53) that William had given Wolverhampton to Samson as a church which belonged fully to the Crown ('sicut illam que proprie et absolute ad coronam regiam pertine-bat').[5] After Samson became bishop of Worcester, the church was given by him to the prior and monks of Worcester. Whatever privileges the church possessed remained intact, for Henry I gave his consent to the grant whereby the prior and monks were to hold the church 'with its lands and possessions as liberally and

---

[1] For what follows, see esp. Styles 1936, pp. 58–69, 80–5, and *The Chartulary of Worcester Priory (Register I)*, ed. R. R. Darlington (*PRS*, new ser., xxxviii), pp. xlvii–xlix, 138–41.

[2] F. E. Harmer, *Anglo-Saxon Writs* (Manchester, 1952), pp. 403–7.

[3] See V. H. Galbraith, 'Notes on the career of Samson bishop of Worcester (1096–1112)', *EHR*, lxxxii (1967), esp. 88, 90.

[4] *Regesta* i, no. 210 (= xxvi), and see *The Chartulary of Worcester Priory*, p. xlviii, n. 1.   [5] Ibid., no. 267.

freely as William gave them to Samson'. Of particular interest is
the confirmation made in 1102 × 1113 by the bishop of Coventry
Robert de Limesey, for he conceded that the monks of Worcester
should hold the church 'by perpetual right and without any perturbation'. If this was not actually interpreted as a direct grant
of immunity from the bishop's control, then it at least prepared
the way for immunity. And the terms of the grant are also an
early indication that the king's own chapels were regarded as
having a distinct and unmistakable status of their own: 'hec
quidem ecclesia de Wlfr[unehamptona] una erat antiquitus de
propriis regiis capellis que ad coronam spectabant'.[1]

Roger of Salisbury unjustly held the college for a time, and
then Roger de Clinton, bishop of Coventry; but King Stephen
restored it to Worcester probably between 1148 and 1153,[2] taking
care to ensure that no rights had been lost to the bishop of
Coventry. Before the accession of Henry II, Wolverhampton had
reverted to the Crown, and Henry granted to the church all the
freedom which it had enjoyed in the time of Henry I. The royal
chapel of Wolverhampton was declared to be free and exempt
from all customs and exactions: '. . . precipio ut eadem ecclesia,
capella mea, libera sit et quieta ab omnibus consuetudinibus et
exactionibus cum omnibus pertinentiis suis, et canonici omnia sua
libere et quiete possideant, ne quis eis dampnum vel molestiam
vel injuriam aliquam facere presumat'.[3] A letter from Peter of
Blois to Pope Innocent III sheds further light upon the position of
Wolverhampton.[4] Peter had resigned as dean because of the
complete indiscipline of the canons and in expectation of the conversion of the church into a Cistercian abbey. The preamble to his
letter is of interest: 'I was the dean of the church of Wolverhampton in the diocese of Chester, which, however, was not
accountable nor subject to any pontiff, except to the archbishop of

---

[1] *The Chartulary of Worcester Priory*, no. 265.

[2] Ibid., no. 263, and *Regesta* iii, no. 969.

[3] *Recueil des Actes de Henri II*, ed. L. Delisle and E. Berger (Paris, 1909-27),
i, 66, and *Regesta* iii, no. 962.

[4] *Patrologia Latina*, ed. J. P. Migne, 207, ep. clii (partly translated in Styles
1936, pp. 67-8); and see C. R. Cheney, *Hubert Walter* (London, 1967), p. 154.
The letter did not escape Prynne's notice (i, 1167-8).

Canterbury and the king. For by a most ancient custom, considered by many as a right, the kings of England always possessed the donation of the deanery. To the dean belonged the donation of and institution to the prebends.' The claim that the church was subject only to the archbishop and the king, however reminiscent of a closer alliance of the interests of archbishop and king than now obtained, need not surprise us. In other cases exemption from the diocesan did not necessarily imply exemption from the metropolitan. In the early bulls of exemption for St Etienne of Caen and for Bury St Edmunds the authority of the metropolitan had been reserved;[1] and the exempt abbey of Evesham was stated in a bull of Innocent III to be under the protection of the archbishop of Canterbury, and here the archbishop retained the right to visit.[2] The letter of Peter of Blois, while in the nature of a supplication for the pope's blessing upon the changes at Wolverhampton, undoubtedly implies that the church as a royal college was outside the jurisdiction of the diocesan.

The privileges enjoyed by Wolverhampton were clarified in 1224—not, of course, by a papal bull, but by an agreement between the dean, Giles of Erdington, and the new bishop of Coventry, Alexander Stavensby.[3] The agreement was certainly a confirmation of freedom. The right of the dean to present and institute to the prebends and to correct the clergy within his parish and the freedom of the church from the payment of procurations were acknowledged; but the college was certainly not to be isolated completely from the diocese. In some important particulars the bishop's authority was recognised: the bishop was to receive canonical obedience from the dean; oil and chrism were to be provided by the bishop, who was to receive the customary payment on the occasion of the pentecostal procession; the bishop was to be free to 'celebrate, preach, confirm and enjoin public penance' in the church; and in the exercise of ecclesiastical law not only were matrimonial cases and cases concerning sacrilege reserved to him, but also his court was to act as a court

[1] Lemarignier 1937, pp. 145, 147.
[2] *Letters of Innocent III*, ed. C. R. and Mary G. Cheney, no. 675, and Cheney 1931, p. 47.   [3] Appendix II.

of appeal. And the church was not exempt from the payment of Peter's pence. At Wolverhampton, as elsewhere, compromise was necessary. Receiving canonical obedience and providing oil and chrism, the bishop had certainly not lost all his rights in the church. From a legal point of view a gap had not been made in the diocese. But from a practical point of view the church was in many essentials free. While Wolverhampton was to have a smoother history than many other chapels, even here the solution was not an easy one. The balance between the exercise of freedom from episcopal customs and the prevention of the dismemberment of the diocese was always a fine one. Not every bishop would agree 'to put away all ill-feeling' towards the church and its clergy; and the claims of complete freedom from the diocesan became more and more insistent.

Bosham

The history of the college of Bosham in Sussex, which begins in the seventh century, provides another quite distinct example of the development of a royal chapel.[1] In pre-Conquest times Bosham was 'one of the greatest non-episcopal churches'.[2] Its lands had apparently been rated at 147 hides, and its parish was the hundred of Bosham. It was given by Edward the Confessor to his Norman chaplain, Osbern, who still held it after he became bishop of Exeter in 1072, and it was served by a group of royal priests. It became the centre of a separate honour,[3] with the whole chapelry held of the king in return for a *servitium debitum* of seven and a half knights.[4] Not until 1320 was the chapel declared free of scutage.[5] Apart from a brief period when it was held by Arnulf of Lisieux,[6] the bishops of Exeter retained possession of the

[1] For what follows, see especially *VCH Sussex*, ii, 109–12, iv, 182–7.

[2] Barlow 1963, p. 190, and see R. V. Lennard, *Rural England, 1086–1135*, p. 398. [3] *Regesta* ii, no. 1872.

[4] *VCH Sussex*, iv, 185, and H. M. Chew, *The English Ecclesiastical Tenants-in-Chief* (Oxford, 1932), pp. 4–5.

[5] *Cal. Charter Rolls*, iii, 431 (see *Report on MSS in Various Collections* (HMC, 55), iv, 9), and *CCR 1318–23*, p. 277.

[6] Dom. A. Morey, *Bartholomew of Exeter* (Cambridge, 1937), pp. 32, 42.

church throughout the middle ages. The bishop of Exeter possessed the patronage of the church and was himself regarded as the dean of Bosham. Strictly speaking, each prelate exercised rights at Bosham as a royal chaplain, not as bishop of Exeter.[1]

At the beginning of the thirteenth century documentary evidence sheds light upon the position at Bosham, and a fascinating picture emerges. It is clear, from the first, that the bishops of Chichester—and Chichester itself is only three and a half miles from Bosham—had not failed to make their authority felt in the parish of Bosham. As King John's charter of 1200 indicates, there was no doubt that the *capellaria* of Bosham was, by the king's gift, in the hands of the bishops of Exeter.[2] But the bishop of Chichester nevertheless claimed that the church was subject to his own diocesan jurisdiction, and the king himself confirmed (on 27 June 1204) that the gift of the chapelry to the bishops of Exeter was not in any way intended to prejudice the diocesan rights of the bishops of Chichester in the church of Bosham and its appurtenances.[3] This unusual and unexpected statement seems to betray the lack, as yet, of any consistent royal policy towards the royal chapels. Or perhaps the fact that Bosham was not held in free alms cast serious doubts upon any pretensions as a demesne chapelry. Bosham—permanently in the hands of a tenant-in-chief—was not seen in the same light as St Martin-le-Grand or Wolverhampton. On the other hand, it is probably significant that the new bishop of Chichester, Simon FitzRobert, consecrated 11 July 1204, had been in the service of Hubert Walter and of the king.[4] To allow the local bishop to exercise ordinary jurisdiction in the parish of Bosham was to create an extremely difficult situation. The college itself was free from episcopal interference; to this extent royal policy was unmistakable. But the nave of the collegiate church

---

[1] It is thus incorrect to mark the chapelry as a peculiar of Exeter: see the *Map of Monastic Britain* (south sheet) (Ordnance Survey, 1954), on which very few of the royal peculiars are marked.

[2] *Rot. Chartarum*, p. 40, and see *Letters of Inn. III*, no. 405.

[3] *Rot. Lit. Pat.*, p. 43b, *Chichester Chartulary*, p. 302, and Prynne iii, 7.

[4] H. Mayr-Harting, *The Bishops of Chichester, 1075-1207* (The Chichester Papers, no. 40, 1963), p. 17.

was the parish church, and the vicar of the parish church was the vicar of one of the canons of the college. The dispute at the very beginning of the thirteenth century[1] was resolved by an agreement (1204 × 1206) between the two bishops, with Bishop Eustace of Ely acting as mediator.[2]

The agreement concerning the college of Bosham was in the diocesan's favour; it is a clear reflection of papal policy towards a bishop's authority. The problem was how to reconcile the exercising of a double authority at Bosham. It was agreed that the chapelry, 'cum omni populo suo et ministris suis et possessionibus et pertinentiis eius in Cicestrensi diocesi', should be subject to the ordinary jurisdiction of the bishop of Chichester, with the exception only of the canons of the church. Jurisdiction over the canons was to be exercised by the bishop of Exeter, who was to collate to the prebends and correct faults. Although the college was free, the cure of souls was reserved to the diocesan. But this dividing line between the two jurisdictions could never in practice be an easy one to respect. The canons, it was stated, were to attend the synods of the bishop of Chichester. Any canon who had cure of souls (and the parishes of Chidham, Funtington and Appledram were annexed to prebends and served by vicars or chaplains)[3] owed obedience to the bishop of Chichester, and the canon who had the obventions of the parish of Bosham owed an annual procuration to the archdeacon of Chichester. While the bishop of Exeter was given cognisance of civil actions between the canons, the bishop of Chichester was given cognisance of any criminal action brought against a canon. The agreement distinguished between the parish church of Bosham and the secular college of Bosham; but the situation invited further disputes, and these were to begin in earnest early in the fourteenth century[4]

---

[1] *Annales Monastici*, ed. H. R. Luard (RS, 1864–9), ii, 255.

[2] *Acta of Chichester 1075–1207*, ed. H. Mayr-Harting (CYS, 1964), no. 149.

[3] *Chichester Chartulary*, p. 313, and *The Liber Epistolaris of Richard de Bury*, ed. N. Denholm-Young (Roxburghe Club, 1950), p. 113.

[4] See esp. *The Register of W. de Stapeldon*, ed. F. C. Hingeston-Randolph, passim, *The Register of John Grandisson*, ed. F. C. Hingeston-Randolph, passim, and *Select Cases in the Court of King's Bench*, ed. G. O. Sayles (Selden Soc., 74), iv, 111–22.

after the policy of complete exemption for the royal chapels had been fully worked out by Henry III and Edward I. At the beginning of the thirteenth century the college alone, and not the deanery, was free. While the king had referred to Bosham as 'nostra capellaria', he had made no claim as yet concerning the freedom of the whole chapelry, its people and its ministers, from the jurisdiction of the bishop of Chichester. And the composition of 1204 × 1206 was, for the time being, an acceptable solution.

Bromfield

Some secular colleges became Augustinian or Benedictine houses. Four examples of royal chapels which did not remain collegiate (the priories of Bromfield, St Oswald's Gloucester and St Martin's Dover, and the abbey of Waltham) will illustrate the changes which obedience to a rule implied. On the whole the maxim 'once royal demesne always royal demesne'[1] seems to have held good for the demesne chapels. The church of Bromfield with its twelve canons was a secular college of some note in the late Anglo-Saxon period.[2] A writ of Edward the Confessor of 1060 × 1061 had safeguarded the church from any kind of interference; what is so interesting about this grant is that the college was specifically protected from episcopal interference: 'And I will not suffer anyone to take anything therefrom, neither bishop nor any other person, save whomsoever they may themselves desire.' If genuine, this is the earliest known direct reference to the freedom of a royal free chapel from the interference of the local bishop. But the clause is so unusual that it cannot fail to arouse suspicions, and the possibility that it was interpolated is increased by the fact that the writ survives only in a late copy, entered into the register of Bishop Swinfield (1283–1317) at a time when the

---

[1] F. Pollock and F. W. Maitland, *The History of English Law* (Cambridge, 1923), i, 385.

[2] Barlow 1963, pp. 135, 239n, R. V. Lennard, *Rural England*, pp. 396–7, and F. E. Harmer, 'A Bromfield and Coventry writ of King Edward the Confessor' in *The Anglo-Saxons*, ed. P. Clemoes and presented to B. Dickins (London, 1959), pp. 90–8.

privileges of royal free chapels were much in dispute.[1] The
specific reference to freedom from the bishop is more unusual
than Miss Harmer has implied,[2] and the nearest parallel seems to
be the clause in the charter of William I to St Martin-le-Grand.[3]
But in the absence of further contemporary charters to royal
minsters it is probably unreasonable to expect comparable
clauses. And in the final analysis it is difficult to challenge the
writ's authenticity if the grant of freedom from the bishop is
itself credible.[4]

It was in 1155 that Bromfield became a Benedictine priory and
a cell of St Peter's Gloucester.[5] The terms of Henry II's gift[6] of his
church of St Mary Bromfield to the prior and monks of Bromfield
are significant. The church was still to be held in free alms of the
king and of his heirs 'sicut meam dominicam capellam'. The prebendaries (as, for example, 'Fredericus clericus de Bureford, et
Robertus Colemon de Pautesburi, et Edricus presbiter de Brum-
feld, et Robertus presbiter de Feltuna') were to continue to hold

---

[1] Harmer, *ubi supra*, pp. 101–2, and *Registrum Ricardi de Swinfield*, ed. W. W.
Capes (CYS, 1909), p. 425

[2] Op. cit., 96.   [3] Above, pp. 30–1.   [4] Below, pp. 137–8.

[5] The mention of canons still at Bromfield in 1155 (A. Saltman, *Theobald
Archbishop of Canterbury*, p. 336) indicates that the house had not become
Benedictine before this date. The suggested foundation date of 1105 in *Monasticon*, i, 537 and n. c., is a misprint for 1155 (see R. Atkyns, *Gloucestershire*
(London, 1712), p. 129); and the 1115 suggested by D. H. S. Cranage (*Churches
in Shropshire* (Wellington, 1901), i, 170) is derived from a reference (unspeci-
fied) to Osbert, prior of Bromfield. The early mention of a prior of Bromfield
(see R. W. Eyton, *Antiquities of Shropshire* (London, 1854–60), v, 210) presents
a problem, and suggests either that confusion has arisen between Bromfield
and Brimpsfield, or that the college had already become a priory of Augustinian
canons, or that there was a priory at Bromfield before the college was merged
with it in 1155. At least we can be confident that the gift by Henry II (see next
note) of his church to the prior and monks at Bromfield and the gift (in 1155)
by the canons of their church to St Peter's Gloucester refer to two necessary
and closely consecutive stages in the transformation of the community of canons
into a Benedictine priory dependent upon St Peter's Abbey.

[6] *Historia et Cartularium Monasterii Sancti Petri Gloucestriae*, ed. W. H. Hart
(RS, 1863–7), ii, 213–6 (and *Monasticon*, iv, 155, *Cal. Charter Rolls*, i, 210,
and *Registrum R. de Swinfield*, pp. 425–6); and see R. W. Eyton, op. cit., v,
211–2.

their prebends for life; but at their deaths the prebends were to revert 'ad proprios usus et dominium predictae capellae et fratrum illius loci, cum omnibus libertatibus, et quietantiis, et liberis consuetudinibus et regiis dignitatibus'. 'Free customs and royal privileges' is certainly a striking phrase. The king confirmed the complete freedom of the lands belonging to the chapel and ordered the protection of all its possessions 'sicut meas dominicas et proprias res'. Although the abbey of Gloucester was not an exempt house, it thus possessed a dependent cell which was exempt because of its status as a royal chapel. At about the time of Henry II's confirmation of the gift of the church to the prior and monks, the bishop of Hereford, Gilbert Foliot, conceded that the church was exempt from his own jurisdiction: 'Because this church is the king's own demesne chapel, the king desires and orders that it should enjoy complete freedom like the other entirely similar chapels in England. And the king does not permit me to exercise any jurisdiction over the said prior or any successor to him, nor to collect procurations except by permission of the prior should I happen to pass through that place.'[1]

In 1155 Robert of Haseley, a monk of Gloucester, became both prior and parson ('persona') of Bromfield.[2] Although it was a few years before all the canons of Bromfield died[3] and the changes of 1155 finally took effect, a distinction between the priory of Bromfield and the parish of Bromfield probably followed directly upon those changes. The description of the prior as parson of Bromfield has been taken to imply that the prior himself served the parish.[4] But a parson was a rector, often a corporate rector: to take only one example, a contemporary letter, probably from Archbishop Theobald, describes the canons of

---

[1] *The Letters and Charters of Gilbert Foliot*, ed. A. Morey and C. N. L. Brooke (Cambridge, 1967), no. 303 (and *Registrum R. de Swinfield*, p. 426); and see A. Morey and C. N. L. Brooke, *Gilbert Foliot and His Letters* (Cambridge, 1965), p. 223 (but the priory was certainly not 'made a royal chapel... by Henry II').

[2] *The Letters and Charters of G. Foliot*, loc. cit.

[3] *Materials Becket*, ed. J. C. Robertson, v, 401–2.

[4] M. Chibnall, 'Monks and pastoral work: a problem in Anglo-Norman history', *Journal of Ecclesiastical History*, xviii (1967), 170n.

St Martin-le-Grand as the parson of the church of Maldon.[1]
And it is possible—in both these cases perhaps likely—that the
parson appointed a clerk to serve the parish. Bulls of 1190 and
1191 permitted the appropriation of the church of Bromfield to
the priory,[2] and a vicarage was ordained in the church. While we
learn that the prior retained possession of the church,[3] it was the
abbot and convent of Gloucester who were the patrons, for it was
they who presented to the vicarage.[4] The church of Bromfield
had become a vicarage which was subject to episcopal visitation[5]
and to which the bishop of Hereford instituted.

The parish of Bromfield had quickly lost its freedom from the
bishop, but the priory of Bromfield held on to its privileges as a
royal chapel for some time. In the new age of episcopal visitation
these privileges became more and more difficult to support. In
1350 the official of the court of Canterbury cited the bishop of
Hereford to appear before the court of Arches for proposing to
visit Bromfield which as a royal free chapel was stated to be
subject only to the spiritual jurisdiction of the abbot of Gloucester
and of the pope. But five years later an agreement was made
between the abbot and bishop (the pope was in no way party to
the agreement) to bring an end to the disputes about the bishop's
right to visit the priory. Evidence had been found showing that
two bishops, Thomas Cantilupe and Richard Swinfield, had
visited the priory, and without any mention that the house was a
royal chapel—and apparently without any interference from the

---

[1] A. Saltman, *Theobald Abp. of Cant.*, p. 394.

[2] *Historia et Cartularium*, iii, 11, 15.

[3] *Registrum J. de Trillek*, ed. J. H. Parry (CYS, 1912), p. 228, *Registrum E. Lacy*, ed. J. H. Parry and A. T. Bannister (CYS, 1918), p. 78 and *Registrum T. Spofford*, ed. A. T. Bannister (CYS, 1919), p. 23.

[4] *Registrum R. de Swinfield*, p. 525, *Registrum L. de Charltone*, ed. J. H. Parry (CYS, 1914), p. 69 and *Registrum R. Mascall*, ed. J. H. Parry (CYS, 1917), p. 187. The relationship between the dependent priory and the abbey was not a settled one. In 1325 the abbot of Gloucester petitioned the king, it seems without success, for the monks of the priory of Bromfield to be allowed to live in the abbey of Gloucester itself, and the king ordered a full inquiry into the condition and rights of the priory: *Rotuli Parliamentorum*, i, 436.

[5] *Registrum J. de Trillek*, pp. 155-6.

king—the abbot agreed that the bishop should be allowed to exercise rights of visitation there.[1] In this small and remote monastery ancient rights, now of no advantage to the king, were apparently allowed to lapse. As far as spiritual jurisdiction was concerned, Bromfield had eventually lost all sight of its traditional status.

St Oswald's Gloucester

Two other colleges which became priories—St Oswald's Gloucester and St Martin's Dover—did not lose sight of their privileges. The early history of both these houses is obscure, but their later claims to be royal free chapels had historical foundation. The history of St Oswald's Gloucester has been unravelled by A. Hamilton Thompson.[2] It was built as a monastery in the reign of King Alfred by Ethelred, ealdorman of the Mercians, and Aethelflaed, daughter of King Alfred, and the body of Oswald, king of Northumbria, was lodged there.[3] At the beginning of the fourteenth century the prior of St Oswald claimed that the church of York possessed an original charter of the first year of King Athelstan (924 or 925) which granted the house complete freedom and confirmed that it had been founded and built by Ethelred.[4] The monks were apparently driven away from the monastery, and were replaced by canons some time after 972, when Oswald, as archbishop of York, also held the see of Worcester.[5]

The link between St Oswald's and the archbishops of York no doubt goes back in the first place to the close ties between the two sees. When Archbishop Ealdred withdrew from exercising direct jurisdiction in the diocese of Worcester in 1062, he retained

---

[1] *Reg. J. de Trillek*, pp. 236–40.

[2] See Hamilton Thompson 1921, which supersedes the account in *VCH Glouc.*, ii, 84–7.

[3] Hamilton Thompson 1921, p. 129 (and see p. 91), citing *Willelmi Malmesbiriensis Monachi de Gestis Pontificum*, ed. N. E. S. A. Hamilton (RS, 1870), pp. 263n, 293, and *Symeonis Monachi Opera Omnia*, ed. T. Arnold (RS, 1882–5), i, 369–70.

[4] *Select Cases King's Bench*, ed. G. O. Sayles, iii, 141–2.

[5] *Willelmi Malmesbiriensis*, loc. cit.

E

for himself and his successors twelve vills from the lands of the see of Worcester ('de episcopatu Wigorniae'); 'in this appropriation', wrote Thompson, 'we have the primary origin of the peculiar jurisdiction of the archbishops of York in Gloucestershire.'[1] But at this stage the college itself does not appear to have been in the hands of the archbishop of York, and at least some of the manors which Archbishop Ealdred held had belonged to the abbey of St Peter.[2] Land which had formerly belonged to St Oswald's and which was in the hands of the archbishop of York in 1086 had passed from Stigand, archbishop of Canterbury, to Thomas, archbishop of York. The entry in Domesday Book gives precise information only about the manor of Swindon; but the fact that the priory had appropriated to it at a later date the churches (or rather chapels), for example, of Churchdown, Norton and Compton Abdale,[3] indicates that St Oswald's had probably held the manors of the same names before they passed first to Archbishop Stigand, then to Archbishop Thomas.[4] The college, in common with other similar churches,[5] had suffered a decline in its landed wealth. It held two small manors (Widford and North Cerney) from the archbishop of York as tenant-in-chief, and was otherwise left in possession only of the property adjacent to the church itself, along with its small prebends.[6]

St Oswald's, greatly depleted, seems to have remained in royal hands until William Rufus (c. 1093) gave the church with all its rights to the archbishop of York and his successors.[7] While H. W. C. Davis regarded the charter of c. 1093 as spurious, there is no reason to doubt that William II gave the church to the archbishop of York. The gift was ratified by Paschal II, and the

---

[1] Hamilton Thompson 1921, p. 87.   [2] *DB*, i, 164v.

[3] *The Register of Wm. Greenfield*, ed. A. Hamilton Thompson, i, 206.

[4] See also Hamilton Thompson 1921, p. 94, and C. S. Taylor, *An Analysis of the Domesday Survey of Gloucestershire* (Bristol & Gloucs. Archaeological Soc., 1887), pp. 94–5.

[5] St Oswald's can be added to R. V. Lennard's list of minsters and collegiate churches in decline: *Rural England, 1086–1135*, app. IV.

[6] Hamilton Thompson 1921, p. 95.

[7] *Regesta* i, no. 341, and *Early Yorkshire Charters*, i, ed. W. Farrer (Yorks. Archaeological Soc., Record Ser., Extra Ser., 1914), 116–17.

archbishops were confirmed in their possession of the house by a succession of bulls during the twelfth century.[1] While it is no doubt true to maintain that St Oswald's and the churches belonging to it now 'came under the direct jurisdiction of the archbishops of York and formed an outlying part of their diocese',[2] it seems clear that the archbishops' rights over the college and its annexed chapels were exercised by reason of their guardianship of a royal chapel. St Oswald's was comprised essentially of spiritual rights, whereas the lands transferred at an earlier date to the church of York formed the temporal barony of Churchdown.[3] And however much the archbishops possessed St Oswald's as their own, the church and its parish remained until the dissolution of the monasteries a royal peculiar.[4] Henry I gave (1108 × 1111) some of the land belonging to the canons to the sheriff of Gloucestershire, Walter of Gloucester, and ordered Walter to give in exchange equivalent land from the royal demesne.[5] When Henry I confirmed (1106 × 1135) St Oswald's in the possession of the schools of the whole of Gloucester (by which was probably meant possession of the 'ius scholarum'), a gift made to the church by the bishops of Worcester, he referred to St Oswald's specifically as 'mea capella'.[6]

The college was apparently well maintained by Archbishop Thurstan (1119–1140),[7] but before its conversion by Archbishop Murdac into an Augustinian priory in 1152 or 1153 it seems to have suffered a decline in its collegiate organisation. Archbishop Murdac chose as head of the newly founded priory a canon from

[1] *The Register of Wm. Greenfield*, i, 215–18, *Historians of the Ch. of York*, ed. J. Raines (RS, 1879–94), iii, 28, 41–3, 85, and *Regesta Pontificum Romanorum*, ed. P. Jaffé and S. Loewenfeld (Leipzig, 1885–8), nos. 6831, 7227, 12871; and see *Anglia Sacra*, ed. H. Wharton (1691), i, 295.

[2] Hamilton Thompson 1921, p. 98.

[3] Ibid., 101–4.

[4] *Three Chapters of Letters Relating to the Suppression of the Monasteries*, ed. T. Wright (Camden, old ser. 26, 1843), p. 124.

[5] *Ancient Charters*, ed. J. H. Round (PRS, x, 1888), p. 4 (*Regesta* ii, no. 998).

[6] *Regesta* ii, no. 1936.

[7] *Historians of the Ch. of York*, ii, 386, and *Willelmi Malmesbiriensis Gesta Pontificum*, p. 293, cited in *VCH Gloucs.*, ii, 84–5.

the nearby house of Lanthony; two of the secular canons resigned their prebends, two were dispossessed because they had received their prebends from a lay hand, one received a prebend at Beverley, and the sixth became a regular canon at St Oswald's.[1] As a peculiar—in the province of Canterbury, but in the hands of the archbishop of York—St Oswald's was in no easy position. A dispute between the bishop of Worcester and the archbishop of York began during the early years of Henry II's reign. Archbishop Becket took a strong line on the matter, for in a letter to the bishop of Worcester he ordered his suffragan to do nothing concerning the excommunicated men of St Oswald's and to absolve no one, whether at the entreaty of king or cardinal, without the archbishop's advice.[2] The dispute flared up again in 1174, when the status of the priory became a major issue in the conflict between the new archbishop of Canterbury, Richard of Dover, and the archbishop of York, Roger de Pont l'Évêque.[3] When Richard of Dover, as primate and legate, undertook a visitation of his province in 1174 he included St Oswald's priory in his itinerary. The canons there claimed, according to Ralph of Diceto, that they had been exempted from the archbishop's jurisdiction by a special papal decree; if the account is accurate this is a very early indication of the insecurity of the royal free chapels when faced with the need to demonstrate their spiritual freedom. St Oswald's certainly possessed no bull of exemption. Richard of Dover ignored their claim and excommunicated the canons for their contumacy; as a result, Roger de Pont l'Évêque appealed to Rome. This was no simple dispute about rights of visitation. Clearly, St Oswald's posed the problem of primacy. At Winchester in 1175—no doubt with the aid of the newly arrived papal legate, Hugh of Pierleone —the king spent a number of days considering the dispute between the churches of Canterbury and York. These discussions

---

[1] Hamilton Thompson 1921, pp. 98–9, 112–13, 131.

[2] *Materials Becket*, ed. J. C. Robertson, vi, 194.

[3] R. Foreville, *L'Église et la Royauté, 1154–89* (Paris, 1942), pp. 518–19; see *Gesta Regis Henrici Secundi Benedicti Abbatis*, ed. W. Stubbs (RS, 1867), i, 90, 104, and *Radulfi de Diceto . . . Opera Historica*, ed. W. Stubbs (RS, 1876), i, 396.

at Winchester were perhaps of an informal kind, but it was more of a royal than an ecclesiastical occasion; acting on the king's advice, Richard of Dover agreed to absolve the excommunicated clerks of the archbishop of York and to surrender his claim to jurisdiction over St Oswald's. The chapel of St Oswald's was to be regarded as free from his jurisdiction 'sicut dominicam capellam domini regis'.

But the difficulties at St Oswald's could not simply be solved at the highest level. The bishop of Worcester was himself involved. The parishioners of Sandhurst had apparently begun to pay their customary dues and their tithes to the church of Worcester rather than to the church of St Oswald. In three separate letters Henry II protected his 'capellaria'.[1] He ordered that the parishioners of Sandhurst should render all their customary dues to the prior and ministers of St Oswald's, and that, in respect of the rights belonging to his chapelry, no support should be given to the bishop of Worcester in his dispute with the archbishop of York. All the clergy and laity who held lands within the parish of St Oswald, no matter whose lands they were ('de cuiuscumque feudo sint'), should render all rights and tithes to the chapelry. The king was declaring the freedom not just of the priory but of the whole parish; the canons, the clergy and the parishioners were protected from any interference; the chapelry was to enjoy the freedom which it had enjoyed at the time of Henry I.

Historians have noted the peculiarities of the relationship between the priory of St Oswald and the archbishop of York. The canons possessed no rights of election to the office of prior, who was appointed entirely at the discretion of the archbishop of York;[2] this authority he exercised as 'patron and prelate', and in this respect the relation of St Oswald's to the archbishop of York 'seems rather like that of a cathedral priory';[3] in addition, the archbishop's consent was required before new canons were admitted.[4] Such peculiarities are explicable by reason of the status

---

[1] *CPR 1385–9*, pp. 525–6.   [2] Dickinson 1950, p. 160.

[3] Wood 1955, p. 49, n. 1, referring to *The Register of Wm. Wickwane*, ed. W. Brown (Surtees Soc., 114), p. 234.

[4] Wood 1955, p. 111, n. 3.

of this priory; to combine the functions and privileges of a priory of regular canons which remained also a royal free chapel had necessitated deviation from the normal pattern of Augustinian houses. In 1213, during the vacancy of the see of York, the king ordered Engelard de Cicogny (sheriff of Gloucestershire and Herefordshire) and Walter of Clifford (one-time sheriff of Herefordshire) to go to the priory, take the advice of upright men concerning a new prior, and appoint a suitable man to rule the house ('. . . talem sibi priorem constituatis quem idoneum credideritis . . .').[1] Like the deans in other royal chapels the archbishop was guardian of a royal peculiar, and even the title 'patron and prelate' gives no clear indication of the extent of his control over the priory and parish of St Oswald. It would be of great interest to know whether, during the priory's early history, the prior himself was regarded as exercising spiritual jurisdiction in the parish of St Oswald. Certainly the chapels within the parish—the chapels of Churchdown, Norton, Sandhurst and Compton Abdale—were annexed to the priory, and the prior and convent appointed the stipendiary chaplains to serve in them. Sandhurst was served by a 'vicar', but any real distinction between Sandhurst and the other chapels is not apparent. The position of two other churches, at Witcombe and Lassington, is not completely clear;[2] but in 1309 Archbishop Greenfield confirmed that they, along with the other four chapels, were appropriated ('in proprios usus') to the prior and convent.[3] In the middle of the thirteenth century, at the latest, a distinction was made between the office of prior and the care of the parish or deanery, soon to be known as the deanery or jurisdiction of Churchdown. In Archbishop Walter de Gray's visitation ordinances of 1250 it was decreed that the care and custody of the deanery should be committed either to the 'parochial chaplain' or to some other clerk; if a clerk other than the chaplain were appointed, then he should receive the same

---

[1] *Rot. Lit. Claus.*, i, 149b.

[2] Hamilton Thompson 1921, pp. 95–6, 104–5.

[3] *The Register of Wm. Greenfield*, i, 206; and see the bull of Innocent IV in *The Register of Th. of Corbridge*, ed. W. Brown and A. Hamilton Thompson (Surtees Soc., 138, 141), ii, 47–8.

allowance as a canon of the house.[1] The custodian of the deanery was to hold office at the discretion of the archbishop ('secundum arbitrium nostrum'), and, referred to as dean or official or warden of Churchdown, he is soon much in evidence in the registers of the archbishops of York.[2] Spiritual jurisdiction at St Oswald's was thus exercised by both prior and dean on behalf of the archbishop of York.

St Martin's Dover

After 1131 the archbishop of Canterbury was to St Martin's Dover what the archbishop of York was to St Oswald's Gloucester. But St Martin's was in the diocese of Canterbury itself, and disputes concerning the exercise of ordinary jurisdiction (at least, ordinary jurisdiction as exercised by the archbishop as diocesan rather than by the prior or the archdeacon of Canterbury) were therefore out of the question. Chronicle tradition[3] had it that Eadbald (king of Kent, 616–640) had established twenty-two canons, each with his prebend, to serve his chapel in the castle of Dover; in 696 his great-grandson, King Wihtred, moved the canons, their privileges and liberties intact, to a separate church. That the chapel was in a privileged position from its foundation is very likely; but there was some reading back of the attitudes of the twelfth century or later in at least one account of the minster's history: 'Iste rex Edbaldus ordinavit et induxit xxij canonicos seculares in dicto castro Dovorr' . . . nec dicti canonici cuidam ordinario vel prelato fuerant subjecti, excepta curia Romana, nisi domino regi . . .'[4] Nevertheless it must be stressed that the priests established at Dover had been the *familiares* of the king and not of the archbishop; and the king's priests, like priests of other minsters, had served a large *parochia*.[5]

---

[1] *The Register of Walter Giffard*, ed. W. Brown (Surtees Soc., 109), p. 205.

[2] E.g. Hamilton Thompson 1921, p. 116.

[3] *Monasticon*, iv, 533–5, and see *VCH Kent*, ii, 133, and C. R. Haines, *Dover Priory* (Cambridge, 1930), pp. 16–30.

[4] *Monasticon*, iv, 535b.

[5] Barlow 1963, pp. 131, 133, 135, 156–8, and cf. *The Domesday Monachorum*, ed. D. C. Douglas (Royal Hist. Soc., 1944), pp. 9–11.

Unlike the other minsters of Kent, Dover appears as an independent tenant-in-chief in Domesday Book, where an account of the prebends of Dover occupies a prominent position.[1] Before the Conquest they had been held communally and altogether had rendered £61, but Odo of Bayeux had made separate holdings of them. Just how the churches which were attached to the college were related to the prebends is not clear. There appear to have been almost as many churches as canons,[2] and in all probability more of these churches were specifically annexed to prebends than Domesday Book, in its almost complete silence on this score, might lead us to believe. What is of interest is the fact that the church of Dover was not regarded as completely isolated from the jurisdiction of the archbishop of Canterbury. The account in Domesday Book[3] speaks of 55s paid to the archbishop each year by the college. The lists in Domesday Monachorum[4] make it clear that before the Conquest Dover owed to the archbishop one sester of honey, thirty loaves of bread, two sheep, 7d (chrism money)[5] and 600d. These were the 'spiritual' customs; they were commuted by Lanfranc into a single payment during Holy Week of 55s. Here, then, was no freedom from ecclesiastical dues. And William I confirmed Lanfranc in his possession of the customary dues from the church of St Martin.[6] How far the archbishop's rights were safeguarded because of his superior position in the English Church is a matter for debate.

For some time the Anglo-Norman kings retained control of the college of priests at Dover, as the letters of Henry I to Archbishop Anselm and the canons in 1108 illustrate.[7] Henry was eager to ensure that the prebend which had been held traditionally by

[1] *DB*, i, IV-2r (*VCH Kent*, iii, 204-8).

[2] *The Domesday Monachorum*, p. 78, and G. Ward, 'The list of Saxon churches in the Domesday Monachorum and White Book of St Augustine', *Archaeologia Cantiana*, xlv (1933), 68-71.

[3] *DB*, i, 2rb.

[4] *The Domesday Monachorum*, pp. 77, 79.

[5] Ibid., pp. 6-7, and Barlow 1963, pp. 179-82.

[6] *Regesta* i, no. 176, and app. no. xxii.

[7] *Regesta* ii, nos. 878-9, and app. no. lix, and *Historia Monasterii S. Augustini Cantuariensis*, ed. C. Hardwick (RS, 1858), p. 357.

the abbot of St Augustine's Canterbury should not be taken from him; it is perhaps possible to detect here some conflict between the interests of the king in the royal abbey and in the royal college and the interests of the archbishop of Canterbury. Be that as it may, the behaviour of the canons seems to have left much to be desired: 'Les ditz chanoignes, pour lour franchises devindront trop jolifs; qe nul home ne les poait chastier de lour mesfaitz . . .'[1] Archbishop William of Corbeil, a regular canon, pleaded with the king in 1124, so we are told, that something be done to improve the discipline of the secular canons. How much confidence we should have in the accuracy of this early fourteenth-century source is arguable, but the complaint of the archbishop that he could exercise no control over the canons because of the liberties and privileges they had obtained from the king occupies an important position in the story. And we must not assume that the possession of some customary dues by the archbishop implied the free exercise of ecclesiastical censure. In 1131 Henry gave the church at Dover (specifically referred to as 'capella regia' in the account of Gervase of Canterbury)[2] to Archbishop William and his successors.[3] The gift was confirmed with the consent of the king's council in 1132, and ratified by a papal bull.[4] William of Corbeil began the construction of a new priory to house the canons as regulars, near the town of Dover and within the franchise of St Martin's, but died before the work was completed.[5]

The monks of Canterbury had opposed the introduction of regular canons into the church of Dover, and after the death of William of Corbeil in November 1136 they established Benedictine monks in the house.[6] Archbishop Theobald, himself a monk, accepted this changeover, added substantially to the possessions of the house and ordained that it should be a cell of Christ Church

---

[1] *Monasticon*, iv, 533b.

[2] *The Historical Works of Gervase of Canterbury*, ed. W. Stubbs (RS, 1879–80), i, 96 (*Monasticon*, iv, 534b).

[3] *Regesta* ii, no. 1736.

[4] *Monasticon*, iv, 538b (*Regesta Pontificum Romanorum*, ed. P. Jaffé and S. Loewenfeld, no. 7736).

[5] *Monasticon*, iv, 533b, 535.

[6] *The Historical Works of Gervase of Canterbury*, i, 97–9 (*Monasticon*, iv, 535).

Canterbury and that the priors of Dover must be elected from among the monks of Canterbury.[1] From the early years of the history of the Benedictine priory of Dover there was tension concerning the respective roles of the archbishop and the cathedral priory. From one point of view this can be seen as the continuing struggle of the priory of Dover to be independent of the priory of Canterbury; but one aspect of the struggle was related essentially to the desire to be free from ordinary jurisdiction.

The position was complicated not only by the fact that Dover had been made a cell of Canterbury but also by the terms of the grants of both Henry I and Henry II: they had given the church of St Martin both to the archbishop and to the church of Canterbury. On the other hand, some attempt had been made to define the position of the archbishop in relation to the new priory: 'ecclesia in propria manu et dominio et protectione archiepiscoporum sit, tanquam quae sua dominica est'.[2] The archbishops were to exercise direct and personal control over the house as though it were their own demesne chapel; this is reminiscent of the title 'patron and prelate' which attempted to define the status of the archbishops of York in St Oswald's Gloucester. And Archbishop Theobald himself stated that since the archbishop of Canterbury was the 'rector et dispositor' of the cathedral priory it was only just that he should also be in full control of the church of Dover.[3] This is reminiscent of Susan Wood's telling comment that the relation of St Oswald's Gloucester to the archbishop of York was 'rather like that of a cathedral priory'.[4] Henry II's charter of confirmation stated that the archbishop of Canterbury alone should have controlling rights ('dispositionem [aut] ordinationem') in the church of Dover.[5] Hadrian IV's bull of 1155[6] stated the position even

[1] A. Saltman, *Theobald Archbishop of Canterbury*, pp. 75–9, 306–19.

[2] *Monasticon*, iv, 538.

[3] A. Saltman, op. cit., nos. 83–4.

[4] Above, p. 55.

[5] *Monasticon*, iv, 538–9, and *Literae Cantuarienses*, ed. J. B. Sheppard (RS, 1887–9), iii, 371–2; and see *Monasticon*, iv, 536b: the archbishop (Edmund Rich) 'nec etiam considerans predictam ecclesiam alicui subici vel obedire debere nisi domino Cant.'

[6] *Papsturkunden*, ii, no. 89: 'Prohibemus insuper, ut si aliquando episcopalis

more clearly: during a vacancy in the see the prior of Canterbury should have no authority whatever at Dover, except by the archbishop's decree. In addition, a bull of Alexander III[1] forebade any archdeacon or other ecclesiastic to demand any unwonted customs from the church. The priory's sole prelate was the archbishop of Canterbury, and strictly speaking he exercised rights there as donee of a royal peculiar rather than as diocesan. It is an interesting fact that Gregory IX's concession to the priory in 1234[2] is in very similar terms to the grants which the papacy was to make specifically to the royal chapels[3]: '. . . ne quis ordinarius seu delegatus a sede apostolica excommunicationis, suspensionis, vel interdicti sententias, in vos vel monasterium vestrum absque manifesta et rationabili causa proferre audeat, auctoritate praesentium inhibemus, et eas sententias prolatas decernimus irritandas.'

It is revealing to examine briefly the later position of the priory. During the reigns of Edward I and Edward II, at a time when there were many disputes about royal free chapels, the rights of the priory of Dover were under discussion. The problem was the extent to which the jurisdiction of the archbishop of Canterbury as delegated to his archdeacon, and more especially to the prior and convent of Christ Church Canterbury, could be exercised over the priory of Dover. The situation was somewhat obscure to contemporaries, but it was the position of the archbishop as 'patron and prelate' and not as diocesan that was being defended. Some of the details of the dispute are worth recounting, for the situation is in danger of being interpreted quite simply as a

---

sedes vacaverit, prior Cantuariensis ecclesie nullam in predictam ecclesiam de Dovoria habeat potestatem nisi per Cantuariensem archiepiscopum aliquid disponendi seu ordinandi.' And see no. 145.

[1] Ibid., no. 166, and see no. 291.

[2] *Literae Cantuarienses*, iii, 374–5, and see *Monasticon*, iv, 536b. A section of this bull is missing after 'necessaria ministrare'; comparison with *Les Registres de Grégoire IX*, ed. L. Auvray (BEAR, 1896–1955), no. 1807 (addressed to the prior and convent of Canterbury) provides the missing portion: the gift of the church of Guston is the compensation for the amount of hospitality which the house was required to offer.

[3] See above, p. 19, and below, pp. 93, 147.

struggle between the dependent priory of Dover and the priory of Canterbury.

Apparently because of the particular inability of Prior Anselm of Eastry to cope with the administration of the priory of Dover,[1] Edward I intervened there in an attempt to establish a way of having more suitable priors appointed to the house.[2] The chief justice, Ralph of Hengham, recommended that the way out of the difficult situation whereby priors were always appointed from among the monks of Christ Church Canterbury was to summon the prior of Canterbury to answer for his exercise of rights of advowson at Dover. Hengham recognised that this would prevent the interference of the prior of Canterbury in the appointment of priors at Dover, for Christ Church had no claim to advowson. The prior was summoned before the king's court and proceedings opened in 1286.[3] Much to Hengham's distress, the proceedings did not follow the intended course. In his absence one of his fellow justices heard the case and, since the prior produced no claim to advowson, decided that the royal right of advowson should be re-established.[4] The sheriff of Kent was ordered to take custody of the priory. The decision was clearly irregular, for the archbishop's rights had been for the moment overlooked. And this confusion in 1286 was not new, for three years before, after the death of the prior of Dover, a royal custodian had been appointed to take charge of the house. The order had been quickly rescinded in favour of the archbishop's custodian.[5]

As a result of the royal seizure of the priory in 1286, Archbishop Pecham, as also the prior and convent of Canterbury, complained

---

[1] *Monasticon*, iv, 534 (and Prynne iii, 917), and see *The Historical Works of Gervase of Canterbury*, ed. W. Stubbs, ii, 282–3.

[2] *Literae Cantuarienses*, iii, 378.

[3] *Registrum R. Winchelsey*, ed. R. Graham (CYS, 1952–6), p. 681 (as *Rotuli Parliamentorum*, i, 368b, and *CPR 1313-7*, p. 286).

[4] *Literae Cantuarienses*, iii, 378.

[5] *Calendar of Fine Rolls* (HMSO, 1911–), i (1272–1307), 196, *CCR 1279–88*, p. 249, and *Registrum Epistolarum Fratris Johannis Peckham*, ed. C. T. Martin (RS, 1882–5), ii, 666. And the archbishop of Canterbury was again pleading his rights against the king in 1299: *Select Cases Exchequer of Pleas*, ed. H. Jenkinson and B. E. R. Formoy, p. 160.

to the king. The seizure was acknowledged by Hengham as ill-advised, and discussion of the case re-opened probably in April 1287.[1] The situation was now clarified in the king's court. The ordinance of Theobald, whereby Christ Church claimed rights at Dover, was declared to have had no power after the archbishop's death, for it had not been made valid by the king's assent. It was reaffirmed that all rights at Dover were to be exercised by the archbishop, for Henry II's charter, although it was a grant in general terms to the archbishop and the church of Canterbury, itself declared that all rights in the priory—that is, both temporal and spiritual rights—were reserved to the archbishop and his successors.[2] The royal decision did not contravene in any way the attitude which successive popes had taken towards the priory. Although the ordinance of Archbishop Theobald had often been confirmed,[3] it had not been seen as detracting from the authority of the archbishop at Dover. Papal bulls had affirmed that no jurisdiction over Dover should be exercised by the prior and convent of Canterbury.[4] While the royal statement of 1287 was in clear terms, the relationship between the two priories remained a difficult one. Disputes between the houses broke out again during the vacancy of the see (1313–14)[5] and during a vacancy at Dover itself (c. 1318–20).[6] The judgment of 1287 was used to settle both these disputes. But, once again, the recovery of the advowson of the house by the king (in 1320) compelled the archbishop of Canterbury to reclaim his rights.[7] By special grace of the king the house was re-granted to the archbishop, this time with the

---

[1] *Registrum R. Winchelsey*, p. 684, Prynne iii, 1289, *Literae Cantuarienses*, iii, 378–9, and *Registrum Epistolarum Peckham*, iii, 941–2.

[2] *Registrum R. Winchelsey*, pp. 682–3 (as *Rotuli Parliamentorum*, i, 368b–369a, and *CPR 1313–7*, pp. 286–7).

[3] *Papsturkunden*, ii, nos. 110, 136, 220, 291.

[4] Ibid., nos. 89, 145.

[5] *Rotuli Parliamentorum*, i, 326, and *Calendar of Chancery Warrants*, i (HMSO, 1927), 421–2, 428.

[6] Ibid., 495, 506, *Placitorum Abbreviatio* (Record Commission, 1811), p. 335, *Rotuli Parliamentorum*, i, 368–70, *Sel. Cases King's Bench*, ed. G. O. Sayles, V, cxxxi–ii, and Prynne iii, 1305–6.

[7] *Rotuli Parliamentorum*, i, 369b–370a.

proviso that priors for Dover be chosen from the monks of Dover. Relations between the two priories remained strained until a solution was reached in 1350, when an ordinance of Archbishop Islip was confirmed by the king.[1] The priory of Dover is not often described as a royal chapel,[2] but this is perhaps because of its unique position. There could be no conflict here between the 'patron and prelate' and the diocesan or metropolitan. Although in practice the privileges at Dover amounted to very little, and although contemporaries would perhaps have been surprised to think of it as an exempt house, that is in fact what it was. Here, as elsewhere, the king was defending a royal chapel.

But what of the churches belonging to the priory? What of the 'deanery' of the old secular college? Only the closest analysis could unravel in any detail the history of the nineteen churches listed in Domesday Monachorum. But one fact is immediately striking: a large number of these churches are still listed together within the deanery of Dover in the 1291 taxatio.[3] When the secular college had become a monastery the monks occupied a new building, but the old church of St Martin remained a distinct parish church. At least some, and probably all, of the churches and chapels belonging to the secular college passed to the Benedictine priory. By the very nature of the gift of Dover to the archbishop of Canterbury, its churches also, no doubt, enjoyed a special relationship with the archbishop. Many parishes within the diocese of Canterbury—parishes which had been long regarded, it seems, as in the demesne of the archbishop—became exempt parishes: exempt, that is, from the jurisdiction of the archdeacon and from the sede vacante jurisdiction of the prior and convent.[4] The church of St Martin Dover and the church of Deal (which belonged to the priory from at least 1182) were among

---

[1] CPR 1348–50, pp. 508–9.

[2] See Prynne iii, 1304–5, Calendar of Chancery Warrants, i, 421, Sel. Cases King's Bench, V, cxxxi, and above, p. 1.

[3] Taxatio, p. 2b.

[4] For the exempt parishes, see I. J. Churchill, Canterbury Administration (London, 1933), i, 52, 83–94, 109–10, and B. L. Woodcock, Medieval Ecclesiastical Courts in the Diocese of Canterbury (London, 1952), pp. 21–5.

these exempt parishes. The archdeacons of Canterbury were naturally eager to assert their rights, and in 1284 there was a dispute about the exercise of jurisdiction in the parish church of St Martin Dover.[1] But Dover and Deal appear to have remained exempt. In other parish churches belonging to the priory of Dover it may well be that the archdeacons succeeded in exercising ordinary jurisdiction. In 1319 Edward II forbade the archdeacon to exercise any ordinary jurisdiction in the churches with cure of souls belonging to Dover priory, his 'free chapel'; but the archdeacon, Simon Convenis, protested against this prohibition and it was rescinded.[2]

As we might expect, the papacy did not see fit to sanction the exemption from diocesan jurisdiction of the priory's churches; indeed, the bull of 1182 specifically states that the priory's parish churches must be responsible to the diocesan bishop in spiritualities.[3] Certainly this applied to those churches which had been given to the house after it had become a priory. Episcopal rights had been saved, for example, in the church of Hougham,[4] and no doubt also in Appledore and Coldred, which were appropriated to the priory by Archbishop Langton.[5] But some distinction was made between these parish churches and the churches which had belonged to the minster. It is significant that there are continuing references to prebendal churches and even to a canon of St Martin Dover[6] long after the abandonment of the collegiate organisation. The ordinance of Archbishop Islip in 1350 is particularly illuminating.[7] By reason of the churches of Hougham, Appledore and Coldred, the prior and convent of Dover must render canonical obedience to the prior of Christ Church Canterbury, must not prevent the vicars, chaplains or other ministers of these churches from making processions in Christ Church Canterbury every

---

[1] *Registrum Epistolarum Peckham*, iii, 832–3.   [2] Prynne iii, 1304-5.
[3] *Papsturkunden*, ii, no. 220.   [4] A. Saltman, op. cit., p. 317.
[5] *Acta Stephani Langton*, ed. K. Major (CYS, 1950), p. 138. See the list of the priory's churches in *Papsturkunden*, ii, nos. 220, 291, and *Literae Cantuarienses*, iii, 372–4.
[6] *Letters of Inn. III*, ed. C. R. and Mary G. Cheney, no. 125.
[7] CPR *1348–50*, pp. 508–9.

year on the third day in Whitsun week, and must not prevent each vicar from offering 1*d* on that day and from receiving oil and chrism at Canterbury. But the prebendal church of St Martin Dover and the churches and chapels in the town and borough of Dover which were annexed to the prebendal church or dependent upon it had been given to the prior and convent of Dover by royal grant before the foundation of the monastery, and were exempt from the jurisdiction of Christ Church Canterbury. About other churches (including, at this stage, the church of Deal) there was dispute: 'because between the parties there is doubt about the churches of Deal, Buckland, Guston and St Margaret at Cliffe, whether these are prebendal and like the church of St Martin Dover, and [because] the archbishop is not yet informed touching the right of either party, he reserves judgment in this point'. The priory of St Martin's Dover retained a privileged status, as did some of the churches belonging to it. It was a royal free chapel of some distinction.

Waltham Holy Cross

Another royal free chapel of distinction was the abbey of Waltham Holy Cross. To study Waltham in the thirteenth century is to discover no fundamental distinction between the abbey and other exempt abbeys which were royal foundations. But Waltham was undoubtedly a royal free chapel. From its foundation (*c.* 1060) by Earl Harold, out of a gift of land from King Edward,[1] until 1177 this important royal church had been a secular college. In 1177 it was converted, like St Oswald's in 1153, into a house of Augustinian canons. It soon became the most important of the Augustinian houses.

The documents relating to the changes in this chapel during Henry II's reign are instructive. Two curious charters of confir-

---

[1] See W. Stubbs, *The Foundation of Waltham Abbey* (1861), passim, *VCH Essex*, ii, 166, and Dickinson 1950, pp. 95–6, 135, 145. The spurious charter of Edward the Confessor is printed in *Monasticon*, vi, 61–2, and *Cartae Antiquae*, ed. J. Conway Davies (*PRS*, new ser. 33), no. 356; for further references, see P. H. Sawyer, *Anglo-Saxon Charters* (Royal Historical Soc., 1968), no. 1036.

mation survive, one from the young Henry, the king's son, dated 1177, and the second from the king himself, dated 1178.[1] The two are very similar and read rather like papal bulls, not only because of their elaborate preambles but also because of the final imprecation: 'Si quis autem contra hec statuta scienter venerit [or venire temptaverit], et ammonitus hoc non emendaverit, indignationem omnipotentis Dei et sancte Crucis et omnium sanctorum incurrat.' There is a further peculiarity in the supposed charter of Henry II, for the first person plural changes to the first person singular. It is possible that the charters were put together from the papal bulls of Alexander III and Lucius III which confirmed the installation of regulars, listed and confirmed the possessions of the house, and granted extensive privileges to it. The narrative content of the charters is credible and can to a large extent be verified by the papal bulls, although the initial bull of Alexander III, which gave papal authority to the introduction of regular canons, is not extant. The supposed charter of Henry II refers to the introduction of regular canons by the authority of Alexander III, and this permission to install regulars is also referred to in a papal bull of 1178 or 1180.[2] The royal charter incorporated the claim that Waltham 'had always been from the time of its first foundation a royal chapel free from the authority of any archbishop or bishop and subject only to the church of Rome and to the control of the king'. Lucius III's bull of 1182[3] contains this claim and states the immunities which belonged to the church as a royal chapel: 'your church, which is, as it always was, a chapel of the kings of England, has possessed its freedom of old, in that the clerks serving their lord there were ordained by a bishop of their choice and neither the dean nor the secular canons of the church were instituted at any time by the diocesan bishop.' There are no grounds for disbelieving this statement of practice which the pope had accepted.

Here is some support for the later claims that the royal chapels had been from time immemorial free from the interference of

---

[1] *Cartae Antiquae*, nos. 357, 359, *Recueil des Actes de Henri II*, ed. L. Delisle and E. Berger, introduction, pp. 265–8, and *Monasticon*, vi, 63.

[2] *Papsturkunden*, i, no. 174.   [3] Ibid., no. 208.

F

the local bishop. It should be assumed perhaps that when Archbishop Richard of Dover had visited the house in 1174 and suspended the dean[1] he had done so as papal legate. The bull of 1182 confirmed Waltham's immunities in the fullest possible way: it bestowed upon the house full canonical exemption, a privilege which Waltham alone among the royal free chapels possessed. No archbishop or bishop was permitted to exercise ecclesiastical rights—'. . . nec in aliquo pontificalem exerceat potestatem'—and the pope took prior Ralph and the canons into the 'ius et proprietatem ecclesie Romane'. The bull of exemption, which was only one of a succession,[2] gave full papal backing to the privileges which Waltham seems to have possessed already. The statements of Waltham's privileged position as a royal chapel are the more interesting since there is no clear indication from the documents concerning Waltham before 1177 that the church was regarded as a fully privileged royal chapel. It had certainly possessed 'libertates et consuetudines et quietancias', and it is true that it was described in general terms as free from all customs.[3] But it is no mere quibble to show caution in interpreting grants of freedom from customs. In this case the freedom apparently signified protection from the interference of the diocesan.

Pope Lucius III's bull of 1182 reserved to the king and his heirs in the church of Waltham whatever rights they should possess there 'as in their own chapel'. Yet Waltham became more like the monasteries of royal foundation than the royal chapels. From the many copies of papal bulls concerning Waltham which have survived from the last decades of the twelfth century, one interesting feature of this royal abbey emerges. The many parish churches which were annexed to Waltham were not free from ordinary jurisdiction. It might well be concluded that the papal privileges obtained by Waltham in fact detracted from its liberties, for they ensured that all its churches would be subject

---

[1] R. Foreville, L'Église et la Royauté, p. 518, n. 6.

[2] Papsturkunden, i, nos. 222, 245, 255, 296, 303, and Letters of Inn. III, ed. C. R. and Mary G. Cheney, nos. 156, 158, 162.

[3] W. Stubbs, op. cit., pp. 50–3.

to the authority of the diocesan. The bull of 1182 itself ended with the clause 'salva ... in subiectis vobis ecclesiis diocesanorum episcoporum canonica iustitia'. The abbot never exercised the right of institution to these benefices. During a voidance of the diocese in which a benefice was situated the respective archdeacons should institute the vicars presented by the abbot and convent.[1] The grant of full canonical exemption precluded the possibility in the thirteenth century of disputes about the exercise of ordinary jurisdiction. It was not simply because of its status as a royal chapel that the house now possessed exemption from episcopal jurisdiction. After the twelfth century the fact that Waltham was by reason of its history a royal free chapel had little or no practical effect upon the rights of the house. But its status was not forgotten.[2] In 1380, for example, a royal grant was made to the abbot stating that because his house was a free chapel of the king 'he and his successors are exempt from being made collectors, taxers, assessors of tenths, fifteenths ... or anything granted to the king by the clergy or the commonalty of the realm, or receivers of moneys arising therefrom against their will'.[3]

Gnosall

Bromfield, St Oswald's Gloucester, Dover and Waltham had all become Benedictine or Augustinian houses. Other royal secular colleges, rather than having their position enhanced, underwent a process of disintegration. The cases of Gnosall, Steyning, Blyth and Pevensey will illustrate different ways in which royal chapels declined. It is not possible to determine whether the relatively unimportant church of Gnosall had actually declined in wealth and status during the eleventh and twelfth centuries; but the fact that it was given to the diocesan bishop, the bishop of Coventry, meant that it became difficult to distinguish as a royal free chapel. When a college was given to the bishop of the diocese in which

---

[1] See *Papsturkunden*, i, nos. 222, 229, 253, 271, 291, and *Patrologia Latina*, ed. J. P. Migne, vol. 214 (*Inn. III Opera Omnia*, i), lib. ii, nos. 109, 121 (*Letters of Inn. III*, nos. 155, 157).

[2] See above, p. 1.   [3] *CPR 1377–81*, pp. 438–9.

it was constituted, there is little means of distinguishing between the former royal chapel and other colleges belonging to the diocesan. It is true that colleges given to a bishop other than the diocesan were in a very similar position, but the fact that these latter churches constituted pockets of peculiar jurisdiction in another diocese ensured that their exceptional status could not be forgotten. A clear distinction was made between the archbishop of York as ordinary in his own diocese and the archbishop as 'patron and prelate' of St Oswald's Gloucester. Yet St Martin's Dover, under the control of the archbishop of Canterbury and within his own diocese, retained more tenuous links with its history as a royal chapel. The colleges of Wolverhampton, Stafford and Penkridge might have been submerged in the diocese, for King Stephen gave them to the bishop of Coventry; but, since they were recovered for the Crown, they remained completely distinguishable as royal chapels. But at least one royal chapel in this same diocese was not recovered. The church of Gnosall, with its prebends, its churches and its chapels, was given to the episcopal church of Lichfield by Stephen,[1] and it remained in the hands of the bishop.

Since freedom from the diocesan was the most striking feature of royal chapels, we could easily assume that the privileged status of Gnosall became as nothing. But in fact Gnosall retained some links with its status as a royal chapel. It is described as a royal chapel in one of the returns of the taxation of 1291,[2] and it found its way on to a list of royal chapels entered into the register of Bishop Walter Stapeldon.[3] It is no surprise to find Edward I trying to regain the patronage of the church. In 1293 he sued the bishop of Coventry and Lichfield for the advowson of Gnosall, but a jury understandably found in favour of the bishop.[4] A law suit at the end of the fourteenth century is most revealing.[5]

---

[1] *Magnum Registrum Album*, pp. 79–81, and *Regesta* iii, no. 454.

[2] *Monasticon*, vi, 1466 n. h.

[3] *Register W. de Stapeldon*, ed. F. C. Hingeston-Randolph, p. 99.

[4] *SHC*, vi, pt. 1 (1885), p. 243 (Staffs. Assise Roll, 21 Ed. I).

[5] A. Hamilton Thompson (*inter alios*), 'A Gnosall lawsuit of 1395', *SHC*, 3rd ser. 1927, esp. pp. 107–10.

The bishop acted not as diocesan in the church of Gnosall, but as 'warden and bishop of the spirituality'. The four portioners or prebendaries of the church appointed an official to act for them in spiritual matters, and the official completely superseded the authority of the local archdeacon. Gnosall, like Dover, illustrates the fact that only the authority of the bishop as diocesan could be delegated to an archdeacon. The church of Gnosall was too small to be a fully developed college, with a chapter as its corporate voice, but the bishop acted as 'dean' of the chapel,[1] the possessor of exclusive spiritual jurisdiction in the church. Whether Gnosall could be distinguished from churches on the bishop's own demesne is another question; but it remains true that, even 250 years after Gnosall had been given to the diocesan bishop, it remained in a sense a spiritual peculiar. Exemption from the authority of the bishop was clearly not the only factor which kept the royal chapels alive. The rights of this church had become relatively insignificant; but the case of Gnosall nonetheless illustrates the durability of the privileges of royal free chapels.

Steyning

An inquisition held in 1290 reveals that the church of Steyning in Sussex[2] 'is the king's free chapel, exempt from the jurisdiction of the archbishop of Canterbury or any other ordinary, and the abbots of Fécamp have held it as a free chapel since the time it was conferred on them by King Alfred . . . and the abbots by their bailiffs have had cognisance of marriages and correction of spiritual trespasses, and in times of voidance the king's ancestors have exercised such jurisdiction'.[3] For 'Alfred' we can substitute 'Edward the Confessor', whose gift of Steyning to Fécamp was affirmed by William the Conqueror.[4] The manor and the church

[1] *Valor Ecclesiasticus* (Record Commission, 1810–34), iii, 99.

[2] For which see especially *VCH Sussex*, ii, 121–2, and D. J. A. Matthew, *Norman Monasteries and their English Possessions* (Oxford, 1962), 20–2, 38–41.

[3] *Calendar Inquisitions Misc.*, i, no. 1494.

[4] *Regesta* i, 1, 206, 253, 416, 423–4, and P. Chaplais, 'Une charte originale de Guillaume le Conquérant' in *L'Abbaye Bénédictine de Fécamp, 658–1958*, i (Fécamp, 1959), 93–104.

of Steyning were held together after the Conquest by the abbey of Fécamp. But the area served by the church, known apparently as the parish of St Cuthman, had not remained completely intact; disputes already in the eleventh century show the abbey of Fécamp fighting to retain rights belonging to the church of Steyning, as in the church of Beeding and in the church of St Nicholas in Bramber castle.[1] In Calixtus II's bull of exemption to the abbey of Fécamp in 1119 the church of Steyning was specified as one of the churches over which the abbot possessed exclusive ecclesiastical jurisdiction;[2] there are grounds for suspecting that this was in fact a confirmation of the existing state of affairs, for William I's grant of the manor of Steyning and whatever belonged to the manor had been a grant 'cum legibus et consuetudinibus'.[3] The church of Steyning was now exempt by papal grant, but not, like Waltham later in the century, by the possession of its own bull of exemption. The early history of the church is obscure, but, as D. J. A. Matthew concluded,[4] the indications are that it was an ancient minster. Other churches were clearly within its parish, and evidence in the thirteenth century shows the existence of four prebends.

There can be no doubt that the manor of Steyning, to which the church remained attached, was closely associated with the Crown. The wording of William I's charter had not stated clearly the privileges which the Conqueror had accorded to the abbey of Fécamp, and a charter was later forged apparently to serve this purpose.[5] It was the forged charter which Henry II confirmed: according to this confirmation the land of Steyning, with its appurtenances and with all its liberties and customs, was to be held 'cum placitis et querelis et causis omnibus absque omni subiectione et dominatione baronum vel principum et omnium aliorum, et absque omni inquietatione vel inminutione cuiuslibet secularis vel iudiciarie potestatis, sicuti res ad fiscum dominicum

---

[1] D. J. A. Matthew, locc. citt.
[2] U. Robert, *Bullaire du Pape Calixte II* (1891), no. 96.
[3] P. Chaplais, *ubi supra*, p. 103.
[4] Op. cit., p. 39, n. 1.
[5] P. Chaplais, *ubi supra*, pp. 100-1.

pertinentes'.[1] In 1247 these terms were adopted again, with the claim that the land should be free 'from all domination of or subjection to barons, princes, and all others; and the said abbot and monks of Fécamp and their ministers shall have all royal liberties, custom and justice of all matters arising in their land, nor shall anyone intermeddle except by their authority, seeing that this is a royal fief [quia hoc totum regale beneficium est] and quit of all service'.[2] The manor of Steyning was regarded as ancient demesne.[3]

In common with other royal free chapels, a written agreement became essential to clarify the bishop's rights in the church of Steyning. The bishop of Chichester was naturally concerned about the obedience due to him from the churches which were in the hands of the abbey of Fécamp. In 1231 it was agreed that the church of Steyning and the clerks of Steyning were to be exempt from episcopal rights, but that the exemption was not to apply to other churches in the possession of the abbot and convent of Fécamp.[4] The terms of the papal privilege of 1119 were being upheld; the churches quite separate from the college of Steyning (Bury, Slinfold and Nuthurst) were not to be regarded as exempt. As elsewhere, the problem at Steyning now centred upon the churches belonging to the college; the problem was particularly acute since it is clear that during the thirteenth century, if not before, the collegiate organisation of this church was breaking up. The question probably hinged on the interpretation of the term 'ecclesia de Staninges' of the papal privilege. Could it be taken to include the churches belonging to the college even after the college had ceased to exist? In 1259, when there was a vacancy at Fécamp, the king gave a prebend in the church of Steyning to his clerk, Ralph de Hotot, noting that 'the church of Steyning and its members is a free chapel of the said abbey and exempt from episcopal jurisdiction'.[5] But the abbot and convent took action against Ralph, claiming that the prebend which he occupied (described as the fourth part of the church) had been appropriated

---

[1] *Recueil des Actes de Henri II*, ed. L. Delisle and E. Berger, i, 159.
[2] *Cal. Charter Rolls*, i, 322.   [3] E.g. *CCR 1242–7*, p. 484.
[4] *Chichester Chartulary*, no. 273.   [5] *CPR 1258–66*, p. 28.

to their own uses,[1] and Ralph, with the assent of the king, at length resigned the prebend.[2] The prebend may well have comprised the church of West Angmering, which in 1283 the abbot of Fécamp was described as having 'to his own use of the king's progenitors and of the king's advowson'.[3] It was during the primacy of John Pecham that the exemption of the abbey's churches was once again questioned.[4] But although Steyning was put under interdict, the dispute appears not to have concerned the church of Steyning itself; it concerned the church of West Angmering and the chapels of Warminghurst and Ashurst. Perhaps—though it seems much too simple a solution—these two churches and these two chapels had formed the four prebends of the college. Certainly Warminghurst and Ashurst had been chapels associated with the church of Steyning.[5] Archbishop Kilwardby had apparently visited at Steyning;[6] but Pecham encountered strong opposition. After the archbishop had excommunicated the abbey's bailiff, a certain Vigor, and his associates, and had himself collated to the church of West Angmering, the abbey of Fécamp both secured the king's support and took the matter to Rome.[7] The abbey was in a strong position and appears to have been able, with little difficulty, to override the archbishop's authority. The pope could not turn his back upon the claim that the abbey possessed exemption from ordinary jurisdiction for its churches, and to the king the archbishop's interference represented an attack upon royal rights. After all, if Fécamp's temporalities reverted to the king, he himself had the right to collate to West Angmering.

[1] *Les Registres d'Urbain IV*, ed. L. Dorez and J. Guiraud (BEAR, 1901–4), no. 223 (*Calendar of Papal Letters*, i, 387).

[2] *CPR 1266–72*, p. 388.

[3] *Calendar Chancery Warrants*, i, 12.

[4] Ibid., *Registrum Epistolarum J. Peckham*, ed. C. T. Martin, ii, 604–6, 609–10, 620, iii, 808–9, 821–2, 882–5, *Les Registres de Martin IV* (BEAR, 1901–35), nos. 447–8 (*Cal. Papal Letters*, i, 471–2), and *Les Registres de Nicolas IV*, ed. E. Langlois (BEAR, 1898–1938), no. 1996.

[5] *Chichester Chartulary*, p. 309.

[6] *Calendar Inquisitions Misc.*, i, no. 1494.

[7] See also the abbot's letter to Edward I dated 7 June 1284: P.R.O., SC 1 (Ancient Correspondence) 47/111.

The case was delegated by the pope to the official of the bishop of Amiens in 1284, but in 1289 Nicholas IV ordered that it should be heard in the papal curia itself. Unfortunately no further details concerning the case have come to light. Although the abbey had apparently gained the support of king and pope, it looks very much as though it failed to retain episcopal rights in any churches other than Steyning itself.[1] Steyning, now no more than a parish church, remained exempt. But without the papal privilege and the composition of 1231 it is more than likely that the church of Steyning would have completely lost touch with its freedom, especially in view of its disintegration as a college. The break-up of the ancient minsters, slow though it was, obscures the history of the royal free chapels.

Blyth

The church of Blyth had a history similar to that of the church of Steyning. It is easy to dismiss Edward I's attempts to create a royal chapelry attached to Tickhill castle as a usurpation of ecclesiastical rights, but his claim that a royal free chapel existed here is not as wild as it first appears. This royal free chapel was known as the chapelry of Blyth in the twelfth century, but usually as the chapelry of Tickhill in the thirteenth century.[2] And the honour of Tickhill, also, had been known as the honour of Blyth.[3] The chapelry had been in royal hands in the twelfth century, for it was given by King Stephen to Lincoln cathedral,[4] and later by Henry II to his clerk Walter of Coutances.[5] After Walter became archbishop of Rouen, it passed to the cathedral church of Rouen; four prebends were created out of the extensive possessions of the

[1] See (for Steyning) *CPR 1348–50*, p. 332, *CPR 1354–8*, p. 171, and *CPR 1358–61*, p. 460; and (for West Angmering) *CPR 1377–81*, pp. 445, 553, and *VCH Sussex*, ii, 124.

[2] It is referred to as the chapelry of Tickhill in 1206 and 1228: *Rot. Lit. Claus.*, i, 70 (as *Monasticon*, vi, 1118), and *CPR 1225–32*, p. 195.

[3] F. M. Stenton, *First Century of English Feudalism* (Oxford, 1961), p. 63.

[4] *Regesta* iii, no. 485, and *Papsturkunden*, ii, no. 55.

[5] *Calendar of Documents in France 918–1206*, ed. J. H. Round (HMSO, 1899), p. 7, and *Recueil des Actes de Henri II*, ed. L. Delisle and E. Berger, ii, 11–12.

chapelry.[1] The complicated story of its reversion to the Crown during the thirteenth century and of Edward I's attempts to re-create the royal free chapel need not concern us here, but it is important to stress that, whatever liberties this chapelry may have possessed in the twelfth century or earlier, the rights of the arch-bishop of York had been firmly established there in the course of the thirteenth century.[2] The churches of the chapelry were still linked together as a group, while the college of canons had long since disappeared; but the normal pattern of ecclesiastical develop-ment—the organisation of parishes under the control of the arch-bishop—had been established, apparently unopposed, during the church of Rouen's possession of the royal chapelry.

Pevensey

The royal chapelry of Pevensey ('mea dominica capellaria'), with its churches, tithes and lands, was given by King Stephen to the bishop of Chichester at some date between 1147 and 1154.[3] The bishop and his successors were to be chaplains of the queen and her successors, and were to 'be invited to her feasts as former chaplains were, and do her the service thereof'. Henry II confirmed the gift, and specified that the bishops should be 'chaplains of the kings and queens of England'.[4] That the gift was not intended to detract in any way from the rights of the chapel cannot be doubted; Henry II ordered that the chapelry should be just as free from interference as any of his chapelries throughout Eng-land.[5] Two of the churches belonging to the chapelry (St Nicholas

[1] *Rot. Chartarum*, I, i, 75–6 (as *Monasticon*, vi, 1118–9), *Acta Pontificum Romanorum*, ed. J. v. Pflugk-Harttung (Tübingen, 1881–8), i, no. 357, *Cal. of Docs. in France*, pp. 12–13, 16, and J. F. Pommeraye, *Histoire des Archevesques de Rouen* (Rouen, 1666), pp. 419, 436.

[2] *York Minster Fasti*, ii (*Yorks. Archaeological Soc.*, Record Series, cxxiv), 146–8.

[3] *Regesta* iii, no. 184, *Chichester Chartulary*, nos. 62, 110 (and see 292), and *Report on MSS in Various Collections* (HMC, 55), i, 182.

[4] *Chichester Chartulary*, nos. 114–15.

[5] Ibid., no. 122 (from Chichester Diocesan Record Office, Liber B, fo. 25v: '. . . volo quod libera et quieta sit ab inquietationibus et exactionibus sicut aliqua mearum capellariarum per Angliam liberior est et quietior').

Pevensey and St Pancras Arlington) were assigned by Bishop Hilary to the newly founded chancellorship of Chichester;[1] and the church of Pevensey remained in the hands of the chancellors of Chichester.[2] But there is no evidence to indicate for how long the status of Pevensey as a royal chapelry was remembered. It may well be that the chancellor in any case enjoyed some independence from episcopal control by reason of his office. But I have found nothing to suggest that after the twelfth century Pevensey was a peculiar. At the beginning of the fifteenth century the bishop was himself responsible for initiating a full inquiry into the fruits of the church of Pevensey and of its two chapels of Manxey and Horse Eye;[3] and it was the archdeacon of Lewes who instituted the vicar of Pevensey.[4] It looks as though Pevensey as a royal chapelry had simply broken apart. Perhaps the fact that it had first been given to the bishop, and then (in part) to the chancellor, accelerated the detachment of the chapelry from the early status which its title 'dominica capellaria' suggests.

St Bartholomew's Smithfield: a royal free chapel?

The Augustinian priory of St Bartholomew's Smithfield[5] was described as a royal demesne chapel in a series of royal charters reputedly of the twelfth and thirteenth centuries.[6] But, unlike other royal demesne chapels, St Bartholomew's was a new foundation with no early history as a secular college. It was founded in 1123, so tradition had it, by a royal clerk called Rahere,[7] and the land at Smithfield was given by King Henry I.[8] The bishop of

---

[1] *Acta of Chichester*, ed. H. Mayr-Harting, p. 95.

[2] *Chichester Chartulary*, pp. 318, 376.   [3] Ibid., pp. 363–4.

[4] *Register of Bishop Robert Rede*, ed. C. Deedes, ii (*Sussex Record Soc.*, xi, 1910), 276, 282.

[5] See esp. *VCH London*, i, 475–80, and *Monasticon*, vi, 291–7.

[6] For a list of all the charters, see E. A. Webb, *The Records of St Batholomew's Smithfield*, i, 477–89; and see esp. *CPR 1416–22*, pp. 239–45 and *Cartae Antiquae*, ed. J. Conway Davies, nos. 327–35.

[7] For whom see E. A. Webb, op. cit., i, 37–75.

[8] Ratified in charters of Henry II and Henry III: ibid., i, 479, and *Monasticon*, vi, 295b.

London, Richard de Belmeis I, was himself concerned with the foundation. Rahere had gained the bishop's support during the negotiations with the king about the founding of the house, and the bishop had consecrated the church and dedicated a small cemetery ('qui debito jure locum ipsum orientalis partis praedicti campi sanctificavit et episcopali auctoritate dedicavit breve tunc admodum cimiterium').[1] This was an unusual way to proceed if the priory was intended to be exempt from the diocesan. Three charters of Henry I dated 1133 survive; while none of them is beyond suspicion, two of them appear to be offshoots of the first.[2] In the two extremely dubious charters St Bartholomew's is described as a royal demesne chapel: 'que est dominica capella mea' and 'libera sicut dominica capella mea'.[3] And all the subsequent charters of Henry II, Richard, John and Henry III which embody these same phrases cannot be free from suspicion. Despite Johnson and Cronne's belief that the first charter of Henry I 'has obviously been a good deal doctored', faith can perhaps be put in some of its terms.[4] The house had been founded on royal demesne and it is altogether reasonable to assume that it enjoyed the liberties and customs associated with royal demesne. Nevertheless, the charter has extravagant phrases to describe the church's privileges: its freedom is compared with the freedom of the Crown itself ('liberam esse sicut coronam meam'), and the church is to have all customs, whether ecclesiastical or secular, just as fully and freely as the king himself had on his demesne ('omnes consuetudines sive in ecclesiasticis sive in secularibus tam plene et libere sicut ego haberem si essent de meo dominio et mensa'). A key statement of the bishop's rights occurs in this charter alone and, whether it is genuine or interpolated, it is an interesting comment on the exercise of episcopal rights over a priory on royal demesne: '. . . quod sint liberi ab omni terrena servitute et terrena potestate et subiectione preter episcopales consuetudines videlicet tantum consecrationem ecclesie baptismum et ordin-

---

[1] *Monasticon*, vi, 294a, and E. A. Webb, op cit., i, 392.

[2] *Regesta* ii, nos. 1761, 1794–5.

[3] See *CPR 1416–22*, pp. 239–42.

[4] *Regesta* ii, no. 1761, and *Cartae Antiquae*, no. 327.

ationem clericorum . . .' This clause points to freedom from episcopal exactions but dependence upon the bishop for those services which only a bishop could perform.

St Bartholomew's itself was not a parish church, and this limited the extent to which it was exposed to episcopal interference. But in the new age of visitation a bishop's authority began to be felt more directly. And it appears that St Bartholomew's in the middle of the thirteenth century had no grounds for claiming freedom from episcopal visitation. In the dramatic account by Matthew Paris of the attempt of Archbishop Boniface to visit St Bartholomew's in 1250[1] one of the canons is made to object, arguing that the bishop of London, who himself exercised the right of visitation ('qui eos habuit, cum necesse fuerat, visitare'), was both experienced and conscientious.[2] It is clear from the papal letters of 22 April 1252 that it was not simply the extent of the metropolitan's jurisdiction which came under discussion as a result of Archbishop Boniface's attempt to visit; we learn that at the root of the problem were the extensive rights belonging to the priory of St Bartholomew, as also to the priory of Holy Trinity and the dean and chapter of St Paul's ('super visitatione, correctione, exemptione et immunitate ecclesiarum ipsarum').[3] This dispute with Archbishop Boniface may well have occasioned the forgery of charters. The fact that the earliest copies of some of St Bartholomew's charters appear on a Cartae Antiquae roll of the king's Chancery is no guarantee of authenticity. The right of the archbishop to visit as metropolitan was upheld by the pope, but the support which Henry III gave Archbishop Boniface may have been an important factor in the failure of the canons to establish freedom from the archbishop's jurisdiction. The exercise of ordinary jurisdiction in the priory was firmly established. Yet the freedom of the royal free chapels from episcopal and

---

[1] See VCH London, i, 476, Cheney 1931, p. 138, and I. J. Churchill, Canterbury Administration, i, 290.

[2] Matthaei Parisiensis . . . Chronica Majora, ed. H. R. Luard (RS, 1872–83), v, 122.

[3] Les Registres d'Innocent IV, ed. É. Berger (BEAR, 1884–1921), iii, nos. 5670–2 (Calendar of Papal Letters, i, 276).

archidiaconal interference was rapidly becoming one of their most important privileges, and certainly the one privilege which was most in dispute and which called for energy and resources to defend. It was the 'freedom' of which the royal chapels became most conscious, the 'freedom' which came nearest to defining their status. It was a 'freedom' which the priory of St Bartholomew's did not possess.

As with other houses where the possession of churches was separate from the organisation of the religious community, we must enquire separately about spiritual jurisdiction in the parish churches. The churches of particular interest are naturally those given by the king himself. Henry I had given to St Bartholomew's in frankalmoign a group of churches in the manor of Lothingland in Suffolk: the churches of Gorleston, St Nicholas Little Yarmouth, Lowestoft and Belton.[1] It is a curious fact that despite the gift to St Bartholomew's these churches were stated, in 1219, 1226–8 and 1235, as being 'de donacione regis'.[2] In 1209 the king had presented Alan Stokes to the churches of Little Yarmouth, Gorleston and Lowestoft. This was by presentation to the bishop's official,[3] the bishop, John de Gray, being away in Ireland. Belton also came under Alan's control, but it was held by a certain Ralph of Belton for the yearly payment to Alan of a pound of incense. Alan is described, in 1219, as holding all four churches 'per canonicos de Sancto Bartholomeo', which meant an annual payment of ten marks from the churches, valued together at a hundred marks. The advowson may have been in the king's hands because of a vacancy in the priory, and perhaps the donation of the churches was repeatedly said to belong to the king simply because of this one example of the king's presentation. Later the church of Belton became alienated from the priory's possessions, but the other three churches became fully appropriated to the priory, with vicarages ordained in each.[4] The irregular position of these Suffolk churches, held together by one clerk, was not long-lived, nor was it inclusive, at any visible point, of exemption from the bishop or archdeacon.

[1] E. A. Webb, op. cit., i, 101.   [2] *The Book of Fees*, i, 282, 392, 403.
[3] *Rot. Lit. Pat.*, p. 90b.   [4] E. A. Webb, op. cit., i, 322–6, 380, 428–9.

In its charters the priory claimed to be a royal demesne chapel, but there is nothing to substantiate the claim and everything points to the falseness of the charters. St Bartholomew's is never found on any of the lists or groupings of royal free chapels. The charters apart, there are no royal statements that the house was a royal chapel. It was not alone as a new royal Augustinian house. St Mary's Newstead, founded by Henry II, was given extensive privileges, including protection from interference and freedom from every 'custom', and its canons were described as the king's 'dominici canonici'.[1] But St Mary's Newstead was not claimed as a royal demesne chapel. The fact that these houses did not achieve exemption is confirmatory evidence that the exemption which the royal free chapels were to achieve was closely connected with their early rights and with the attitude of the pre-Conquest kings towards the exercise of spiritual rights on their demesne. It is possible to argue that the distinction was more between a monastery and a secular college than between Henry I and the Anglo-Saxon kings. Both distinctions are valid; the reign of Henry I was the age of regular canons. St Bartholomew's was the nearest equivalent to the ancient royal chapels which the new age could produce. The time had passed for the founding of colleges with parochial rights, serving the parishioners of the demesne and providing livings for the royal priests.

Two Augustinian houses, St Oswald's Gloucester and Waltham achieved exemption because of their traditional status as royal free chapels; one new Augustinian priory, St Bartholomew Smithfield, was founded on royal demesne but it was not a royal free chapel and it possessed no exemption. One other Augustinian priory, St Botolph's Colchester, has been regarded as exempt,[2] but it is impossible to put faith in its bull of exemption supposedly granted by Paschal II in 1116.[3] The Augustinian priory of

---

[1] *Monasticon*, vi, 474, and *CPR 1350–4*, p. 1. For St Mary's Newstead, see A. Hamilton Thompson in *Transactions of the Thoroton Society*, xxiii (1919), 33–141.

[2] See esp. Dickinson 1950, pp. 98–103.

[3] *Monasticon*, vi, 106 (and *Patrologia Latina*, ed. J. P. Migne, vol. 163, cc. 443–5).

Tonbridge obtained a bull of exemption in 1192,[1] and on present evidence this priory was the only Augustinian house to possess the greatly prized privilege of freedom from ordinary jurisdiction without having first been a royal college of secular canons.

Battle Abbey: a royal free chapel?

The twelfth century was the age in which the great Benedictine houses fought for full canonical exemption, the age in which the papacy succeeded in establishing a monopoly over the granting (or, more aptly, the reinforcing) of freedom from episcopal jurisdiction in these houses. It was not without a clash between the ecclesiastical hierarchy and the king, especially Henry II, that papal control was established. The classic dispute concerning Battle Abbey,[2] although it cannot in fact be regarded as typical, illustrates particularly well the royal attitude towards exemption.

The chronicle of Battle Abbey leaves little room for doubt that the house considered itself from the first as free from the interference of the bishop. It was the extent and nature of this freedom that was in doubt, and as Eleanor Searle has shown the early abbots 'conformed to episcopal demands', for the freedom was 'customary and ill-defined' until the dispute which began in earnest in 1155. Using the evidence of the chronicle of Battle Abbey requires the greatest care: an apparently reliable account of the early history of the house is interspersed with sections which correspond, often verbatim, with the charters forged after 1154. While it must be conceded that the forged charters were to some extent setting down rights which the house had possessed *de facto*, the chronicle cannot be used to give anything approaching a clear picture of the kind of exemption which the house possessed or claimed to possess before 1154. The free area surrounding the abbey certainly constituted a parish, and it was

---

[1] C. R. Cheney, 'A papal privilege for Tonbridge priory', *BIHR*, xxxviii (1965), esp. pp. 196–7, and *Papsturkunden*, ii, 460.

[2] See E. Searle, 'Battle Abbey and exemption: the forged charters', *EHR*, lxxxiii (1968), 449–80, and for earlier accounts esp. Knowles 1932, pp. 218–25, 431–6, and Lemarignier 1937, pp. 272–5.

claimed, apparently early in the century, that the parishioners were under the immediate control of the abbot, with the spiritualities exercised by a chaplain who lived with his own clerk 'in curia monachorum'. A separate chapel or church was built, perhaps during the early years of Henry I's reign, to serve the parishoners.

The chronicle of Battle goes on to tell us that since the ministers of the bishop of Chichester disputed the freedom of this church of St Mary an agreement was drawn up between the abbot and the bishop. Both the abbey and the church were to be always free from episcopal customs and fines, from payments for oil and from synodals ('de omnibus consuetudinibus et forisfacturis episcopalibus et de denariis olei et synodi'); the priest of the church was never to attend chapters of clergy without the permission of the abbot, and was to attend synods only to hear the bishop's precepts; and the confession and the penance of an offending priest of the church must be in the hands of the bishop, but any penalty went to the abbey.[1] But the terms of this 'agreement' are taken, perhaps directly, from a charter forged after 1157. The 'agreement' appears to represent the position achieved after the dispute. In its parish the abbey was not turning its back on the spiritual guidance of the bishop; but it had established freedom from all exactions and interference. This must certainly have been a situation which prevailed in many other peculiars. While the bounds of the parish appear to have extended beyond the *leuga* of the abbey[2] the two can be regarded as roughly equivalent, and the dispute which began towards the end of Stephen's reign and which came to a crisis in the king's court of 1157 thus concerned the exemption of both the abbey and its *leuga*.

The basic issues at stake during the hearing of 1157 are unmistakable: on the one side the abbey and the king supported the right of the Crown to exempt a royal house from the jurisdiction of the bishop; on the other side Hilary, bishop of Chichester,

[1] *Chronicon Monasticon de Bello* (Anglia Christiana Society, London, 1846), pp. 27, 56–7, and E. Searle, *ubi supra*, 461–2, 475–6.

[2] *Chronicon de Bello*, p. 27.

G

(with some support from Theobald, archbishop of Canterbury) maintained that this right belonged to the pope alone.[1] As in later cases concerning churches claimed as royal free chapels, the very fact that the case was heard in the king's court was a determining factor. The forged charters provided the evidence of exemption, and the exemption clauses of these charters are most revealing. The abbey was not simply stated as free from the interference of the bishop. An effort was being made to find a category for Battle Abbey: the abbey was compared either with Christ Church Canterbury or with the royal demesne chapels. The recurring phrases are 'sicut mea dominica capella' or, much more frequently, 'sicut ecclesia Christi Cantuarie'.[2] These two comparisons appear to have been equated, and this led H. W. C. Davis to suggest, without additional evidence, that Christ Church Canterbury was itself regarded as a royal chapel.[3] He was on much safer ground when he wrote: 'there clearly was a recognised doctrine or tradition concerning the liberties of royal chapels.' While this is true, Battle benefits little from a comparison with the chapels. The liberties of the royal chapels were long-standing rights. Wolverhampton had been described early in the twelfth century as a church which was 'antiquitus de propriis capellis que ad coronam spectabant';[4] and those royal chapels which may have been, at least in effect, established after the Conquest (St Martin-le-Grand and Bridgnorth) were certainly—indeed essentially—in origin secular colleges. Battle could not join the rank of the royal colleges. In addition, the abbey, although endowed with royal lands and royal churches, was apparently not founded on royal demesne.[5] It may well be true, as the chronicle indicates, that both the abbot and Thomas Becket as chancellor claimed during the proceedings that Battle was a royal demesne chapel,[6] but there is

---

[1] See H. Mayr-Harting, 'Hilary, bishop of Chichester, and Henry II', *EHR*, lxxviii (1963), esp. 222–3.

[2] E. Searle, *ubi supra*, 469, 471–3, 476.

[3] 'The chronicle of Battle Abbey', *EHR*, xxix (1914), 433.

[4] See above, p. 42.　　　[5] *DB*, i, 17vb.

[6] *Chronicon de Bello*, pp. 82, 100; the phrase of p. 82 ('capella dominica et signum coronae regiae') is found in a charter of William I forged after 1211 (*Regesta* i, 113 and E. Searle, *ubi supra*, 464).

no evidence to support their claim, and the forged charters themselves might well be interpreted as merely stating that the house was *like* a royal demesne chapel ('sicut mea dominica capella'), just as it was also *like* Christ Church Canterbury ('sicut ecclesia Christi Cantuarie'). This is not to imply that the phrase 'sicut mea dominica capella' can always be interpreted in this way.[1]

Although Battle had none of the characteristics of royal free chapels,[2] the king was attempting to extend to the abbey those privileges which the ancient royal colleges enjoyed. This was one way in which he might himself control the granting of exemption to a royal abbey. The terms of the agreement arrived at in 1157 and confirmed by Archbishop Theobald[3] necessarily shed light upon the privileges enjoyed by the royal chapels themselves, for the rights now secured for Battle were thought to be comparable to the rights enjoyed by a royal demesne chapel. The church and abbey of Battle, with the surrounding *leuga*, were declared free from all subjection and exaction of the church and bishop of Chichester, and the bishop should not without the permission of the abbot and monks claim hospitality in either the abbey or its manors, decree anything or exercise any episcopal rights there, or carry out any ordinations, or establish the bishop's see there. Although, as we have seen, other evidence shows that the abbey could not turn its back completely upon the bishop, nevertheless this agreement of 1157 looks very much like an attempt to exclude the bishop to the greatest possible extent. Unlike the later agreements concerning Wolverhampton (in 1224) and Battle itself (in 1215[4] and 1235), no open concessions were being made to the diocesan.

The contest of 1157 had rested well within the king's control. But had he actually succeeded in creating a permanently exempt abbey? Battle was put under royal protection, and the king acted

[1] Above, pp. 48, 55.

[2] Cf. H. G. Richardson and G. O. Sayles (*The Governance of Medieval England* (Edinburgh, 1963), pp. 287–8, 290–1), who have accepted the abbey's claim on its face value.

[3] A. Saltman, *Theobald Archbishop of Canterbury*, p. 243.

[4] E. Searle, *ubi supra*, 467.

as though he were defending the royal dignity. But the passage of time undermined the privileges of the house. No amount of royal support could make Battle an ancient royal chapel, and the house therefore gained nothing from the clarification of the privileges of the royal free chapels during the thirteenth century. On the other hand, during the crucial years of the twelfth century the abbey had relied entirely upon royal backing for its liberties and, despite its claim to the contrary,[1] had apparently not obtained any papal confirmations of its rights and had certainly not obtained a papal grant of exemption. Indeed, Hadrian IV's bull of 1155 had supported the claims of the bishop of Chichester.[2] Thus Battle fell between two stools. The problem of its exemption was in dispute once again in the second quarter of the thirteenth century,[3] and in 1234 Pope Gregory IX actually confirmed the freedom of the abbey as it had been determined in 1157.[4] But it is a mistake to interpret this as a grant of canonical exemption.[5] Freedom from the interference of a bishop did not amount to complete freedom from ordinary jurisdiction. For one thing, the metropolitan had not been excluded from Battle Abbey. In October 1235—partly, no doubt, as a result of the papal support for the freedom of the house—an agreement was drawn up to which both abbot and bishop gave their assent.[6] It was a compromise settlement which both safeguarded the peculiar jurisdiction of the abbey in its *leuga* and at the same time gave the bishop extensive rights. And it was an agreement peculiar to Battle. While there are some similarities between this agreement and the agreement concerning Wolverhampton,[7] the difference between the two churches is perfectly clear. The freedom of Wolverhampton was strengthened and extended as the liberties of the royal free chapels were re-

---

[1] *Les Registres de Grégoire IX*, ed. L. Auvray, no. 1738.

[2] *Chronicon de Bello*, p. 78.

[3] See R. Graham, *English Ecclesiastical Studies* (London, 1929), pp. 200-1, and Cheney 1931, pp. 41-2.

[4] *Les Registres de Grégoire IX*, nos. 1772, 1776.

[5] Cf. Knowles 1932, p. 224, and *The Monastic Order in England*, p. 591.

[6] *Chichester Chartulary*, no. 274 (and *The Episcopal Register of Robert Rede*, ed. C. Deedes, ii, 440-2).

[7] Above, pp. 43-4.

inforced in the thirteenth century; but Battle was not associated with the royal free chapels in the thirteenth century. The settlement of 1235 was a permanent arrangement which was in fact quite favourable to the bishop, and completely favourable to the archbishop.

To summarise the agreement of 1235 would be to rob it of its distinctions and subtleties—and the very significance of the ordinance is to be found in its distinctions and subtleties. These are the terms. The bishop was to bless the abbots, never in the abbey church and preferably in the church of Chichester; but once canonically elected the abbot-elect should not be opposed by the bishop. If the see of Chichester were vacant the abbot-elect could be blessed by another bishop, even if the chapter of Chichester did not give its assent, but not to the prejudice of future bishops. While the abbot-elect should profess obedience to the bishop, the latter must claim no more jurisdiction than the ordinance itself set out. Monks were to be ordained by the bishop or his deputy, but if there were no local ordinations another bishop could be chosen. The abbot and convent should be subject to episcopal visitation, in normal circumstances every three years, but only by commissaries, that is by two monks, one chosen by the bishop (at the abbot's approval) and one chosen by the abbot, who were to stay no more than two days in the abbey; but no procurations should be paid, and the abbot himself should correct any faults. If the abbot refrained from correcting faults, then the visitors should do so, if the majority of the convent agreed and without prejudice to the abbot's regular discipline. Each bishop was to be received with a procession on his first visit, and might come once every three years to be entertained in the abbey, but without exercising any jurisdiction within the *leuga*. Each chaplain of the church of St Mary was to be presented to the bishop, who was to return him to be instituted as dean of the *leuga* by the abbot himself. This was a singularly subtle arrangement, for it gave the bishop the opportunity to commit the cure of souls to the dean but at the same time gave the abbot the last word in the appointment. The bishop's court could be a court of appeal, but all causes within the *leuga* were to be heard and determined by the dean, except criminal and matrimonial causes; in the hearing of the latter cases by the bishop or his official, the dean should attend as assessor but should not give judgments. Profits from all causes were to go to the abbot. The dean was to attend the bishop's synod only to hear precepts; the correction of the dean belonged to the abbot, and only in the abbot's negligence to the bishop. The narrow way between the maintenance of royal privileges and the exercise of episcopal jurisdiction was being trod with the utmost care. The settlement appears to have been observed,[1] but naturally there were ambiguities which needed further discussion.[2] Despite all the qualifying clauses of the settlement, the abbey was able to persist in its claim of freedom from episcopal interference; all the parishioners of the *leuga*, which comprised the whole township of Battle, remained free from any direct visitation by the bishop, but specifically not free from the visitations of the archbishop of Canterbury.[3] Battle retained its freedom, but never achieved the complete freedom of either the exempt abbeys or the royal free chapels.

In those six Benedictine abbeys which achieved full exemption, the general process was the extension of liberties, which had been gained often by royal grant, by means of papal bulls of exemption. While a number of colleges had themselves developed into large monastic houses (the history of Bury St Edmunds can be traced back to a secular college of the tenth century),[4] a great gulf was nonetheless fixed between the secular colleges and the large Benedictine monasteries. Yet both in the royal college and in the royal abbey the king had exercised the right of granting freedom from all interference. It is true on the one hand that this right was far-reaching, as when the king himself granted that the abbey of St Albans and fifteen of its churches could receive their oil and chrism, and the abbot could receive his blessing, from a

---

[1] R. Graham, op. cit., p. 202.

[2] *Chichester Chartulary*, no. 905.

[3] See also D. L. Douie, *Archbishop Pecham* (Oxford, 1952), p. 156, and I. J. Churchill, *Canterbury Administration*, i, 301, 332, 343.

[4] M. D. Lobel, 'Ecclesiastical banleuca in England' in *Oxford Essays for H. E. Salter*, p. 129.

bishop of their own choosing.[1] On the other hand, to the king in the twelfth century the freedom from all interference signified primarily freedom from exactions. It is this freedom from exactions which appears to be implied by the phrase 'sicut mea dominica capella' or 'sicut mea dominica ecclesia'. The first version was used to describe the freedom of Westminster Abbey and the second to describe the freedom of the abbey of St Albans.[2] Certainly the king saw the privileged royal abbeys (especially Westminster Abbey) as bearing a very close relationship to the Crown, a relationship which was most aptly described by comparison with the king's own demesne chapel, wherever it might be. Westminster was described in a dubious bull of 1133 as the church 'que regni tui extat corona', and in 1286 we find the description 'omnium capellarum nostrarum est domina et magistra'.[3] Yet the sole link between Westminster Abbey and the royal free chapels was in fact the king himself.

The references suggesting that St Bartholomew's Smithfield, or Battle, or Westminster, or St Albans were royal free chapels should be studied together. While the charters which describe St Bartholomew's priory as a royal demesne chapel are probably spurious, the use of this term may have arisen out of a belief in the equivalence of a new house of regular canons founded on royal demesne with the older royal churches of secular canons. But equivalence proved impossible to defend. In the case of Battle the only references to the house as a demesne chapel appear in a few charters forged after 1157 and in dubious passages in the chronicle of the abbey. The references concerning Westminster and St Albans are isolated; and the phrase 'sicut mea dominica capella' or 'ecclesia' is, in any case, difficult to interpret. With those royal colleges which became monasteries in the twelfth century—St Oswald's Gloucester, Waltham, Dover and Bromfield—there are many indications after the twelfth century that they retained links with their earlier position as royal free chapels. No such tradition

[1] *The Registrum Antiquissimum of Lincoln*, i, ed. C. W. Foster (Lincoln Record Soc., 27), p. 65.

[2] Ibid., and *Curia Regis Rolls*, vi, 177.

[3] *Papsturkunden*, i, no. 17, and Prynne iii, 1279.

is found in other royal abbeys or priories. It must be concluded that, although some royal monasteries were seen at times to have a status which was equivalent to that of the privileged royal colleges, it was only those churches which had been royal secular colleges that were regarded as royal free chapels.

Despite the extent of the king's authority over royal churches and monasteries, the large Benedictine abbeys especially had resorted individually to the pope. To fail to resort to the pope was to fail—as at Battle—to gain full exemption. The arrangement at Battle was unique, but in many ways it represents the situation in the royal colleges, for they too had obtained freedom from episcopal interference by royal grace. For the ecclesiastical authorities this freedom became a source of great frustration; the bishops needed to know the exact extent of their powers. In the thirteenth century the Crown sought to reinforce and re-define the liberties of the royal demesne chapels until their customary and royal freedom was accepted as in effect equivalent to canonical exemption. The front-line conflict between Crown and papacy concerning prerogative rights and ultimate spiritual authority in the Benedictine abbeys had gone the papacy's way; but in its defence of the royal chapels the Crown was to fight a strong rear-guard action.

CHAPTER IV

THE EXEMPT ROYAL DEANERIES IN THE THIRTEENTH CENTURY

There are many indications in the twelfth century of the long-standing privileges of a—perhaps greatly diminished—group of ancient chapels, and these privileges had been claimed for two relatively new secular colleges, Waltham and St Martin-le-Grand.[1] The liberties of the royal chapels were well established before the first papal bull relating to them. But it looks very much as though the emphasis had been upon freedom from financial exactions. Freedom from exactions, including secular exactions, had undoubtedly figured large in the history of the demesne chapels. For example, Henry II compared Westminster Abbey to a royal demesne chapel when he declared that the house was free with all its possessions and its men 'de siris et hundredis de geldo et denegeldo et auxilio vicecomitis et de omni seculari exactione sicut capella mea dominica'.[2] The reorganisation of the whole business of episcopal administration in the twelfth century made the problem of freedom from episcopal customs particularly acute. It is clear from the evidence of the early thirteenth century that the newly defined rights of bishops and archdeacons were being asserted in the royal free chapels. St Martin-le-Grand had not achieved complete freedom for all its churches. The composition of 1224 concerning Wolverhampton was extremely favourable to the bishop, especially concerning some of the rights which were generally regarded as inseparable from the episcopal order, with the notable exception of the right of institution. The dean of Wolverhampton did not enjoy the episcopal rights which the

[1] And for Bridgnorth, see below, p. 119.
[2] *Curia Regis Rolls*, vi, 177.

abbey of Evesham possessed in its churches.[1] The composition of 1235 concerning Battle Abbey,[2] which was a most subtle compromise, was clearly not far different from the arrangements which obtained in some of the royal free chapels. And the composition of 1204 × 1206 concerning Bosham was a real attempt to regularise the administration of the college according to the principles of ecclesiastical law; even, it seems, with the support of King John, it was agreed that in matters concerning cure of souls the church should not be free from the diocesan.[3] Only the college itself remained free. Freedom from the interference of the bishop was, however, a firmly entrenched concept, and the composition for Bosham was exceptional. Bosham under the bishop of Exeter was not so directly the concern of the king and his ministers as, for example, St Martin-le-Grand and Wolverhampton. The king's *dominium* over some of his royal free chapels remained largely unimpaired; the right to administer the churches and to partake of their revenues had not passed to the diocesan bishops. And financial rights could never be separated from rights of jurisdiction.[4] In the thirteenth century there was nevertheless room for a re-definition, even an extension, of the liberties of the royal free chapels.

Far from undertaking a direct conflict with the Church, the king adopted the tactics of seeking papal support. After Pope Gregory IX's confirmation of the liberties and immunities of the royal chapels in 1236 we might assume that the papacy was willing to comply with royal policy. This is certainly what the king assumed, or wanted to assume: in 1238 he claimed that St Martin-le-Grand was a free chapel 'exempt by the Apostolic See from all episcopal jurisdiction'.[5] The papal indult perhaps signified complaisance, but it signified little else. As the cases of Wolverhampton, Bosham and St Martin-le-Grand illustrate, local circumstances had already produced an uneven pattern of privileges. No general, or even detailed, statement of exemption could have applied to all the royal colleges, unless it took no account of

---

[1] Above, pp. 43–4, and Barlow 1950, p. 107.
[2] Above, pp. 87–8.　　　　　　　　[3] Above, p. 46.
[4] Below, p. 137.　　　　　　　　[5] *CPR 1232–47*, p. 218.

customary rights. The central theme of royal policy was to be the complete freedom of the chapels from ordinary jurisdiction: freedom from archdeacon, from bishop and from archbishop. But could the pope countenance and could his prelates countenance such an attack upon spiritual government? Could the Church countenance the existence of deaneries within which the ecclesiastical authorities had in theory no authority at all, and in practice very little authority indeed?

The attitude of Pope Innocent IV towards the chapels is even more illuminating than that of Pope Gregory IX. A bull of 21 July 1245 stated that the chapels were immune from sentences of excommunication or interdict promulgated by anyone exercising ordinary authority or by any delegate or sub-delegate, and that they were free from all burdens to the same extent as other exempt churches.[1] Freedom from interdict and from excommunication and freedom from exactions were significant privileges, but they did not amount to exemption.[2] The pope took the precaution of declaring that the chapels were subject immediately to the Roman Church. And the indult was to be effective for only ten years ('presentibus usque ad decennium valituris'); this important clause was omitted from the copies of the bull which Henry III issued under seal to at least two of the deans of royal free chapels (Wolverhampton and Stafford) and to the archbishops and bishops of the realm,[3] and the king, ignoring the temporary nature of the papal grant, ordered 'privilegium illud in perpetua firmitate manere'.[4] The papal inhibition was being given an authority which it was not intended to possess. To Henry III it was concerned with the 'immunitatibus, exemptionibus, et libertatibus capellarum nostrarum'; taken together these are impressive terms. An inspeximus of Henry's letter to the dean of Stafford, reproducing the bull without the 'ad decennium' clause,

---

[1] *Foedera*, I, i, 261 (two sealed originals are P.R.O. SC7 (Papal Bulls) 21/11 and 21/18), and *Annales Monastici*, ed. H. R. Luard, i, 275.

[2] Cf. *Councils and Synods* ii, 446.

[3] Prynne ii, 982–3, *CPR 1281–92*, p. 360 (Prynne iii, 424), and *CCR 1247–51*, pp. 99, 226.

[4] *Annales Monastici*, i, 275.

was issued as letters patent in 1290.[1] The king had also armed himself with another bull of Innocent IV, dated 27 July 1245, which ordered the chancellor of Oxford to hear and decide the complaint of Henry III against the archdeacon of Stafford, who was trying to collect procurations from the chapel of Bridgnorth, and presuming to interdict the chapel and suspend and excommunicate the chaplains. The king's claim—and the bull states it as the king's claim—was that ordinary, or delegated, jurisdiction did not obtain in the chapel of Bridgnorth.[2]

The gulf between papal and royal interests is fully revealed by a third bull of uncertain date.[3] It was issued after the bull of 21 July 1245 to which it refers: 'pridem . . . inhibuisse dicimur.' Writing to the bishop of Coventry and Lichfield, Innocent declared that the privileges he had granted the chapels should not be prejudicial to episcopal and archidiaconal authority. The bishop had complained to the pope that rectors and canons of the churches of Stafford, Shrewsbury, Bridgnorth and Tettenhall, and of other parish churches or of chapels belonging to these churches, were claiming their churches to be royal chapels and usurping the established rights of the bishop and his archdeacons. The ordinaries had, freely and 'ab antiquo', celebrated synods in these parishes, exercised other episcopal and archidiaconal rights, and had taken cognisance of all the ecclesiastical causes of the servitors, ministers and parishioners of the churches or chapels. The rectors and canons were undermining these rights. The pope stated specifically that it was not his intention that the papal indult sent to the king should be used to undermine in any way the bishop's rights; and he gave the bishop authority to fulfil the duties of his office. It is unwise to conclude that the statements of the two bulls, the one to the king, the other to the bishop, are irreconcilable.[4] After all, it was only in recent times that canonical exemption itself had come to imply without question complete

[1] *CPR 1281–92*, p. 360 (Prynne iii, 424).
[2] F. Palgrave, *The Antient Kalendars*, i, 9–10, and *Foedera*, I, i, 261 (P.R.O. SC7 (Papal Bulls) 22/33). And see *CCR 1272–9*, p. 252.
[3] *Annales Monastici*, i, 275–6 (Potthast, no. 11797).
[4] Cf. Styles 1936, p. 86, and D. L. Douie, *Archbishop Pecham*, p. 145.

independence from diocesan control.[1] And it is well to remember Innocent III's protection of episcopal rights in the ducal chapel at Dijon, as also his careful distinction between the freedom of the *locus* and the lack of freedom of the officiating clergy in one of the French royal chapels.[2] While there is no 'salva diocesana lege' clause in the bull of Innocent IV upon which Henry III placed so much trust, it was not the pope's intention to grant away the diocesans' rights in the deaneries of the king's chapels. The bull was concerned only with freedom from sentences of excommunication and interdict and with impositions upon the colleges, and in using the term 'royal chapels' the pope gave no indication that he meant both the colleges and their parishes. It is hardly likely that this is what he did mean. Concerning impositions, the fact that the right to collect procurations may not always signify the right to visit (nor the immunity from procurations signify the immunity from visitation)[3] was perhaps one of the complicating factors in the dispute concerning the college of Bridgnorth's freedom from procurations. The distinction between the colleges and the parishes belonging to them—a distinction which it was extremely difficult in practice to make—was perhaps taken too much for granted by the pope. It was a distinction which the king chose to ignore.

Henry III interpreted the papal concessions as granting complete exemption for his chapels and their possessions from all episcopal interference. In 1246 he appealed to the pope against the holding of ordinations at Stafford by the bishop of Coventry and Lichfield.[4] In 1249 he ordered Innocent IV's bull of 21 July 1245 to be observed, and, in a prohibition against interference at Penkridge, he declared the exemption of all the royal chapels in England.[5] In 1250 he wrote to the council of prelates at Oxford, defending in extreme and emphatic terms the rights of his chapels.[6] This last letter is an indication of the extent to which Henry's attitude

---

[1] See Cheney 1931, pp. 37–8, and W. E. Lunt, *Financial Relations of the Papacy with England to 1327* (Cambridge, Mass., 1939), p. 102.

[2] Above, pp. 19–20, 22.

[3] Cheney 1931, pp. 39, 106–7, 117. [4] *CPR 1232–47*, p. 475.

[5] *CCR 1247–51*, pp. 223, 226. [6] *Councils and Synods* ii, 446–7.

towards the chapels differed from the papal attitude. Both Gregory and Innocent had been careful to point out that in spiritual matters the chapels were subject directly to the authority of the papal see; but the king claimed that 'neither the pope, nor any archbishop, bishop or prelate, should have exercised jurisdiction or authority in the chapels'. This was a freedom even greater than canonical exemption; it was freedom from the Church, local or universal.

Behind the apparent co-operation of king and pope there was a severe clash of interest. The king was effectively achieving direct and sole control of the royal chapels, a control which was particularly apparent in those churches which had not been entrusted to prelates in earlier years (as Penkridge had been given to the archbishop of Dublin, Derby to the dean of Lincoln and Bosham to the bishop of Exeter). The papal concessions had been misrepresented. In 1257, 1259, 1260 and 1261 the king was able to restate the complete exemption of his chapels and of the churches attached to the chapels from the interference of the ordinary.[1] The king used the doctored bull of July 1245 to support his own case. The diocesan was not to hold ordinations in the chapels, nor was he to take cognisance of all causes concerning tithes and offerings. Within the parishes spiritual jurisdiction should not be exercised by the bishops, but rather by the deans of the chapels. Since the deans were under the authority of the king, appointed exclusively by him, the implication was that the king himself exercised ultimate spiritual authority over his chapels and over the parishes which they controlled. No better evidence could be found to substantiate further M. T. Clanchy's recently expressed view of Henry III's policies;[2] his policy towards the royal chapels was a coherent assertion of royal sovereignty and divine kingship. While some would describe his methods as subtle, others would find evidence of deceit. The reaction of the clergy to the royal policy towards the chapels seems to be embodied in one of the formal complaints of 1257.[3] The king, they

[1] Owen and Blakeway 1825, ii, 189n, CCR 1256–9, p. 427, CPR 1258–66, p. 126, and Councils and Synods ii, 688.

[2] M. T. Clanchy, 'Did Henry III have a policy?', History, liii (1968), 203–16.

[3] Councils and Synods ii, 540, c. 6.

claimed, was using force to intrude clerks, against the wishes of the ecclesiastical ordinaries, into parish churches and prebends possessing cure of souls.

The compromise solutions, as they had been reached at Wolverhampton and at Bosham, had become less than satisfactory to the Crown during the thirteenth century. And the increased practice of visitation made a positive decision for or against exemption all the more necessary. The highest concentration of chapels existed in the diocese of Coventry and Lichfield, and any dispute between the king and the bishop concerning one of the chapels of that diocese naturally affected, at least by implication, the chapels as a group. It is clear that all was not peaceful at Penkridge during the middle years of the century,[1] but the first dispute for which sufficient material has survived to illustrate the clash between Crown and papacy concerns the college of St Mary Stafford.

From at least 1244 the college of St Mary Stafford was under pressure to defend its liberties.[2] The king himself was from the first directly involved, and in 1244, 1257 and 1258 he appointed three canons of the church as his proctors to defend the liberties of the chapel.[3] He had already, in 1246, appealed to the pope against the bishop, Roger Weseham, who had held an ordination at Stafford, for 'the church of St Mary Stafford is one of the king's special chapels exempt from the jurisdiction of ordinaries'.[4] Soon there was cause for greater concern. On 21 December 1258 the new bishop, Roger Longespee, took the college by storm.[5] With the assistance of a gang of men, lay and cleric alike, dressed in coats of chain mail and armed with lances and bows and arrows, the bishop broke into the church, beating, wounding and

---

[1] CCR 1247–51, p. 223, CCR 1256–9, p. 427, and CPR 1258–66, p. 40 (Prynne ii, 996).

[2] See Styles 1936, pp. 86–90; and, of the many short pamphlets written by Lionel Lambert on the history of St Mary Stafford, one is particularly useful: Chronological Table of the Principal Events in the History of St Mary's Church, Stafford (Stafford, 1936).

[3] CPR 1232–47, p. 420, and CPR 1247–58, pp. 550, 621.

[4] CPR 1232–47, p. 475.

[5] P.R.O. KB26/161 (Curia Regis Roll for Michaelmas 43 Henry III), m. 7 (translated in SHC, 1st ser. iv, pt. 1 (1883), pp. 140–1).

generally ill-treating the canons, chaplains and clerks of the college. The king tried to hold the bishop in check, claiming that this mother church of Stafford had been free from ordinary jurisdiction, as a church immediately subject to the pope, from the time of the first arrival of the Christian faith.[1] During the Michaelmas term of 1259, action was taken against the bishop in the king's court for damages of £510, a breach of the peace, and an attack against the king's 'crown and dignity'. The bishop presented himself but said that he was not disposed to answer to the charge against him in the king's court, for he was, after all, a clerk; and it looks very much as though the bishop had already appealed to the pope against the dean and chapter of Stafford.[2] In addition, the earl of Gloucester and Hereford, acting on behalf of his son, Bogo of Clare, who was the newly appointed dean of Stafford, claimed (against his son's interests, to all appearances) that no plea concerning the jurisdiction of the chapel of Stafford should be heard in that court.

Proceedings in the king's court never got off the ground. But elsewhere the issue was soon being taken a stage further. During a metropolitical visitation of the diocese of Coventry and Lichfield, Archbishop Boniface of Savoy came to Stafford on 27 September 1260, and discovered that the dean, canons and ministers had usurped episcopal and archidiaconal jurisdiction there over the people and parishioners of the church of Stafford and of the churches or chapels annexed to it.[3] The issue is clearly stated, the Church's point of view carefully defined. Archbishop Boniface made no mention of the exemption of the college. He took the canons and clergy of the church to task for exercising exclusive jurisdiction 'in populum et plebem et parochianos'. It was on the question of parochial rights, the question of cure of souls, that issue was joined. Under penalty of excommunication the arch-

---

[1] *CCR 1256–9*, p. 486.

[2] In the first proceedings directed from the papal curia (see Appendix VI) Simon of Offham is referred to as dean; he had resigned before 10 September 1259 (*CPR 1258–66*, p. 42).

[3] Prynne, iii, 1234–5, printing what is now P.R.O. SC1 (Ancient Correspondence) 11/94.

bishop forbade any continuation of the malpractices. Proceedings opened in the archbishop's court. It was claimed that the canons and ministers of St Mary Stafford possessed papal grants of exemption from any episcopal or archidiaconal interdict, and that these papal grants specifically protected the persons of the canons and ministers. The case was brought before the archbishop at the end of October and again in February 1261, but no papal bulls were produced. This is not surprising, for while the bull of 1245, a transcript of which had been sent to Stafford,[1] certainly exempted the chapels and their clergy from sentences of excommunication and interdict, it concerned the royal chapels in general, bore no specific mention of Stafford, and had been, according to the terms of the bull itself, valid for only ten years. Nevertheless, so much importance had been attached to it that it cannot have been unknown; and, unless it was recognised as now invalid, its existence must have made it all the more difficult for the archbishop to take the dean and canons to task. The proctor of the college of Stafford, declaring that the dean and chapter exercised jurisdiction within the deanery of the college from ancient and approved custom, avoided further proceedings in the archbishop's court by appealing to Rome. The appeal embodied the statement, as approved by the papacy, that the church was subject immediately to the pope. The appeal was in effect a request for some clarification of the claim that a royal chapel was subject in spiritualities only to the pope. The king's court and the archbishop's court had failed to terminate proceedings; the papal curia must decide.

At the papal curia[2] the claims of the bishop of Coventry and Lichfield were put forward: that the right to exercise episcopal jurisdiction at Stafford and the right to take cognisance of the ecclesiastical causes of all the officials, ministers and parishioners of the church belonged to him. He and his predecessors had been in virtual possession ('in quasi possessione') of these rights from ancient times. Because the dean and chapter opposed these rights, the bishop had suspended the chapter and excommunicated the dean and major canons. On the other hand, the dean and chapter claimed that, as one of the special chapels of the king, Stafford had

---

[1] Above, p. 93.   [2] For what follows, see Appendix VI.

H

been exempted by special papal privileges from all ordinary jurisdiction, and pleaded with the pope that they should be freed, while the case was being heard, from the sentences of excommunication and suspension, and that the bishop should be constrained from making any exactions. Urban IV delegated the case to the bishop of Worcester, the abbot of Bury St Edmunds and the precentor of St Paul's London, requiring them to return the case to the curia if a decision had not been reached within a year. As the senior of the judges delegate, the bishop of Worcester certainly took steps to collect evidence. And the case for the bishop of Coventry and Lichfield was presented to the judges delegate; but there is now no mention of a *libellus* of the dean and chapter. The case was returned to the curia, and the pope appointed as auditor Richard, cardinal deacon of St Angelus, who in turn appointed first Andrew Spiliaci and later Nicholas de Sanctis, both his chaplains. But term after term the dean and chapter failed to appear, even by proxy. The bishop had avoided the issue in the king's court; the dean and chapter were avoiding the issue in the papal court. After consultation the papal auditor terminated the case, condemning the dean and chapter to £50 costs and decreeing that the bishop's sentence of excommunication against the dean and chapter must remain and that the dean and chapter must obey the bishop as their diocesan until such time as they could show themselves to be exempt. On 3 August 1267 the mandate of Clement IV commissioned the bishop of Worcester and the prior of St Thomas's near Stafford to execute the decisions of the papal court. The pope was in effect reaffirming the principle that the royal chapels were free as colleges but not as churches with cure of souls.

An attempt was apparently made to provide the royal chapels with a papal bull which would demonstrate their complete exemption to intending visitors once and for all. A. J. Kempe and, separately, H. Owen and J. B. Blakeway printed in 1825 inaccurate texts of an indult of Clement IV dated 22 June 1266,[1] that is, before the Stafford case was terminated and during the actual hearing by the papal auditor. It is known to have existed in

[1] See Appendix V.

two copies (one at St Martin-le-Grand and the other possibly at Bridgnorth), but I have been able to trace only the first of these. This indult shows a remarkable advance in the papal attitude towards the chapels. Issued in response to a plea from Henry III, the bull embodies a re-wording of the claim which the dean and chapter of Stafford had put forward at the very beginning of the papal proceedings:[1] that the king's predecessors had founded the royal chapels before bishops had been ordained in England, and that from the time of their foundation they had been free from the jurisdiction of archbishops, bishops and lesser ordinaries. The king's plea was that by issuing ecclesiastical censure in these churches the archbishops, bishops and other ordinaries had exercised the office of visitation; and the pope, protecting the churches and their clergy and the king as their patron, conceded that visitation was a usurpation of established rights. The papal grant was not simply in favour of the college or the 'locus': it was in favour of the churches, their clergy and their possessions. If it is genuine we must regard it as a short-lived *volte face*. No original has survived; as the most important concession of all, and addressed to the king, it would have had, we might think, a good chance of finding its way to the collection of bulls in the royal treasury. It was not there in 1323.[2] The papal judgment of 1267 itself goes a very long way towards invalidating this 'indult' dated 1266. In fact, it is impossible to put any faith in it. It answered the needs of the dean and chapter of Stafford perfectly, and it may well be that they themselves inspired the forgery. It set down the royal policy towards the chapels, not the papal policy. Whether it was ever used does not appear; but the Crown and the royal chapels continued to act as though the pope had made concessions in their favour rather than judgments against them. For years the dean and chapter of Stafford remained under a ban of excommunication, but it is hard to believe that this had any important practical effects.

Royal policy was firmly established during the reign of Henry III. The Crown recognised the deans of the royal chapels as

[1] See Appendix VI, pp. 165–6.
[2] F. Palgrave, *Antient Kalendars*, i, 9–10.

ecclesiastical superiors in their deaneries. Although bishops, archdeacons, abbots and all ecclesiastical judges could exercise the right of excommunication, only the residential bishop could signify an excommunication to the king and thus, through the royal Chancery, empower the caption of the excommunicate by the sheriff. There were exceptions to this rule, so that some abbots and archdeacons by special royal grace were at times given the right to signify excommunications without reference to the diocesan bishop; but the notable exceptions were at least five of the deans of the royal free chapels—the deans of St Martin-le-Grand, Stafford, Tettenhall, Penkridge and Shrewsbury.[1] The deans exercised quasi-episcopal power. St Martin-le-Grand provides many examples of this process of obtaining secular aid for dealing with the contumacious. In 1253 Master Hugh, the proctor of the dean of St Martin-le-Grand, who was himself on business overseas, issued a signification concerning two excommunicates, requesting that they be compelled by arrest to give satisfaction.[2] In March and again in June 1314 Edward II wrote to the sheriff of London[3] instructing him to bring to justice Richard de Medhurst, 'vicar' of St Botolph without Aldersgate, which church, Edward claimed, was subject to the immediate jurisdiction of the royal chapel of St Martin-le-Grand. The 'vicar' had been excommunicated by the dean and would not submit to correction by ecclesiastical censure.

But constant vigilance was clearly necessary to maintain the exempt status of the chapels and their churches. When authentic bulls of exemption could not be produced, it was natural that ecclesiastical officials should be antagonistic towards claims which cut across the routine of ecclesiastical government. In 1250 Henry III had summoned the bishop of London, Fulk Basset, to appear before him to answer for exercising jurisdiction in the churches

---

[1] See F. D. Logan, *Excommunication and the Secular Arm in Medieval England* (Toronto, 1968), pp. 25, 33–5, 177–8.

[2] W.A.M., Book 5, fo. 28r.

[3] W.A.M., Book 5, fo. 21v (the first letter is translated in Kempe 1825, p. 92); a surviving signification of the excommunication of Richard de Medhurst (P.R.O. C85/214/25) is dated 27 July 1313.

of Newport and Chrishall, which were prebendal churches of St Martin-le-Grand;[1] and in 1287 and 1288 it was the archdeacon of Colchester whom Edward I was taking to task for visiting Chrishall and levying procurations.[2]

Edward I inherited and extended his father's policy towards the royal chapels. In defending royal rights the young king took special action. Between at least 1275 and 1287 he employed a proctor, a certain Master Ralph of Marlow, who acted for him 'in all causes and transactions affecting the king and his free chapels in England'.[3] Describing himself as proctor and warden of the king's free chapels, Ralph issued (in 1286) a set of rules to be observed by the college of Hastings,[4] which the king was now claiming as a royal free chapel. This claim was a novel one and has no rightful place in a discussion of the ancient chapels proper;[5] but with Edward I novel claims went hand-in-glove with a defence of ancient rights.

Although some of the royal chapels had firmly established their rights (and St Martin-le-Grand, as one of the most important, and Wimborne Minster, as one of the smallest, stand out in this respect), in other cases precise agreements between the deans and the bishops were needed before a peaceful settlement could be hoped for. After all, the papal interdict upon the college of Stafford had not been lifted. No general statements of principle, whether from the pope or from the king, could settle the local disputes. Without doubt, royal policy was for the most part already respected; but it was only after strenuous opposition to the Crown that a working agreement was achieved for the chapels in the diocese of Coventry and Lichfield. The strenuous opposition came from John Pecham shortly after he became archibishop of Canterbury. His fight for the rights of the church universal in

[1] W.A.M., Book 5, fo. 26r.

[2] Ibid., fo. 27r-v, and Prynne iii, 1288.

[3] CCR 1272–81, pp. 88, 91, Rôles Gascons, ed. Ch. Bémont, ii. no. 529 (and Prynne iii, 240), and Prynne iii, 324 (CPR 1281–92, p. 135).

[4] C. Dawson, The History of Hastings Castle (London, 1909), i, 114–15 (from what is now P.R.O. C 47 (Chancery Miscellanea) 21/2 mm. 2–3).

[5] See below, p. 116, n. 2.

these royal peculiars in fact strengthened the hand of the king and his deans.

After visiting his own diocese and the diocese of London, Pecham, with amazing energy and resolution, set out for the diocese of Coventry and Lichfield. His letters to the king following his attempt to visit the royal chapels of this diocese highlight the anomalous position of the king's deaneries.[1] To the archbishop a royal 'liberty' could not mean a 'liberty' which derogated from the rights of the church of Canterbury; it was *his* duty as archbishop to defend royal liberties. To possess chapels which were exempt by royal grants represented in his opinion no gain at all to the Crown, for it meant that the king himself would be charged with their sins. While the archbishop admitted that at various times working agreements had been drawn up concerning the chapels, he stressed that the canons of the churches could produce nothing but frivolous evidence to support actual exemption. Exemption by the king's grace amounted to unauthorised exemption ('sanz auctorite par vostre poer'), and the archbishop claimed that he had been disseised without judgment of rights which former archbishops had possessed. Pecham was genuinely shocked that the churches should claim exemption from episcopal control; he saw the claim as a sinful usurpation of rights and an attack upon the liberty of the Church. It thwarted the cure of souls and fostered both plurality and non-residence. No doubt there was some truth in his assertions, but just how well the parochial work was being carried out despite the freedom from the diocesan and the non-residence of the canons is impossible to ascertain.

Pecham censured without restraint. He set himself the task of restoring ecclesiastical rights in the peculiars of the diocese, and not one of the royal colleges escaped his attention. His visitation of the diocese began on 3 March 1280, and on the following day he

---

[1] The following account is based very largely upon the letters entered in Pecham's register: *Registrum Epistolarum Peckham*, ed. C. T. Martin, i, 91, 109–13, 130–1, 147–50, 155–6, 178–85, 196, 384–7, 392g (letters in French translated in appendix II), and *The Register of J. Pecham*, ii, ed. D. L. Douie (CYS, 1968), p. 140. For other accounts of Pecham's opposition, see D. L. Douie, *Archbishop Pecham*, pp. 145–7, and Styles 1936, pp. 88–91.

issued a general sentence of excommunication against all who opposed him. The king prohibited the archbishop from visiting the chapels,[1] but Pecham disregarded the prohibition, attempted to visit and found that the colleges were defended against him by armed guards (armed at the king's order, as the archbishop rightly claimed). The deans and canons thereby incurred the sentence of excommunication. Pecham knew of the earlier dispute concerning St Mary's Stafford, knew Boniface of Savoy had visited the college and knew that the outcome was papal support for the rights of the bishop. As he himself pointed out to the king, he learned that the college of Stafford was under an interdict and that its clerks were excommunicated[2] from the prior of St Thomas near Stafford and from the bishop of Worcester; they were the executors of the papal mandate of 1267. Acting with speed, the king ordered the sheriff of Stafford to go in person to the free chapel of Stafford and to prevent the archbishop or his men from entering it.[3] But a church under papal interdict in any case needed special treatment; and it was because of the interdict, so Pecham maintained, that he held ordinations in the church of the friars minor rather than in the mother church of St Mary. The archbishop was simply attempting to follow the papal lead in defending diocesan rights.

The chapel of Penkridge posed a particular problem, for the dean there was the archbishop of Dublin, *pro tem*. John de Derlington, and Pecham rightly regarded the clerks of Penkridge as not holding directly of the king ('ne se tenent pas a vostre furme'). The process concerning Penkridge was referred to the court of the Arches, but, after a chaplain of the archbishop of

[1] A prohibition had already been received on 1 April 1280, as Pecham's letter of the same date indicates (*Registrum Epistolarum Peckham*, i, 109); the undated prohibition in *The Liber Epistolaris of Richard de Bury*, ed. N. Denholm-Young, pp. 35–6, was the king's reply to this letter.

[2] Pecham's letter (*Registrum Epistolarum Peckham*, i, 111) states that the royal chapels of the diocese were under an interdict. It is certainly true that the papal mandate of 1267 concerned by implication chapels other than Stafford, but Pecham's statement is the only evidence that I have found to suggest that interdict was widespread.

[3] *Calendar of Chancery Warrants*, i, 5–6.

Dublin had represented his interests before Pecham, the case was prorogued pending future discussion between the two archbishops. Pecham was presented with a letter of Henry III, of a very familiar sort, which prohibited any interference at Penkridge and cited the papal indult of July 1245. The sustained propaganda of the Crown (and 'propaganda' is no loose term when the papal attitude was so completely twisted in favour of the Crown's case) was having its effect, for the bull even took Pecham by surprise. But he was not convinced of its relevance, for he pointed out that it was a concession 'in genere', and that the mention of Penkridge was made by the king alone 'proprio consilio'. What Pecham wanted from the archbishop of Dublin was clear evidence of exemption ('exemptionis solidum fundamentum'), evidence which royal letters could never supply, especially since, as Pecham believed, the chapels possessed no prescriptive rights. While the archbishop showed great consideration to the archbishop of Dublin himself, the clerks of the chapel of Penkridge remained under a sentence of excommunication and appealed to Rome against the archbishop's attack. Understandably, it proved difficult to stay the exercise of spiritual jurisdiction by the dean and canons pending a legal decision; and in July 1280 Pecham complained to the king that certain men whom he claimed as parishioners of the church of Lichfield had been imprisoned following action taken against them by the dean and canons of Penkridge.[1]

For three of the royal chapels (Derby, Shrewsbury and Tettenhall) we know only that Pecham initiated proceedings against the 'deans, canons, ministers or vicars'. At Wolverhampton the dean and canons were excommunicated and attempts were made to bring both to justice in the archbishop's court. The action against the dean, Tedesius de Camilla, became a separate issue,[2] unrelated to the dispute concerning the rights of the chapel itself;

[1] The signification of excommunication from the archbishop of Dublin dated 18 May 1280 (P.R.O. C85/214/15a) is in all probability evidence of the action to which Pecham referred.

[2] *Registrum Epistolarum Peckham*, i, 384-7, ii, 558-60, and *The Register of Pecham*, ii, 44-5, 68-9, 153, 158-9.

among several charges brought against Tedesius was one of
simony, for he had apparently tried to sell the church of Wengham
to the notorious Bogo of Clare (dean of St Mary Stafford, and
outstanding pluralist) in exchange for land valued at eighty
marks. And Pecham also charged him with having been invested
with the deanery of Wolverhampton by lay hands. This particular breach of canon law seems in general to have been ignored,
for no other specific charge of 'lay investiture' concerning the
appointments to the royal deaneries has come to light.

Undeterred by the opposition which he had encountered in the
diocese of Coventry and Lichfield, the archbishop proceeded in
November 1280 to offend the dean and canons of St Martin-le-
Grand.[1] When he was at Saffron Walden, men (including a clerk,
Richard Osgot) from the nearby parish of Newport (which
was a prebendal church of St Martin-le-Grand) came to the
archbishop 'pur le salu de lur almes', and as a result either the
dean of St Martin-le-Grand himself or his officials took action
against the men (imprisoning the clerk) and made them swear
that they would never approach the archbishop again. Pecham
in turn excommunicated those who thus usurped his authority.
The king was quickly on the defensive and wrote to the sheriff
of Essex instructing him to allow no sentence of excommunication issued by the authority of the archbishop to prevent men of
those parishes belonging to St Martin-le-Grand from hearing
divine service and taking the sacraments. There must be no
breakdown in communications with the canons and ministers
of the royal chapel and no interruption in the holding of markets.[2]
Less had actually happened than Edward seems to have feared;
far from putting an interdict on St Martin-le-Grand or its churches,
Pecham had merely excommunicated unnamed offenders. But
his policy here, as in the diocese of Coventry and Lichfield,
represented for the Crown an attack upon the royal dignity.

In response to the many letters of Edward I to his archbishop
(of which only one copy has survived)[3] Pecham made a single

[1] *Registrum Epistolarum Peckham*, i, 184–5, and *The Register of Pecham*, ii, 124.
[2] W.A.M., Book 5, fo. 25v (translated in Kempe 1825, pp. 96–7).
[3] Above, p. 105, n. 1.

concession: he agreed to suspend the publishing of the sentences of excommunication against the royal clerks in the king's chapels of the diocese of Coventry and Lichfield (excepting the clerks of the chapel of Penkridge), and to suspend also the sentence against the offenders at Newport, until negotiations could be entered into at the parliament of Easter 1281. One concession was more than enough. Pecham had been pleading a lost cause. No record of the actual negotiations following the Easter parliament has survived, but it is difficult to imagine any significant opposition to the reaffirmation of royal policy. The archbishop himself was not present, but was represented by the archdeacon of Canterbury and the dean of the Arches,[1] and the chapter of Lichfield was also represented by two proctors.[2] Before the negotiations took place it was understood that an agreement was to be drawn up between the bishop of Coventry and Lichfield and the deans and chapters of the royal chapels. The problem was seen as essentially a diocesan rather than a provincial matter; but there is no doubt that the intention of the king and his deans was to prevent the archbishop, quite as much as the bishop, from exercising jurisdiction in the chapels. Far from exercising special rights over the royal peculiars as may have been the case a century before,[3] the archbishop of Canterbury exercised no rights at all, not even rights of arbitration. The archbishop did not enter into the agreement of 1281.

A composition, dated 27 May 1281, was drawn up between the bishop of Coventry and Lichfield and the dean and canons of St Mary Shrewsbury,[4] and this was possibly one of a group of separate agreements with the chapels. A composite agreement

---

[1] *Registrum Epistolarum Peckham*, i, 196.

[2] Oxford Bodleian Lib., Ashmole 1527, fos. 72v–73r, noted in Owen and Blakeway 1825, ii, 306. In this instrument (dated 26 April 1281) proctors of the dean and chapter of Lichfield were appointed to assist at an agreement between the bishop and the deans and chapters of Stafford, Wolverhampton, Bridgnorth, St Mary Shewsbury and Tettenhall. The reason for the exclusion in this context of the two royal free chapels which had been given away in perpetuity, Derby and Penkridge, is not apparent.

[3] Above, pp. 42–3.

[4] Owen and Blakeway, ii, 307, n. 2. See Appendix VII.

followed on 3 June between the bishop and the deans and chapters of Stafford, Derby, Penkridge, Tettenhall, Wolverhampton, Bridgnorth and St Mary Shrewsbury.[1] The terms of the separate and the composite agreement are identical. By the will and assent of the king, who was known to be patron ('patronus') of these churches, it was agreed that the deans, canons, servitors, ministers and parishioners of the churches and of the chapels attached to the churches should remain free from all ordinary jurisdiction and that they should be immediately subject to the church of Rome. The king himself, with the consent of the parties concerned, was declaring the colleges to be exempt. Bishops or other ecclesiastics exercising ordinary jurisdiction must not visit these deaneries, take cognisance of any causes, or do anything that would not be done in other exempt churches. It was added, however, that for the sake of good relations the deans and canons should receive the bishop with a procession and all due honour when he happened to pass through the deaneries, and that by their good grace he might preach in their churches, celebrate orders, bless the oil and chrism and confirm the young. Whenever he celebrated orders or blessed chrism in one of the churches the bishop might ordain the clerks presented to him following their examination by the dean and might himself present the oil and chrism to the churches if he so wished. These concessions were not thought to compromise the 'exemption, liberty, and immunity' of the royal chapels, but, at least, it is still possible to say that the deaneries were within the diocese of Coventry and Lichfield. The links with the diocese remained. Some essential functions could be performed by a bishop alone, and there are no indications that the deans and canons were empowered to choose their own bishop. The seals of the bishop, the king, and the deans and chapters were appended to the composition. There had been no earlier indications that Bishop Longespee—a kinsman of the king—would give his consent to the exemption of the colleges. The declaration that the agreement should be sent to the pope so that his confirmation might he sought was probably to satisfy the bishop's doubts about its validity. Or perhaps this was a way of taking into

[1] Appendix VII.

account the objections of Pecham's representatives. There was of course little chance that any pope would confirm a document which so blatantly disregarded the Church's control over spiritual matters.

The agreement of 1281 is found in the Magnum Registrum Album of Lichfield (compiled 1317 × 1328); the printed translation of this copy of the agreement bears no reference to the fact that Derby has been carefully erased. It has therefore been wrongly concluded that the dean and canons of Derby were not party to this composition. And the suggestion has been made that the agreement copied into the Carte Decani of Lincoln was a new agreement drawn up in 1292 which included Derby for the first time. Yet this is in fact a copy of the 1281 composition which was found among the king's 'privileges' in 1292.[1] It is understandable that the possession by the dean of Lincoln (who was dean of Derby) of an exempt deanery within the bishopric of Coventry and Lichfield was particularly galling to the bishop of that diocese. The situation had caused some animosity, and this probably explains the erasure of Derby in the Lichfield cartulary. There are no grounds for suspecting that Derby had not been a party to the composition of 1281, nor for suspecting that the church was not a royal chapel.[2] Domesday Book records that there were two churches in the town of Derby, one with seven clerks and another with six clerks.[3] The entry is important, for both churches are specifically noted as being 'in dominio regis'. The record of a dispute with the abbey of Darley in the middle of the thirteenth century establishes that the two churches had by this time been united, and that the boundaries of their parishes corresponded with the boundaries of the royal demesne. Apart from the complication of being formed from two churches, the college of All Saints Derby appears to have followed a regular pattern of development. It was given by Henry I to the church of Lincoln, and this was confirmed by Henry II as a gift which included all

[1] Appendix VII.

[2] *VCH Derby*, ii, 87–90 (as J. C. Cox and W. H. St John Hope, *The Chronicles of All Saints Derby* (London, 1881), pp. 1–6).

[3] *DB*, i, 280b.

the liberties and free customs which the college possessed.[1] Far
from being held in common by the chapter of Lincoln, the college became the immediate possession of the dean, so that the
dean of Lincoln was also dean of All Saints Derby. The thirteenth
century brought a familiar round of disputes, along with the
familiar claims from the king that as a royal chapel Derby was
exempt from the jurisdiction of the bishop of Coventry and
Lichfield and of the archdeacon of Derby. For this chapel, as
for others, Henry III asserted that exemption had been secured
through 'privileges' of the apostolic see.[2] The claim was re-asserted
by Edward I.

Despite the agreement of 1281, the bishop exercised jurisdiction at Derby; but he was prohibited from doing so and a case
against him was brought before the king's court during 1284–5.[3]
Understandably, Bishop Longespee first sought justice to establish whether in fact he should be made to answer in the king's
court concerning the exercise of spiritual jurisdiction; but the
case proceeded at least as far as determining what the customary
practices had been at Derby. Strange though it seems, the 1281
composition had apparently been forgotten—by the bishop
probably deliberately. He claimed that the church was within
his bishopric and fully within his jurisdiction; the dean of Lincoln
claimed that the bishop had no jurisdiction there, that he himself
had visited, corrected and instituted to the prebends. A jury of
twenty-four was summoned, and gave evidence in 1285. Their
declaration shows, predictably enough, that the exercise of jurisdiction at Derby had been divided between bishop and dean.
The working arrangement which had developed there apparently
gave to the bishop the right to collect synodals, to celebrate orders
and to make corrections (with the implied right of visitation)
concerning the chaplains, clergy and parishioners of the deanery;
but at the same time the dean of Lincoln certainly exercised

[1] *Registrum Antiquissimum of Lincoln*, i, ed. C. W. Foster, pp. 29, 93 (as
Lincoln Dean and Chapter Archives, Carte Decani (A.1.7), fo. 48r, nos. 126–7).

[2] *Registrum Antiquissimum*, i, 185–6 (and *CPR 1266–72*, p. 512), *Reg. Antiquis.*,
iii, 100–1 (as Carte Decani, fos. 48r–49r), and *CCR 1268–72*, pp. 30, 110.

[3] See Appendix VIII.

the full right of institution to the prebends. This was clearly not a declaration in line with royal policy. For the time being the matter rested there: a decision of complete exemption could hardly follow immediately upon this statement from a sworn jury. Whatever had been the 'free customs' of the royal college of Derby in the twelfth century, the diocesan had come, by a process in which no doubt both expediency and deliberate Church policy played a part, to exercise a large degree of spiritual control. How far Edward I was able to halt, in a sense to reverse, this process is not at all clear. There is reason to suspect that there were obstructions at Derby which the king had not had to face in the other chapels of the area. The fact that the copy of the 1281 composition in the Carte Decani of Lincoln is noted as being found at Westminster in 1292[1] perhaps suggests that the dean was attempting at this time to enforce its terms. While it is impossible to be certain, the indications are that this chapel, like the others of the diocese, gained recognition of its claim to be free from the bishop. The holding of ordinations there, which is within the terms of the agreement, appears to be the only evidence of the continued exercise of episcopal jurisdiction,[2] and Derby was included on three out of four of the lists of royal free chapels which have survived from the reigns of Edward I and Edward II.[3]

What was the state of play with regard to the royal free chapels at the beginning of the fourteenth century? A large number of churches had developed away from their early condition as royal chapels.[4] Pevensey had completely disintegrated. Gnosall, Steyning and Blyth had each undergone processes of change which detracted from their status and rights. And Bromfield was only clinging to its former liberties; its link with the past would soon be broken. While some parishes in the town of Dover remained free, the priory of St Martin Dover had not retained close contact with the parish or parishes it had served as a secular college. At

[1] See below, p. 172, n. 7.

[2] J. C. Cox and W. H. St John Hope, op. cit., p. 6.

[3] *Councils and Synods* ii, 1146, *CCR 1313–8*, pp. 172–3, 596, and *Register of W. de Stapeldon*, ed. F. C. Hingeston-Randolph, p. 99.

[4] For all these royal chapels see chapter III.

Waltham exemption was closely associated with the early status of the church and in a sense the abbey's position as a royal free chapel had not been lost; but it had become an exempt abbey conforming to a pattern quite different from that of the royal chapels.

Finally, we must exclude Bosham from a list of the fully privileged. Poised as this college was between the jurisdiction of the bishop of Chichester and the bishop of Exeter, its position remained precarious, and efforts on the part of the Crown and the bishop of Exeter to establish the full freedom of the parishes which Bosham served led to a bitter dispute in the fourteenth century.[1] The problem here was simply that neither of the bishops would give way; the only agreement remained the compromise settlement of 1204 × 1206.[2] A petition to Pope Martin IV in 1282, which may or may not have been sent, shows Edward I trying to obtain a papal declaration of Bosham's exemption.[3] The king's letter was an attempt to override the compromise solution ('non obstantibus quibusdam pactis, compositionibus . . .') and to secure by papal bull full ordinary jurisdiction for the bishop of Exeter in the whole chapelry of Bosham. The plea was for the full exemption of Bosham 'cum canonicis et personis ecclesiasticis predictis canonicatibus et praebendis et annexis ecclesiis et capellis, et ministris, clero et populo eorundem'. But the matter remained unresolved, and conflict began in earnest after Walter Stapledon was elected to the bishopric of Exeter in 1308. The lengthy proceedings in the king's court during Edward II's reign against the archdeacon of Chichester and his official and against the bishop of Chichester and his official could, in the end, only determine whether or not royal prohibitions had been contravened. The decisions of the court, however much they implied the freedom of the whole chapelry, could not themselves constitute a decision against the extent of a bishop's jurisdiction. This is why the king had concentrated in other cases upon bringing the parties to agreements

[1] See esp. *Select Cases King's Bench*, ed. G. O. Sayles, iv, 111–22, *The Register of W. de Stapeldon*, passim, and *The Register of J. Grandisson*, passim.

[2] Above, p. 46.

[3] Prynne iii, 1266 (source now untraced).

favourable to the Crown and to the clerks who enjoyed royal patronage. Bosham was a fully acknowledged royal free chapel for which the Crown had failed to gain full exemption. It was exempt as a college, but not as a college with cure of souls. The chapel and the deanery of Bosham remained under the control of two bishops, and the disputes continued.

Leaving aside Pevensey, Gnosall, Steyning, Blyth, Bromfield, Dover, Waltham and Bosham, we are left with ten royal free chapels which in 1300 possessed exemption for themselves and for their churches. These chapels fully enjoyed, as Archbishop Pecham expressed it, a spiritual freedom by royal grace ('par exempcion doneye si come len dist par le reisum de vostre reaute').[1] The privileges of St Martin-le-Grand and of Wimborne Minster (the only chapel for which I have found no evidence of a clash with the diocesan)[2] were now beyond dispute. And Edward I had succeeded in establishing the exemption of seven colleges in the diocese of Coventry and Lichfield: St Mary Shrewsbury, Bridgnorth, Stafford, Tettenhall, Penkridge, Wolverhampton and probably Derby. To make the tenth, a dispute concerning St Oswald's Gloucester, which led to proceedings in 1304 and 1305, re-established this Augustinian priory, with its deanery of Churchdown, as an exempt house with the status of a royal free chapel.[3]

But there is no doubt that it was part of Edward I's policy to increase the number of his royal free chapels. He was not content simply to consolidate the achievements of his father; he tried to extend his free deaneries beyond those which had a just, or at least an intelligible, claim to ancient customary rights. In his attempt to establish spiritual control over St Mary's Hastings, St Buryan's Cornwall and Tickhill, the king was in one form or another going against established custom. Long and fascinating disputes followed all three claims. Hastings castle came under the Crown's direct control when Edward became king, and it is at the beginning of his reign that we find the first statement that the college in

---

[1] *Registrum Epistolarum Peckham*, ii, 547. [2] Above, pp. 27–8.
[3] See esp. *Select Cases King's Bench*, iii, 138–44, and below, pp. 116, n. 2, and 141-2.

the castle is a royal free chapel.[1] Although the rights of the bishop of Chichester in the churches attached to this college were firmly established, Edward tried to usurp them. This college was now a chapel in a royal castle. The dispute dragged on until the last weeks of Edward's reign, and in June 1307 the king's court came to the only possible conclusion: that ordinary jurisdiction must continue to be exercised by the bishop in the churches which possessed cure of souls, reserving only the castle-chapel itself *qua* chapel.[2] As a royal college, and a well-endowed one, Hastings remained free, but the churches belonging to it were not free. In this respect Hastings was of the same status as Bosham, although Bosham had some claim to ancient rights. The bishop's parochial rights had been safeguarded. After 1307 the king presented his nominees to vacant prebends to the bishop of Chichester, the bishop admitted the presentation, and the king then instructed the dean and chapter to assign a stall in the choir and a place in the chapter.[3]

The castle of Tickhill also became a royal castle at the beginning of Edward's reign, and the king made an audacious bid to re-create the ancient chapelry of Blyth[4] by amalgamating it to the chapel of Tickhill castle. The chapelry was very extensive, consisting of the churches of East Bridgford, Lowdham, East Markham, Markham Clinton, Walesby, Wheatley and Harworth in the diocese of York. Although there was now no college at Blyth or at Tickhill and although the archbishop of York had established his rights as diocesan over the churches which formed the chapelry, the royal claim to the complete freedom of the royal free chapel of Tickhill may be thought at least to have an historical basis. But, despite renewed claims of complete freedom from ordinary jurisdiction in 1343 and 1344,[5] the newly established free chapelry of Tickhill seems in fact to have had a short history and to have outlived Edward I by only a few years.

---

[1] *CPR 1272–81*, p. 9, and C. Dawson, *The History of Hastings Castle*, i, 104.

[2] *Select Cases King's Bench*, ed. G. O. Sayles, iii, 190.

[3] E. Gibson, *Codex Iuris Ecclesiastici* (2nd ed., Oxford, 1761), p. 211 (tit. ix, 12), citing *Registrum Omnium Brevium* (London, 1531), p. 307b.

[4] See above, pp. 75–6.   [5] *CPR 1343–5*, pp. 117, 171, 388–9.

In the college of St Buryan the king became patron when Edmund of Cornwall died in 1300, and immediately Edward claimed the church as a royal free chapel.[1] Here the Crown, and the Black Prince, eventually secured the freedom of the college and its churches, with the aid of a charter of King Athelstan forged in all probability during or shortly after 1352. Edward's attempts to create new royal free chapels at length brought St Buryan's fully, and Hastings only partly, into line with other exempt royal colleges. With the exception of St Buryan's, the number of exempt deaneries was established by the end of the thirteenth century. Although the history of Tickhill can be traced back to the royal free chapel of Blyth, there are no adequate grounds for including Hastings, St Buryan's or Tickhill in a list of 'genuine' royal free chapels. They were all in some degree Edward I's creations, and a study of them belongs elsewhere.[2]

Three new 'royal free chapels' of the fourteenth century (St Edith's Tamworth, St George's Windsor and St Stephen's Westminster) possessed no exempt deaneries. Although little evidence concerning Tamworth survives, it is clear that the bishop of Coventry and Lichfield continued to exercise the right of institution to both the deanship and the prebends.[3] The church became a royal college but not a royal peculiar. The college in Windsor castle, founded in 1348, obtained a papal privilege in 1351 (specifically referred to as a grant of exemption and liberty), which conceded complete freedom from ordinary jurisdiction,[4] and placed the college under the pope's immediate authority ('ad jus et proprietatem beati Petri'); but this freedom applied only to the 'capellam, collegium, canonicos, presbyteros, clericos, milites et ministros'. There was no hint that the churches appropriated to

---

[1] See C. Henderson, *Essays in Cornish History* (Oxford, 1935), pp. 93–107.

[2] See my forthcoming *Robert Winchelsey and the Crown* for these and also for the dispute concerning St Oswald's Gloucester.

[3] See Hamilton Thompson 1947, p. 82n, and *The First Register of R. de Stretton*, ed. R. A. Wilson (*SHC*, new ser. x, pt. 2, 1907), passim. A case between a prebendary and the dean concerning tithes was heard in the consistory court of Lichfield in 1359 (ibid., p. 9).

[4] *Monasticon*, vi, 1355–6, and see A. K. B. Roberts, *St George's Chapel Windsor Castle*, p. 49.

the college[1] should be regarded as exempt. Indeed, Clement VI's bull stressed that the warden of the college should be subject to the diocesan, the bishop of Salisbury, in respect of the exercise of cure of souls within the college. In practice, however, it appears that in all spiritual matters within the college there was to be no interference with the warden's authority. He was responsible only to the Crown. This college followed the established pattern of colleges in royal castles, but it was no longer possible to create parochial enclaves outside the college walls. However important the privileges of exemption for a large royal college, the warden or dean of Windsor was not a petty bishop to the same extent as, for example, the dean of Wolverhampton.

The position of St Stephen's in the palace of Westminster, also founded in 1348, was very similar.[2] Once again Clement VI declared that, while the canons and clerks should be exempt from ordinary jurisdiction, 'the dean is to receive cure of souls from the bishop and to be subject to him in all things relating to it'.[3] But the terms of the bull were not strictly observed. The pope required the annual payment of one mark to the papal camera. It is no surprise to discover that this census was never paid from the royal chapel.[4] And once again it is quite clear that the creation of the college had not amounted to the creation of a spiritual peculiar concerned with parishes and parishioners. A quarrel between St Stephen's and the abbey of Westminster from 1375 to 1393 reveals the very limited extent to which the college can be said to have possessed its own spiritual rights.[5] In the many royal colleges outside England (as St Stephen's Vienna)[6] the situation was much the same. An act of 1396 defines in similar terms the extent of the jurisdiction of the dean and chapter of the French royal college of St Wulfran of Abbeville.[7] Even the most

---

[1] Roberts, op. cit., pp. 14–27.   [2] See *VCH London*, i. 566–71.

[3] *Calendar of Papal Petitions*, i (HMSO, 1896), 187.

[4] W. E. Lunt, *Financial Relations of the Papacy with England 1327–1534*, pp. 60–1.

[5] *VCH London*, i, 568, and for the documents concerning this dispute see esp. W.A.M., Muniment Book 12, fos. 31r–87v.

[6] N. Grass in *Festschrift K. S. Bader*, esp. p. 172.

[7] Mollat 1951, p. 8.

prestigious of the English 'royal free chapels' created in the later middle ages must be set apart from the exempt deaneries.

But this does not complete the survey of the royal chapels which were ecclesiastical peculiars. No mention has been made of some well-endowed chapels in royal castles. It is clear from Edward I's attempts to create royal deaneries attached to the newly acquired castles of Hastings and Tickhill that the chapels in royal castles formed a very important category of free chapel. Castle-chapels as a group merit separate discussion. Some, like St Mary's Hastings and Bridgnorth, were important colleges; very many were mere buildings, were not benefices and were not endowed. Other castle-chapels were well endowed and had been—or possibly had been—collegiate in the twelfth century or earlier. For example, the clergy's list of royal free chapels[1] included the chapel of St George in Oxford castle, and the king's list of 1315[2] included the chapel of St Michael in Shrewsbury castle. We shall find no more large exempt deaneries. But how far did St George's and St Michael's, and other royal castle-chapels, possess rights which set aside the jurisdiction of the diocesan?

[1] Above, p. 1.   [2] *CCR 1313–8*, pp. 172–3.

Chapter V

CASTLE-CHAPELS

The chapels of royal castles naturally enjoyed a special relationship with the king. And early in their history the royal free chapels were often associated with fortified towns, as at Dover and almost certainly at Pevensey, and as also in Mercia, for example at Derby and Stafford.[1] Clerical minsters had been established at centres of population. Yet during the centuries after the Conquest only one of the fully privileged royal colleges—St Mary Magdalene Bridgnorth[2]—was, and remained, a castle-chapel. It had been founded by the earl of Shrewsbury at Quatford in 1086. The earl's son, Robert of Belesme, transferred both his father's castle and the secular college to Bridgnorth in 1098. When the property was forfeited to the Crown in 1102, Henry I became patron of the college, and it was Henry I who was regarded in the later middle ages as the founder of the college of Bridgnorth.[3] The church retained its collegiate status and was the centre of an extensive deanery. Some other churches in royal castles of the twelfth and thirteenth centuries seem to have been fully collegiate only at an early stage in their history; but is there any evidence that royal castle-chapels other than Bridgnorth had exempt parishes attached to them?

The college of St George was founded in the castle of Oxford by Robert d'Oilli and Roger d'Ivri in 1074.[4] The patronage rights

---

[1] See *Beverley Chapter Act Book*, ed. A. F. Leach (Surtees Soc., 98), p. xxxii.

[2] See Hamilton Thompson 1927.

[3] *Calendar of Inquisitions Misc.*, v, no. 353.

[4] See J. Parker, *The Early History of Oxford* (Oxford Hist. Soc., 1884), *VCH Oxford*, ii, 160, *Cartulary of Oseney Abbey* (Oxford Hist. Soc., 1929–36), i, 1–10, and *The History of the King's Works*, ed. H. M. Colvin (HMSO, 1963), ii, 771–2.

of the second founder of the college apparently passed to the king early in the twelfth century, and thereafter d'Oilli himself was always stated as sole founder. But d'Oilli appears to have held Oxford castle not in fee but as royal custodian. Privileges were granted by the king to St George's,[1] and the king claimed for the canons of the college that they held their lands in frankalmoign. The provost, Walter archdeacon of Oxford, possessed the church of St Mary Magdalene Oxford as part of his prebend.[2] There is no indication that St George's was regarded as possessing the full spiritual liberties of a demesne chapel, but it is possible that the provost and canons of the college exercised virtually exclusive jurisdiction within the parishes they served. St George's was perhaps comparable with the church of St Martin-le-Grand. Had it remained in royal hands it may well have developed, like St Martin-le-Grand, towards a defined and recognised spiritual freedom. But the college with all its possessions (including the church of St Mary Magdalene Oxford, the churches of Stowe, Buckinghamshire, and Cowley, Oxfordshire, and a claim to part of the tithes of many manors) was granted to Osney abbey, a royal house, in 1149.[3] And from this time forward it is difficult to trace its separate history.

The church of St George's Oxford not only lost its collegiate status, but it also lost its direct relationship with its parishes. There are references in the thirteenth century to small non-parochial royal chapels at Oxford, as elsewhere;[4] these are not references to St George's. It is clear that during the thirteenth century the church was not regarded as a spiritual peculiar, for the churches which had belonged to it were not being claimed as exempt from episcopal jurisdiction. The abbot of Osney made presentations

---

[1] H. E. Salter, *Facsimiles of Early Charters in Oxford* (Oxford, 1929), nos. 57–8, and *Cal. Charter Rolls*, iii, 418–19.

[2] *VCH Oxford*, iii, 1.

[3] *Annales Monastici*, ed. H. R. Luard, iv. 26, H. E. Salter, *Early Charters in Oxford*, nos. 59, 61–3, and H. E. Salter, 'Geoffrey of Monmouth and Oxford', *EHR*, xxxiv (1919), 385.

[4] *Rot. Lit. Claus.*, ii, 61b ('capellam nostram extra castrum nostrum Oxon'), 104b, *CCR 1256–9*, p. 397, and *Calendar of Liberate Rolls* (HMSO, 1916–), vi, nos. 119, 2007.

to the bishop of Lincoln for these churches.[1] As a chapel within a royal castle, the church remained of importance to the king. At the beginning of the fourteenth century it still had some kind of corporate existence, and was being claimed as the king's free chapel: in a petition to the king the abbot and convent asserted that 'from the foundation of their abbey there had been a free chapel of St George in the castle of Oxford for which the abbot finds thirteen ministers and two canons for daily service, for whose sustenance divers parcels of tithes were given, under royal confirmation, to the said chantry . . .'[2] The king assisted Osney abbey in its efforts to retain intact the tithes belonging to the chapel.[3] The freedom from diocesan control of St George's itself and its ministers never appears to have been challenged, but this was a freedom enjoyed by other chapels *non curate* in royal castles. It had lost its collegiate, and to some extent its independent, status; and, at least after 1149, it does not appear to have been a royal chapel of great standing.

Even less is known about the chapel of St Michael in the castle of Shrewsbury. Perhaps, as A. Hamilton Thompson implied,[4] this was one of the Anglo-Saxon minsters at Shrewsbury; but the historians of Shrewsbury, Owen and Blakeway, regarded Roger of Montgomery, earl of Shrewsbury, as its founder.[5] While no evidence can be cited to confirm Hamilton Thompson's suspicions that it had been a college, the possibility remains.[6]

[1] *Rotuli Hugonis de Welles*, i, ed. W. P. W. Phillimore, 179–80, *Cartulary of Oseney Abbey*, iii, 62, and *Rotuli R. Grosseteste*, ed. F. N. Davis, pp. 347, 444, 446–7, 481, 485.

[2] *Collectanea*, iii (Oxf. Hist. Soc., 1896), 94–5 (from P.R.O. SC 8 (Ancient Petitions) file 329 E904); and see *Calendar of Liberate Rolls*, v, 213. That canons of Osney celebrated divine service daily in the chapel is shown also in *Calendar of Memoranda Rolls (Exchequer) 1326–7* (HMSO, 1968), p. 364.

[3] *Cal. Chancery Warrants*, i, 288, 475, *Cartulary of Oseney Abbey*, iv, 524–6, v, 253–9, and Lincoln Diocesan Record Office, Reg. Dalderby III, fos. 161v–162r.

[4] Hamilton Thompson 1917, p. 182, and see *Monasticon*, vi, 1463–4.

[5] Owen and Blakeway 1825, ii, 420, and see 416–17.

[6] A royal letter of 1261 addressed to the constable of the castle (*CCR 1259–61*, p. 441) refers to the 'canons of the free chapel of Shrewsbury', but this is no doubt the college of St Mary Shrewsbury.

After the Conquest the castle of Shrewsbury was in the hands of the earl of Shrewsbury and, like the castle of Bridgnorth, was forfeited to the Crown in 1102.[1] Thereafter, St Michael's was in royal hands. While there is very little evidence concerning the chapel, it is clear that it became very closely associated with another royal chapel at Shrewsbury, the chapel of St Juliana.[2] In 1342, for example, the king granted both chapels at the same time to the same royal clerk.[3] St Juliana's, undoubtedly a chapel with a parish, was perhaps an older foundation than St Michael's. There is mention in the thirteenth century of portions or pre-bends in the church of St Juliana, and it is probable that it had been collegiate early in its history. Indeed, this small church of St Juliana merits inclusion among the royal free chapels. It was claimed as a 'libera capella regis', and the very scant evidence suggests that the 'rector' or his official enjoyed freedom from episcopal jurisdiction. In 1390 and 1446 the official of the 'rector' of this royal chapel was exercising the right of probate of wills.

The references concerning St Michael's are usually to the 'rector'[4] or the 'parson'[5] of the castle-chapel. Only a few refer-ences, in Edward II's reign, are to the 'dean'.[6] There was only one

---

[1] *Hist. of the King's Works*, ed. H. M. Colvin, ii, 835.

[2] See T. Auden, 'The church and parish of St Juliana in Salop', *Shropshire Archaeological Soc.*, 1st ser. x (1887), esp. 158–62, and J. E. Auden, 'The local peculiar courts of Shropshire', *Shropshire Arch. Soc.*, 4th ser. xii (1929–30), 285–6. A royal writ printed in *Registrum Omnium Brevium* (London, 1531), pp. 40b–41, as an example of a royal prohibition ('Ne quis intromittat se de libera capella regis prohibitio'), concerns St Chad's Shrewsbury. But unless this represents a temporary and ill-conceived claim that St Chad's was a royal free chapel, it must be an error; the church was an episcopal college (see Owen and Blakeway 1825, ii, 185–8). The king exercised rights of presentation here (not collation) when the bishopric of Coventry and Lichfield was vacant (*CPR 1358–61*, p. 190, and *CPR 1381–5*, p. 565).

[3] *CPR 1340–3*, p. 479.   [4] *CPR 1247–58*, p. 411.

[5] *CPR 1292–1301*, p. 154, *CPR 1307–13*, pp. 98, 139, 198, *CPR 1313–7*, pp. 2, 28, and *Cal. Chancery Warrants*, i, 283. For further references and a list of incum-bents, see W. G. D. Fletcher, 'The church of St Michael within the castle, Shrewsbury', *Shropshire Arch. Soc.*, 4th ser. viii (1920–1), 254–9.

[6] *CCR 1313–8*, p. 173, Owen and Blakeway 1825, ii, 422, n. 4 (citing the Pipe Roll of 14 Edward II), and *Cal. of Memoranda Rolls 1326–7*, no. 1708.

'parson' in the chapel of St Michael, and he was assisted by 'chaplains and clerks'. The chapel was free from diocesan interference for the clerk appointed to hold the chapel was not presented to the bishop of Coventry and Lichfield; the king himself ordered either the constable of the castle or the sheriff of Shropshire to institute. There is one important indication that the castle-chapel of St Michael had parochial responsibilities attached to it: the chapel or parish of Ford was held by the incumbent of the castle-chapel.[1] St Michael's, like St Juliana's, was apparently a small spiritual peculiar. Although it had remained in royal patronage, in its endowments it was probably not even comparable to the chapel in Oxford castle. Towards the end of the fourteenth century the chapel fell into a state of severe disrepair,[2] and Henry IV granted it, with the chapel of St Juliana, to the new college established in 1409 at Battlefield.[3] Owen and Blakeway, puzzled by the claim that St Michael's enjoyed exemption from episcopal jurisdiction, offered the explanation that the chapel had derived its land from the royal free chapel of St Mary Shrewsbury

We have stated above some reasons for supposing the parish of St Michael's chapel to have been an excerpt from the parish of St Mary. If this were the case, it was already exempt from episcopal jurisdiction, and would be likely to retain that peculiarity after its separation. It certainly could not acquire it after its foundation by Roger de Montgomery; for by this time the papal and episcopal authorities were sufficiently consolidated to prevent the creation of such an anomaly.[4]

While they put too much faith in the extent of the Church's control, it is possible that the parish of St Michael enjoyed special rights as an offshoot of St Mary Shrewsbury. On the other hand, the chapel of St Michael may have become a small royal peculiar after, and because, the castle of Shrewsbury became a royal castle; and it clearly derived some of its importance from the fact

[1] R. W. Eyton, *Antiquities of Shropshire*, vii, 192–3.

[2] Ibid., 254–6.

[3] *Monasticon*, vi, 1427.

[4] Owen and Blakeway 1825, ii, 424–5.

that it was linked with the royal chapel of St Juliana. The two chapels were hardly royal peculiars of great size or significance, and they were overshadowed by the large college of St Mary Shrewsbury; but notice must be taken of them, for they were royal peculiars in their own right.

The prebends in the church of St Nicholas in the castle of Wallingford appear to have been founded by Miles Crispin,[1] who died in 1107.[2] The college of St Nicholas probably passed into the hands of Miles's wife Maud and her second husband Brian fitz Count, and then into the hands of Henry II.[3] Wallingford was henceforth regarded as a royal chapel. As the evidence of the early thirteenth century shows, at least three prebends of Wallingford had churches attached to them (North Stoke, Chalgrove and All Saints Wallingford); and, although the advowson of Chalgrove was in some dispute, the king himself possessed the patronage of North Stoke and All Saints, as well as the patronage of the deanship of the chapel.[4] But there is every indication that the jurisdiction of the bishops of Salisbury and Lincoln was being asserted in these churches.[5] In 1229 the castle and the honour of Wallingford were given to Richard, earl of Cornwall;[6] although the record of the gift states specifically that patronage of the prebends in the chapel of Wallingford was to remain in the king's hands, this was not the final arrangement. The complete absence on the Chancery rolls of any indication that the king continued to appoint either deans or canons in the chapel suggests that Richard earl of Cornwall, and in 1272 Edmund his son, had full possession of the college of St Nicholas. The advowson of the churches of North Stoke and Chalgrove certainly passed into the

[1] *Cartulary of Oseney Abbey*, iv, 415.

[2] W. Kennett, *Parochial Antiquities* (Oxford, 1818), i, 105–6.

[3] *VCH Berks*, iii, 523–4.

[4] *The Book of Fees*, i, 251, 252, 255, 385, and *CPR 1216–25*, p. 27.

[5] North Stoke: *Rot. Chartarum*, I, i, 200, *Rot. Lit. Pat.*, i, 118b, *CPR 1225–32*, pp. 113–14, and *Rotuli Hugonis de Welles*, ii, ed. F. N. Davis etc., 24. Chalgrove: *Calendar of Papal Letters*, i, 347, and see *Rot. Chartarum*, I, i, 11b. All Saints Wallingford: *Rot. Chartarum*, I, i, 75b, and *The Registers of R. Martival*, i, ed. K. Edwards, 350.

[6] *CCR 1227–31*, p. 258.

hands of the earls of Cornwall.[1] By 1278 the chapel of St Nicholas —re-endowed in that year by Edmund earl of Cornwall[2]—was no longer prebendal; it had no canons and henceforth consisted of a dean, five chaplains (six by 1356),[3] six clerks, and four acolytes. The churches which had belonged to the prebends had apparently become dissociated from the chapel, and when two churches (one of which was All Saints Wallingford) were appropriated to the chapel in the fourteenth century[4] they were given for the support of the dean and his chaplains, not for the founding of prebends.

Since it is clear that the local bishops exercised the right of institution to the churches which had belonged to the college, it would be easy to conclude that, at least by the thirteenth century, no peculiar jurisdiction remained at Wallingford. But this would be wide of the mark. Evidence from the rolls of parliament[5] shows that close links between the chapel of St Nicholas and the church of All Saints remained, and they enjoyed some freedom from the jurisdiction of the ordinary in respect of cognisance of cases arising within their boundaries. This freedom meant that John Bray, a royal clerk who held the church of All Saints, was not in a position to appeal to his ecclesiastical ordinary about the usurpation by 'men of the castle' of income and tithes which belonged to the church of All Saints—a usurpation connected, perhaps, with the responsibility of the parson of All Saints for providing one chaplain to serve in the castle-chapel. John Bray's complaint therefore took the form of a petition to parliament in 1315, and a full inquiry was set in motion. Ever since 1229 the

---

[1] *Rotuli R. Grosseteste*, ed. F. N. Davis, pp. 449, 452–3, 456, and *Rotuli R. Gravesend*, ed. F. N. Davis, pp. 216, 226.

[2] *Cal. Charter Rolls*, ii, 209, 269, and *Monasticon*, vi, 1330.

[3] *CPR 1354–6*, p. 471.

[4] Ibid., and *CPR 1388–92*, p. 4. The dean already possessed the advowson of St Mary at Stall, and St Peter, Wallingford (*Registrum S. de Gandavo*, ed. C. T. Flower and M. C. B. Dawes, p. 786, and *The Registers of R. Martival*, i, 152, 161, 359).

[5] *Rotuli Parliamentorum*, i, 344b: '. . . nec ordinarii loci illius pro exemptione domini regis libertatis cognitionem habent, que post fundacionem dictarum ecclesie et capelle solebant semper dictis capelle et ecclesie pertinere . . .'

castle-chapel—although still in the hands of the royal family—
had been rarely under the king's direct control (the possessions
of the late earl of Cornwall were in the king's hands between
1300 and 1307), but the chapel of St Nicholas retained a privileged
status as a royal chapel.[1]

It must be remembered, of course, that it was not simply royal
castles which possessed 'free chapels'.[2] But when the term 'libera
capella' was used to describe non-royal chapels, it cannot have
carried with it implications of privilege and exemption. It signified the extra-parochial status of the chapel.[3] The chapel of St
Clement in the castle of Pontefract was in the hands first of the
de Lacy family and then, from 1311, of the house of Lancaster.
It had been founded by Ilbert de Lacy c. 1090,[4] and was endowed
as a collegiate church, with many portions of tithes (but no
churches) annexed to its prebends. As revealed by the taxatio of
Pope Nicholas, the endowments were divided into four prebends,
one of which was held by the dean of the college and another by
the prior of St John's Pontefract.[5] The chapel remained in the
hands of the de Lacy family throughout the first two centuries
of its history; it was not a royal chapel until 1399. The king from
time to time exercised influence over it. In 1241, during the minority of Edmund de Lacy, the king possessed the patronage of
the chapel, to the advantage of a physician and a chaplain of the
queen.[6] Later, during the minority of Henry de Lacy, another
queen's physician was granted, in 1262, a prebend of Pontefract,[7]
as also was the royal clerk Anthony Bek, in 1267.[8] After the

---

[1] The Registers of R. Martival, locc. citt.

[2] For example, the 'free chapel' of St Nicholas in the castle of Stafford:
see Monasticon, vi, 223, 232; T. J. de Mazzinghi, 'Castle Church' (SHC, viii,
pt. 2, 1887), pp. 21–2, 83–4; and The First Register of R. de Stretton, ed. R. A.
Wilson (SHC), pp. 136, 220.

[3] See above, pp. 8–9.

[4] Monasticon, v, 128, and Early Yorkshire Charters, iii, ed. W. Farrer, 185–6,
248. W. E. Wightman (The Lacy Family (Oxford, 1966), p. 24) favours a later
date.

[5] Taxatio, p. 298b.

[6] CPR 1232–47, pp. 258, 382, and CCR 1237–42, pp. 291, 329.

[7] CPR 1258–66, pp. 202–3.   [8] CPR 1266–72, p. 83.

treason and execution of Thomas of Lancaster the chapel seems to have been in the hands first of Queen Isabella and then of Queen Philippa.[1] St Clement's had no parish attached to it and was described as a free chapel. It is hardly surprising that there is no evidence of an archbishop of York attempting to visit the chapel, but this is not an indication that it was considered to be outside his jurisdiction. There appears to have been no set procedure for the king to follow concerning appointments to the prebends during minorities. In 1241 the constable of the castle was ordered to institute to the prebends conferred by the king, but in 1267 it was the archbishop of York who was ordered to assign Anthony Bek 'a stall in the choir and place in the chapter'.[2] Perhaps it is significant that in 1267 the archbishop, Walter Giffard, was the recently resigned royal chancellor, and the new chancellor was his brother, Godfrey Giffard. But there had been no conflict about the rights of the college, and the archbishop may have had an established right to have a hand in the appointments to the prebends.

A castle-church at Leicester is another example of a non-royal college. Probably in 1107 a college had been founded and richly endowed by Robert Beaumont in the castle of Leicester, and the endowments appear to have included six churches; but in 1143 Robert's son gave the college in its entirety to the abbey of St Mary de Pré, Leicester.[3] Unlike St Clement's Pontefract, the college at Leicester had parochial rights belonging to it. Although it was in the hands of St Mary de Pré, St Mary *de Castro* retained, or perhaps regained, some form of collegiate organisation, while at the same time serving as a parish church in the hands of a vicar presented by the abbot and convent.[4] As a college St Mary's appears to have been free from ordinary jurisdiction, the abbot

---

[1] *Calendar of Papal Letters*, ii, 407, and see R. Somerville, *The Duchy of Lancaster*, i (London, 1953), 35.

[2] *CCR 1237-42*, p. 329, and *CPR 1266-72*, p. 83.

[3] See *VCH Leic.*, ii, 45-6, Hamilton Thompson 1917, p. 154, and A. Hamilton Thompson, *The Abbey of St Mary of the Meadows Leicester* (Leicester, 1949), pp. 1-2.

[4] Ibid., 144-5, 165-8, and *A Calendar of Charters . . . belonging to the Hospital of Wyggeston*, ed. A. Hamilton Thompson (Leicester, 1933), no. 552.

of St Mary de Pré being its ordinary; but as a parish church with cure of souls it was certainly subject to the bishop of Lincoln's spiritual control. In its collegiate capacity St Mary *de Castro* was exempt. But it is doubtful whether this college should be called a chapel. It was not referred to as a chapel. It was not dependent upon any church. It was not a 'free chapel', for it had its own parish. Yet if it had been a royal college in a royal castle, like St Nicholas Wallingford, it would have been called a 'free chapel'. The term carried two meanings, describing a non-parochial chapel on the one hand and a privileged royal chapel on the other. St Mary *de Castro* belonged to neither category.

The fact that the non-royal college of St Mary *de Castro* was exempt makes it an exception. The case of a college at Exeter shows that we cannot conclude that non-royal colleges in castles were as a matter of course exempt from the jurisdiction of the bishop. The college of St Mary in the castle of Exeter, with its four prebends, had probably been given by the Conqueror to Ralph Avenil,[1] who in turn gave it to the priory of Plympton. But later it came into the hands of the earls of Devon, and remained in their possession, even though the castle of Exeter was itself under direct royal control after 1154.[2] At the beginning of the fifteenth century it is described as a free chapel.[3] The bishops of Exeter had exercised the right of institution to four prebends without cure of souls (the prebends of Hayes, Carswell, Cutton and Ashclyst),[4] and at the beginning of the fourteenth century Bishop Stapledon was not prepared to regard the college as free from his jurisdiction. In 1322 he visited the chapel. It had been the custom for divine service to be celebrated there each day, but Stapledon found that 'to all appearances services had been completely abandoned; the chapel was in a ruinous condition, open

---

[1] *Monasticon*, vi, 54, and for Ralph see *Regesta* i, no. 146.

[2] *History of the King's Works*, ed. H. M. Colvin, p. 648.

[3] *CPR 1408–13*, p. 117.

[4] *Register of W. Bronescombe*, ed. F. C. Hingeston-Randolph (London, 1889), p. 139, and see the 1291 *taxatio* in G. Oliver, *Monasticon Dioecesis Exoniensis*, p. 474, and *Register of J. Grandisson*, ed. F. C. Hingeston-Randolph, p. 377n.

to the sky in many places and its doors broken down'. He ordered
that something be done about it as quickly as possible.[1] The
bishop took with him into Exeter castle a large band of men,
including William of Malmesford, who was acting sheriff, and
it is perhaps doubtful whether any of Stapledon's successors were
confident enough to interfere to the extent of exercising the right
of visitation.

Every castle had a private chapel. Many had more than one:
Dover, for example, had three chapels within the castle.[2] Most
castle-chapels were simply private altars. Where a castle-church
was a secular college, as at Bridgnorth and at Leicester, it is no
surprise to find that the castle had a separate private chapel.[3]
Between the large college and the small private altar there were
chapels at every stage of development. Some examples of royal
castle-chapels will show the diversity. The royal chapels in the
castles of Windsor and Nottingham illustrate two quite different
kinds of organisation in chapels of intermediate status. From the
time of Henry I there was a chapel in Windsor castle, and there
were four chapels there by the time of Henry III.[4] One of these
was a new chapel dedicated to Edward the Confessor. This chapel
became a college of canons in 1348, when it was re-dedicated as
St George's Chapel. Until 1348 the castle chaplains of this new
chapel were paid wages from the royal revenues and had no
endowments. New ordinances were drawn up in 1313 and they
provided for an establishment of four chaplains, which was later
increased to eight.[5] The ordinances declared that the king's
chancellor, if able, should visit the chapel every year to ensure
that it was properly equipped ('servie des ornomentz, de libraire et
de chanterie'), that the chaplains and clerks received their wages and
that a full complement of chaplains and clerks was maintained.
But it is unlikely that annual visits from the chancellor became
the rule. In 1339 the chapel was visited by royal commissioners.[6]

[1] *Register of W. Stapeldon*, ed. F. C. Hingeston-Randolph, p. 155.
[2] *Calendar of Liberate Rolls*, iii, 123.
[3] Ibid., vi, no. 1625, and Levi Fox, *Leicester Castle* (Leicester, 1944), pp. 18–19.
[4] A. K. B. Roberts, *St George's Chapel Windsor Castle*, pp. 3–4.
[5] *Foedera*, II, i, 193.   [6] *CPR 1338–40* p. 354

Here was a small community of chaplains, with no prebends and no parochial rights. And there is no doubt that this royal chapel was free from the bishop's control. The 'free chapel' in the royal castle of Nottingham[1] was described during Edward I's reign as a single prebend. It was fully in the king's gift. Whatever the nature of the religious organisation in this castle-chapel (which was served by at least two chaplains in the middle of the thirteenth century),[2] it must have been quite well endowed, for it helped to support a succession of royal clerks.[3] Some castle-chapels were served by a chaplain from a nearby religious house. In the castle of Marlborough it was the master of the hospital of St John who celebrated divine service.[4] The Cistercian monks at Scarborough appear to have had some rights in the king's chapel in the castle there.[5] Where the king had lost the patronage of an early castle-chapel, as was the case with the chapel of St Martin in the castle of Hereford, the loss made particularly necessary the building within the castle of a private chapel which was under the king's control.[6] And the number of royal castle-chapels tended to increase. Conquests outside England brought both castles and their chapels into his possession, as is illustrated by the appointments to the castle-chapel of Roxburgh[7] and also to the college established in the ancient castle of Holyhead (Anglesey).[8] We should expect

[1] For the four royal chapels at Nottingham, see *History of the King's Works*, ed. H. M. Colvin, p. 758, n. 3.

[2] *Calendar of Liberate Rolls*, i, 441, iv, 424, and v, 135.

[3] *CPR 1272–81*, pp. 83, 199, *CPR 1301–7*, p. 98, and *CPR 1307–13*, p. 11.

[4] *Calendar of Liberate Rolls*, vi, no. 951.

[5] *Calendar of Chancery Warrants*, i, 386.

[6] *History of the King's Works*, pp. 675–6. St Martin's had been founded by the de Lacy family, and had passed first to the bishop of Hereford and then to the priory of St Guthlac (*Registrum R. de Swinfield*, ed. W. W. Capes, pp. 47–8, W. W. Capes, *Charters and Records of Hereford Cathedral* (Cantilupe Soc., 1908), pp. 13, 22, and S. H. Martin, 'St Guthlac priory and the city churches', *Transactions of the Woolhope Field Club*, xxxiv (1952–4), 227). King John tried, apparently without success, to retrieve the advowson of the chapel (*Curia Regis Rolls*, vi, 28, 60, 103, and *Placitorum Abbreviatio* (Rec. Commission), p. 75).

[7] *CCR 1307–13*, p. 96, and *Rotuli Scotiae* (Record Commission, 1814–19), i, 67.

[8] Hamilton Thompson 1917, p. 183, A. Hamilton Thompson in *Journal of*

all the royal castle-chapels to be exempt from the bishop, and there is no evidence to suggest otherwise. But parochial responsibilities were associated with only a few castle-chapels. Some parochial rights had been attached to the royal castle-chapel at Oxford and some were still attached to the royal castle-chapels at Shrewsbury and Wallingford. Because of these parochial rights they merit consideration, along with St Juliana's Shrewsbury, as royal free chapels. Yet, with the exception of Bridgnorth, the royal castle-chapels of the thirteenth century do not augment in any substantial way the list of royal spiritual peculiars.

Hist. of the Church in Wales, i, 104–5, and G. Williams, *The Welsh Church from Conquest to Reformation* (Cardiff, 1962), p. 63.

CHAPTER VI

THE SURVIVAL OF SPIRITUAL FREEDOM

By common consent and without any dispute, royal chapels possessing no parochial responsibilities enjoyed freedom from episcopal control. But Bracton had said not only that chapels might enjoy special privileges but also that the king's chapels might have churches belonging to them.[1] Setting aside the newly claimed royal free chapels of Edward I's reign (Hastings, St Buryan and Tickhill), there were at least twenty-two royal chapels which possessed parochial rights in one parish or many parishes at some stage during the twelfth and thirteenth centuries: St Martin-le-Grand, Wimborne Minster, Wolverhampton, Stafford, Penkridge, Tettenhall, St Mary's Shrewsbury, Bridgnorth, Derby, St Oswald's Gloucester, Bosham, Bromfield, St Martin's Dover, Waltham, Gnosall, Steyning, Blyth, Pevensey, St George's Oxford, St Michael's Shrewsbury, St Juliana's Shrewsbury and St Nicholas's Wallingford. With the exception of Pevensey and St George's Oxford, all these churches retained some links, however tenuous, with liberties which were related to their parochial rights. The first ten in the list were fully exempt deaneries at the beginning of the fourteenth century. I have used the term 'royal free chapel' to signify a royal chapel with parochial responsibilities, and I began by saying that 'it appears that only the most important royal chapels—the royal secular colleges—could in fact possess parishes'. And I have suggested that in the absence of further evidence the existence of prebends within a church might be taken as an indication of collegiate status.[2] The

[1] Above, p. 13.   [2] Above, pp. 2, 13.

existence of secular canons at a large number of the royal free chapels can be demonstrated; at others there is only the mention of prebends. In some cases (Blyth, Pevensey and St Michael's Shrewsbury) the existence of a secular college at an early stage in the history of the chapelry or chapel can only be inferred. Despite these three cases and despite the fact that the list of twenty-two royal free chapels cannot be regarded as conclusive, the evidence strongly suggests the equivalence of royal free chapels and royal secular colleges.

The evidence which this study has brought together poses many questions. For example, the royal free chapels merit separate and detailed examination as centres for royal patronage—as centres, so it often seems, for the training of royal clerks for episcopal office. The deanships were valuable positions, and distinguished members of the royal court are to be found enjoying them. But before the reign of John was passed much of the patronage had gone out of the hands of the Crown. Bosham had gone to the bishop of Exeter, Blyth to the church of Rouen, Steyning to the abbey of Fécamp, St George's Oxford to the abbey of Osney, Pevensey to the chancellor of Chichester, Gnosall to the bishop of Coventry, Derby to the dean of Lincoln and Penkridge to the archbishop of Dublin. In the eleventh century there were probably many other royal colleges or minsters alienated from the Crown.[1] The examination of royal patronage in the royal colleges of the twelfth and thirteenth centuries is necessarily a narrower study than the study of privilege. Another question is the later history of the royal free chapels. The royal deaneries, exempt from the control of the ecclesiastical hierarchy, continued to thrive, but how important were they to the pre-Reformation kings? And their history continued after the sixteenth century, for ecclesiastical peculiars were not finally abolished until 1847.[2] We learn,

---

[1] The minster at Axminster appears to have been a royal college. It was granted by Edward the Confessor to Ealdred, the 'deacon' of Archbishop Ealdred, to be held 'as fully and completely as ever any priest before him had it, as a pious benefaction for St Peter's minster at York': F. E. Harmer, *Anglo-Saxon Writs*, pp. 415–19.

[2] *Public General Statutes 10 and 11 Victoria* (London, 1847), cap. 98.

for example, that in 1837 St Mary's Shrewsbury was still a peculiar exempt from the jurisdiction of the bishop:

The minister, or official, of St Mary is not only exempt from the bishop of the diocese, but possesses many of the powers and privileges of a prelate. He appoints his own surrogate, holds his court for proving wills etc. of persons dying within his parish, which is indeed very extensive, comprising not only about one fourth of the whole town of Shrewsbury, but extending itself into the country—includes Great and Little Berwick, Newton, Leaton, Bomer Heath, Great and Little Wolascot, part of Harlescot, and the three parochial chapelries of Albrighton, Astley and Clive.[1]

But one question posed by this study is directly relevant to its own theme. In the thirteenth century it was claimed that the royal free chapels were founded and endowed in ancient times, even before bishops had been established in the kingdom of England, and that they had been free at all times from episcopal jurisdiction.[2] Does the evidence suggest that this claim had some historical basis? A large number of the royal free chapels were churches of ancient standing; but could it be that the category 'royal demesne chapel' or 'royal free chapel' and the privileged status associated with the titles were in fact created in the twelfth century? Some of the royal free chapels were relatively new creations or were recently constituted, as Waltham and St Martin-le-Grand. And with the use of different terms, as 'capella regia' and 'capellaria regis' and 'dominica capella regis', it is not easy to prove conclusively the existence even in the twelfth century of a coherent group of privileged royal churches. The use of the phrase 'sicut dominica capella' in relation to religious houses which were not secular colleges, as Battle Abbey and Westminster Abbey, could be thought to confirm these suspicions. It is indeed difficult to avoid the conclusion that in England the use of the term 'capella' or 'capellaria' to refer to royal privileged churches began in the twelfth century. These terms appear to have had no Anglo-Saxon equivalents. And it is difficult also to

[1] T. Phillips and C. Hubert, *The History and Antiquities of Shrewsbury* (Shrewsbury, 1837), i, 84.
[2] Below, pp. 160, 165.

avoid the conclusion that royal claims for the royal free chapels took precise shape in the twelfth and, even more, in the thirteenth centuries.

Yet the argument for the novelty of the royal claims hardly gets off the ground. Most of the royal colleges of the twelfth and thirteenth centuries were the survivors of an ecclesiastical organisation which was already decaying in the late Anglo-Saxon period. The importance of many of them as royal churches—for example Dover, Bromfield and Steyning—belonged to the past rather than to the future. It is wrong to assume that all Anglo-Saxon minsters were the parochial outposts of a bishop's see. Many had been royal minsters:

As the hundred, either individually or grouped, often represented some earlier district originally dependent on a royal *tun*, or vill, it seems that kings had founded in their *tuns* churches to serve the area governed from those centres. These are the 'old minsters' of the tenth and eleventh centuries, churches with large endowments, sometimes still served by a community of priests or canons, and with parochial rights over a wide area.[1]

This is at least part of the story; and, of such minsters, Bosham, although founded much earlier than the tenth century, is an outstanding example. Some royal minsters became monasteries, and some were given in perpetuity to monasteries; they had all been faced with the challenge of an increasing number of manorial churches. With the outstanding exception of St Martin-le-Grand the twelfth century was a period of decline for the royal colleges. Of the few new colleges which came to be regarded as royal free chapels because they belonged to royal castles (Bridgnorth, St George's Oxford, St Nicholas's Wallingford and the more doubtful St Michael's Shrewsbury) not one was a royal foundation. And after these colleges came into the king's hands there was nothing automatic about the extension of the privilege of exemption to their annexed parishes. Bridgnorth became an exempt deanery, but the fact that the deanery served by the college of Bridgnorth was a compact area surrounding the town suggests

[1] Barlow 1963, p. 184.

that the college may in fact have been of pre-Conquest origin. All the colleges of pre-Conquest origin, or probably of pre-Conquest origin, (with the exception of Blyth) possessed compact areas of jurisdiction. Three colleges were given scattered parish churches during the twelfth century: of these St Martin-le-Grand enjoyed exemption for most of its parish churches, but St George's Oxford and St Nicholas's Wallingford gained no exemption for their churches (with the exception of All Saints Wallingford). Leaving aside the unusual St Martin-le-Grand, it is the lack of any new or constructive policies on the part of the Crown that is so striking about the history of the royal free chapels in the twelfth century. There is an absence of innovation and little evidence of novel claims.

It cannot be denied that the last decades of the twelfth century, when the growth of diocesan government was particularly marked,[1] were very important in the history of the royal colleges. It was a crucial time for some churches. Bosham, for example, emerged with apparently depleted rights. But there seems to have been little change in the customary position of other churches; certainly the central right of free appointment—that is, collation—was firmly entrenched. The position of the royal free chapels had become distinctive very largely because episcopal jurisdiction was beginning to operate fully in all other churches in lay hands. There was a policy of defence, because established rights were there to be defended. It is unlikely that the chapels actually gained any appreciable privileges as a result of a defensive policy in the face of increased episcopal vigilance. The rights of the royal colleges must appear all the more entrenched when we learn that 'the times were no longer favourable to local immunities and peculiars' and that 'the growing centralisation of church government and law rendered the creation of new immunities difficult and encroachment on old ones comparatively simple'.[2]

But it is no easy task to specify the rights which the royal colleges enjoyed before the thirteenth century or to trace them

[1] See E. John, 'The litigation of an exempt house, St Augustine's Canterbury, 1182–1237', *Bulletin of the John Rylands Library*, xxxix (1956–7), 392–3.
[2] Ibid., 413.

through any stages in their early development. A lack of precise information in the charters bedevils the study of episcopal customs and freedom from episcopal customs. No doubt local variations in practice and different attitudes to customary rights were protected by the generalities of charter form. The alienation of episcopal customs to religious houses had been a commonplace, and their extensive alienation to lay lords—for example in Normandy—has been demonstrated conclusively.[1] Episcopal customs should not be thought of as merely financial; profits could not be enjoyed without jurisdiction.[2] The customs may have been essentially financial, but it was difficult to separate procuration from the right to visit, and the payment of synodals from the duty to attend synods. The possible nature and extent of episcopal customs are illustrated in a charter cited by Haskins: 'aecclesiam S. Marie de Berlo et altare et omnes reditus eorum, decimas scilicet, primitias, sepulturam, sinodalia, circada, et omnes forfacturas ad ipsam aecclesiam pertinentes, hoc est: sacrilegium, latrocinium, infracturam cimiterii, et cum omnibus commissis episcopo pertinentibus.'[3] Freedom from episcopal exactions and episcopal interference must have been equivalent to freedom from episcopal customs. We may regard as possibly interpolated the statement in the charter of 1060 × 1061 that the church of Bromfield was free from the bishop's interference and the statement in the charter of 1068 that St Martin-le-Grand should be free from all exactions and interference of bishops, archdeacons, deans and their ministers;[4] but there are soon very clear indications that this kind of freedom was enjoyed by the royal free chapels.

In Henry I's reign the bishop of Coventry confirmed that Wolverhampton should be held 'by perpetual right and without perturbation'; in Henry II's reign freedom from the control of the local bishop was clearly stated with regard to St Oswald's

---

[1] Lemarignier 1937, pp. 67–71, C. H. Haskins, *Norman Institutions* (Cambridge, Mass., 1918), pp. 6–7, 32–5, and C. Morris, 'William I and the church courts', *EHR*, lxxxii (1967), 452–3.

[2] See Lemarignier 1937, pp. 64–117, and Cheney 1956, pp. 149–54.

[3] C. H. Haskins, *Norman Institutions*, p. 33, n. 129.

[4] Above, pp. 30, 47–8.

Gloucester, Waltham and Bromfield, in which last case the bishop of Hereford confirmed the freedom of the church from his jurisdiction.[1] This is strong evidence of established liberties. To discover that royal colleges on royal demesne were free from episcopal interference is in a sense to discover the expected. That ecclesiastical franchises had existed before the Conquest is not to be doubted,[2] and few churches can have been more likely to enjoy immunities than the royal minsters. So strong is this probability that it begins to look like pedantry to regard with suspicion the terms of the Bromfield and the St Martin-le-Grand charters.

But it would be dangerous to assume that evidence of freedom from procuration (as at Bromfield) or freedom from episcopal interference in appointments to prebends (as at Waltham) are indications of complete freedom from the bishop. The fact that the bishop of Hereford was not permitted by Henry II to exercise jurisdiction over the prior of Bromfield is, it is true, suggestive of important liberties. But even if freedom from the bishop meant not simply freedom from exactions but also freedom from the bishop's *potestas jurisdictionis*—that is, his power to 'govern, legislate and administer justice for his diocese'—there still remained his *potestas ordinis*: the bishop was 'the primary dispenser of the sacraments, especially baptism at Easter and Whitsun (but without the exclusive right), confirmation, ordination of priests, and dedication of ecclesiastical buildings, altars, vessels, and chrism'.[3] To exclude the bishop's *potestas ordinis* meant to seek the services of another bishop. This had happened at Waltham, for the clerks there had been ordained by a bishop of their own choice. But there is nothing to suggest that this practice was common in royal free chapels. Freedom from episcopal customs was one thing, but complete exemption from the bishop was another.[4] The whole question of the exercise of cure of souls was

---

[1] Above, pp. 49, 55, 67.

[2] Barlow 1963, p. 250.   [3] Ibid., p. 243.

[4] This theme is worked out fully with many examples from French charters by J. Vendeuvre, 'La *libertas* royale des communautés religieuses au XIe siècle: la *libertas* vis-à-vis des évêques', *Nouvelle Revue Hist. de Droit Franç. et Étranger*, xxxiv (1910), 332–76.

undergoing a profound change in the twelfth century. Freedom from the bishop at the beginning of the century was the possession of *episcopalia*; freedom from the bishop at the end of the century was canonical exemption. The one sometimes developed into the other, but the two kinds of freedom belonged to two different worlds.

In 1092 there was litigation concerning the rights of the cathedral priory at Worcester over its churches, and the prior and monks appear to have established their right to collect the episcopal customs from all the churches of Oswaldslow.[1] The customs still belonged to the bishop, but no archdeacon or rural dean was allowed to intervene. The evidence suggests that a greater privilege may have been enjoyed by royal minsters over their churches. The royal minsters may have possessed episcopal customs. What is so striking about the post-Conquest evidence is that the royal free chapels can be studied convincingly as a group, and this despite the many varied ways in which the churches developed. The clergy at the end of the thirteenth century were able to list the most important of them.[2] The fact that the status of a royal chapel was so durable argues not only for an ancient origin but also for an early coherence of the royal minsters, if not exactly as a group at least as a genus. The bishop of Coventry's statement in 1102 × 1113 concerning the church of Wolverhampton carries some weight: 'Hec quidem ecclesia de Wlfr[unehamptona] una erat antiquitus de propriis regis capellis que ad coronam spectabant.'[3] The association of some of the royal priests of the period 1024–66[4] with Dover, Bromfield, Bosham and St Martin-le-Grand suggests, as we should expect, an early connection between the royal chapels and the royal court. Although the English Chapel Royal cannot be compared with the Carolingian Chapel Royal,[5] yet the English royal chapels bear a distinct resemblance to the Carolingian *Pfalzkapellen* with

---

[1] Barlow 1963, pp. 198, 252–3, and E. John, 'An alleged Worcester charter', *Bulletin of the John Rylands Lib.*, xli (1958–9), 75–80.

[2] Above, p. 1.   [3] Above, p. 42.

[4] Barlow 1963, pp. 156–8.

[5] Ibid., 120–1, 133.

their subordinate and perhaps prebendal *Fiskalkapellen*.[1] It is worth noting too that the early royal chapels or chapelries seem to provide a clearer indication of ancient demesne than can be deduced from the 'ancient demesne' claims of the Angevin monarchs.[2] In the Carolingian tradition, we are told, the principle of exemption was directly associated with the king's own possessions.[3] The tradition was not exclusively Carolingian. But to reject episcopal rights altogether would be to reject the right to provide chrism, the right to ordain and the right to consecrate. There is no indication whatever that Church unity was broken to this extent.[4] Complete isolation from the bishop was not a principle of the system of proprietary churches. Nor, apparently, had it been a principle of parochial minsters. Yet it would be rash to imagine the minsters fitting into a strictly hierarchical scheme of ecclesiastical authority, beneath the bishop, who was himself beneath the archbishop. In his letter to the king of the Mercians in 802, Pope Leo III asked the king to respect the archbishop Aethelheard's authority in the dioceses 'tam episcoporum quam monasteriorum'.[5] The bishop of Lichfield's own diocese had been in effect the parish of a minster; yet it is difficult to escape the implied distinction between the dioceses of bishops and the dioceses of minsters. How far distinction meant separation is quite another question.

The royal chapel of Dover, before and after Domesday Book, like the other minsters of Kent, paid customary dues to the archbishop of Canterbury.[6] These appear to have been essentially spiritual dues, payments for chrism and wine and perhaps contributions for the poor and hearth-pennies.[7] But it would hardly

---

[1] J. Fleckenstein, *Die Hofkapelle der deutschen Könige*, i, 101–3.

[2] See R. S. Hoyt, 'The nature and origins of ancient demesne', *EHR*, lxv (1950), 145–74.

[3] N. Grass in *Festschrift K. S. Bader*, p. 159, and Fleckenstein, op. cit., esp. i, 110–11.

[4] Barlow 1950, pp. ix, xv, and E. John, 'The litigation of an exempt house', *Bulletin of the John Rylands Lib.*, xxxix (1956–7), 392–3.

[5] M. Deanesly, 'Early English and Gallic minsters', *Transactions of the Royal Historical Soc.*, 4th ser. xxiii (1941), 32–3.

[6] Above, p. 58.　　　　　　　　　　　[7] Barlow 1963, p. 180.

be wise to use the position of the royally endowed minsters of Kent as a yardstick; the archbishop's exclusive spiritual rights in a group of them, including Dover, Folkestone and Lyminge, had been safeguarded from the time of King Wihtred (696–716).[1] No doubt there were many distinctions between the seventh-century minsters of Kent and the later minsters of Mercia.

The defence of the royal chapels in the twelfth and thirteenth centuries was asserted as a defence of customary rights. This being so, we should expect, on present evidence, that in some matters, as the provision of chrism and the right to ordain, the bishop's position would be respected; and this is true of the composition for Wolverhampton in 1224 and also of the later composition for all the chapels of the diocese of Coventry and Lichfield in 1281.[2] It is nonetheless understandable that in a royal deanery where an outside bishop or archbishop was 'patron and prelate' separation from the diocese in which the church was situated could be even more complete. One of the claims against the freedom of St Oswald's Gloucester had been that the diocesan had held ordinations in the priory; it was also asserted that the canons had been accustomed to go in procession to the abbey of Gloucester and pay their pentecostals there, and that they received their oil and chrism from the archdeacon of Gloucester. After the king's court had settled the case in favour of the freedom of St Oswald's, the bishop of Worcester, William Gainsborough, tried to compel the house to continue its payments to the diocesan by a petition to the parliament held at Carlisle in 1307; but following the instructions of the archbishop of York, Thomas Corbridge, the priory began to pay pentecostals and Peter's pence to the dean of the jurisdiction of Churchdown, and under the instruction of Corbridge's successor, William Greenfield, it received its oil and chrism from Southwell Minster.[3] Here a complete peculiar had been established; in fact the deanery of Churchdown was in the diocese of York rather than in the diocese of Worcester. This

---

[1] M. Deanesly, *ubi supra*, 41–4.

[2] Above, pp. 43–4, 109.

[3] *Register of Wm. Greenfield*, ed. A. Hamilton Thompson, i, 32–3, 38–9, 181–5.

was possible because another bishop replaced the bishop of Worcester. The sinews of episcopal authority could not be severed; but this is not to underestimate the extent to which kings had influenced and shaped the exercise of episcopal jurisdiction.

It is only during the thirteenth century that a clear picture emerges of what freedom from ordinary ecclesiastical jurisdiction signified in the royal free chapels. What were the privileges which the Crown and the deans and canons possessed in the exempt deaneries? The changes which took place in the royal colleges during the twelfth and thirteenth centuries can be described in terms of a development towards full 'canonical exemption'. The few monasteries which were exempt by papal privilege—and especially the two (Evesham and St Albans) with fully exempt deaneries—provide us with the exemplars of 'canonical exemption', and our evidence has from time to time upheld the equivalence of the privileges of the exempt abbeys and of the royal free chapels.

But the comparison in fact suggests contrast much more than equivalence. For the exempt monasteries, direct dependence in spiritual matters upon the pope was a claim of practical significance. Papal delegates could visit and correct; the houses were never automatically exempt from papal taxes; and direct recourse to Rome had become an undeniable feature of their spiritual, as of their political, condition. But, as I have been at pains to show, there is no hint of papal consent to the liberties of the royal free chapels as these were interpreted by the Crown. The papacy stood quite apart from the development towards full exemption in the royal deaneries. The general papal indults relating to the royal chapels appear to have taken for granted their status as private chapels and ignored their status as churches with annexed parishes. It is true that Innocent IV had claimed that the king's private chapels and oratories were subject immediately to Rome.[1] The pope was stressing his role as universal ordinary. He conceded as a temporary measure that even his own delegates should have no authority, unless with papal licence, to promulgate sentences of interdict or excommunication against the chapels or their canons

[1] *Annales Monastici*, ed. H. R. Luard, i, 275, and see above, p. 93.

and ministers. Yet the immediate subjection to Rome of the king's private chapels (colleges or otherwise) was a legal nicety; papal interference there, except on rare occasions and in the defence of episcopal jurisdiction, can hardly have been seriously considered. The Crown at times paid lip service to the spiritual overlordship of Rome, as also did the dean of St Martin-le-Grand.[1] And there is evidence of one case arising out of Innocent IV's nomination of the abbot of Westminster as *conservator* of the privileges granted to the king concerning his chapels.[2] A notarial instrument of January 1294 reveals that a dispute between the dean of St Martin-le-Grand and the 'perpetual vicar' of St Botolph without Aldersgate concerning the payment of a pension had been heard before the commissary of the abbot of Westminster.[3] The abbot had been empowered to protect the royal chapels. In this case an issue concerning a royal free chapel was being determined before what was in fact a papal court. Yet despite these examples of papal authority being used to serve the ends of the king and his clerks, the Crown aimed to preserve the freedom of the royal free chapels from papal control.

The distinction between the exempt monasteries and the exempt secular colleges is underlined by the fact that the privileged abbeys were exempt from patronage relations; for a monastery to become exempt was a distinct disadvantage to the patron, since the pope's control was exclusive.[4] In the royal chapels it was the patron who claimed all rights. The freedom of the chapels from financial exaction became quite distinctly a freedom from papal as well as diocesan exaction. This was true also of the French royal chapels.[5] Only when the proceeds from papal taxes

---

[1] For example, in two significations of excommunication of 1314 and 1315 William de Melton describes himself as dean of the royal free chapel of St Martin-le-Grand 'sedi apostolice in spiritualibus immediate subiecte': P.R.O. C 85/214/26 and /27.

[2] *Les Registres d'Innocent IV*, iii, no. 5655, and F. Palgrave, *The Antient Kalendars*, i, 103.

[3] W.A.M., MS 13484.

[4] See Wood 1955, p. 14, and W. E. Lunt, *Financial Relations of the Papacy with England, 1327–1534*, p. 57.

[5] Mollat 1951, p. 7.

were being directed to the royal coffers are there clear signs that the colleges made their contributions.[1] The simple fact is that the actual collection of taxes in the chapels remained the Crown's prerogative. No taxation other than taxation levied by the king and collected by the king's ministers was thus possible;[2] but the Crown could, of course, itself organise the collection within its own deaneries of papal tenths, as also no doubt the collection of subsidies granted independently by the English clergy. In the matter of recourse to Rome, Edward I, as we should expect, had been fully prepared (in 1279) to prohibit an appeal to the pope, since it constituted an attack upon the liberties of one of his chapels (All Saints' Derby);[3] but when it was a question of petitions to Rome in favour of the freedom of the royal colleges, then naturally the king would himself sponsor the appeal. The churches were given the king's, rather than the pope's, overall protection.

The papal attempts to exercise the right of provision in royal colleges illustrate further the pope's lack of control over churches which were in theory immediately subject to his authority. Before July 1238 the pope had ordered the papal legate, Cardinal Otto, to find a church in the diocese of London for a certain Roger de Sancta Trinitate, and the cardinal had demanded the reservation of a prebend of St Martin-le-Grand. The king responded by appealing to the pope against his conferring any prebend in this church.[4] Here is an early example of an attitude which hardened as the century progressed. Many of the colleges were, however, in the king's direct patronage, and the protection of the rights of lay patrons was itself sufficient to exclude the possibility of papal provision.[5] When attempts were made to execute a provision,

[1] See Styles 1950–1, pp. 27–8, CPR 1266–72, pp. 220–1, 329, CCR 1268–72, pp. 30, 110–11, and Calendar of Fine Rolls, iii, 39–40.

[2] See Royal Letters of Henry III, ed. W. W. Shirley, ii, 60, and Calendar of Memoranda Rolls (Exchequer) 1326–7 (HMSO), no. 614.

[3] CPR 1272–81, p. 313; for similar prohibitions see G. B. Flahiff in Medieval Studies, vi (1944), 268–9.

[4] CPR 1232–37, p. 227 (Prynne ii, 557).

[5] A. Deeley, 'Papal provision and royal rights of patronage', EHR, xliii (1928), 504–6.

as at St Martin-le-Grand, Wolverhampton or Tettenhall,[1] the Crown had little difficulty in overriding the papal claim. The difficulties arose when the patronage of prebends was in the hands of prelates, as at Derby (the dean of Lincoln) and Penkridge (the archbishop of Dublin). Here the statement of royal prerogative rights needed greater emphasis.[2] Bosham, in the hands of the bishop of Exeter, was in a peculiarly equivocal position, for this college had been unable to secure complete freedom for its prebends as *prebende curate*. Nevertheless, the Crown persisted, here also, in its policy of protection from interference with the rights of collation.[3] Edward I even claimed, in 1279, that several papal 'privileges' had themselves declared the royal free chapels to be exempt from provision.[4] He perhaps sought comfort and prestige in this pretence.

Despite the fact that disputes which concerned the royal chapels had often been taken to Rome, the spiritual superior of these deaneries was without doubt the Crown. The king's chancellor, whose responsibility for the Chapel Royal was apparently long established,[5] came to be regarded as the ecclesiastical ordinary of the royal peculiars. And after 1340 the chancellor was not always a clerk. From at least the early years of the fourteenth century it was the chancellor who possessed the right of visitation in the royal hospitals[6] as well as in the royal free chapels; visitation followed complaint and appears not to have been a regular procedure.[7] The chancellor often commissioned others to visit on his behalf.[8] Visitations were commissioned at St Martin-le-Grand in

---

[1] Prynne iii, 228, *VCH London*, i, 559, n. 73 (W.A.M., Book 5, fos. 27v–28r), *Select Cases King's Bench*, ed. G. O. Sayles, iii, 120–2, and Styles 1936, pp. 92–3.

[2] Styles 1950–1, pp. 31–5, W. E. Lunt, *Accounts Rendered by Papal Collectors*, pp. 201, 370, 507–8, and *The Liber of Ric. de Bury*, ed. N. Denholm-Young, p. 21.

[3] *Register of W. de Stapeldon*, ed. F. C. Hingeston-Randolph, p. 101, *The Register of Th. de Brantyngham*, ed. F. C. Hingeston-Randolph (London, 1901–6), pp. 185, 457, and W. E. Lunt, *Accounts Rendered*, pp. 106, 211.

[4] Prynne iii, 228.   [5] Above, p. 4.

[6] See *CCR 1302–7*, p. 225, and I. J. Churchill, *Canterbury Administration*, i, 149.

[7] But see above, p. 129.   [8] Wood-Legh 1934, pp. 33–59.

1323, at Shrewsbury in 1329 and at Penkridge in 1334.[1] And, as the order to visit Penkridge illustrates, the rights of the chancellor were already well defined: 'Le chaunceller qi est ordeiner de fraunches chapeles le roi & a qi atteint par reson de son office a visiter meismes les chapeles.' In visiting at Penkridge the chancellor was exercising a jurisdiction superior to that of the dean, who was the archbishop of Dublin. The chancellor had come to possess rights which set aside not merely diocesan but in effect also papal jurisdiction. Later in the century the principle was stated in relation to St Stephen's Westminster, for this royal chapel was specifically declared to be 'exempt from all jurisdiction ordinary and delegate except that of the chancellor'.[2]

The distinction between ecclesiastical and lay control must not be exaggerated: chancellors were almost always prelates, the visitors whom they commissioned were important monks or clerics, and the deans of the chapels, if not prelates in their own right, were usually royal clerks of a high standing in the realm. Yet the rights of the royal deaneries had certainly not developed out of an alliance of papal and royal policy, as successive kings would have us believe. The real attitude of the Crown had been revealed when Henry III declared in 1250 and again in 1254 that the royal free chapels were exempt even from the pope's jurisdiction.[3] When St Buryan's fought to join the privileged chapels in the fourteenth century its parishioners claimed that they recognised no superior except the lord king.[4] But naturally it was in the interests of the Crown to uphold the fiction that the chapels were immediately subject to the court of Rome.[5] Apparent co-operation suggested, to all parties, a position of strength.

When a period of alliance between pope and king began with the pontificate of Clement V, new bulls were issued in favour of the royal free chapels. In 1306, and again in 1309, Clement granted

---

[1] CPR 1321–4, pp. 355, 385, CPR 1327–30, p. 478, and Rotuli Parliamentorum, ii, 77b.   [2] CPR 1377–81, p. 95.

[3] Above, p. 96, and Prynne iii, 110 ('Placit. 38 Hy III rot. 7').

[4] Register of J. Grandisson, ed. F. C. Hingeston-Randolph, p. 43.

[5] E.g. Select Cases Exchequer of Pleas, ed. H. Jenkinson and B. E. R. Formoy, p. 133, and CPR 1272–81, p. 313.

the exemption of the chapels from sentences of excommunication or interdict declared by any papal delegate except by the special mandate of the pope.[1] There was nothing new in this. Nor was there anything new in John XXII's bull of 1317;[2] in fact it was no more than a re-issue of Innocent IV's bull of 21 July 1245, except that it was now intended as a concession of permanent value. While the papacy had held its ground, it had little choice but to tolerate a completely erroneous interpretation of its own indults. Pope John XXII was, however, eager that the king should set down clearly the rights of the chapels, so that the papal collector could carry out his duties 'without hindrance from the king and his officials'.[3] The papacy had shown no inclination to treat the ancient royal colleges as churches meriting specific bulls of privilege, like the ones of 1304 and 1317 for the Sainte-Chapelle;[4] but then the French colleges were extra-parochial. The bull of exemption for Waltham had effectively separated that house from the royal free chapels as a coherent group; it had in fact ensured that the abbey's churches would not be exempt from the diocesan. Despite the apparent predilection of the royal Chancery for the term 'exemption',[5] it was, as Thomas Corbridge, archbishop of York, fully realised,[6] a term with unfortunate implications, for how could a church be declared exempt from a jurisdiction which it had never acknowledged? The Crown retained for the chapels more extensive rights than a pope would ever have granted. Since 'canonical exemption' implies exemption by papal sanction, it would be difficult to find a term less apt. The Crown sought not simply to be its own bishop in the royal

---

[1] *Foedera*, I, ii, 979 (P.R.O. SC7 (Papal Bulls) 10/29), and F. Palgrave, *The Antient Kalendars*, p. 10; and *Foedera*, II, i, 74 (P.R.O. SC7 11/20), and see *Register of W. de Stapeldon*, p. 81.

[2] *Lettres Communes de Jean XXII*, ed. G. Mollat (BEAR), no. 3357, and *Foedera*, II, i, 322 (P.R.O. SC7/24/9).

[3] *Calendar of Papal Letters*, ii, 426, cited in W. E. Lunt, *Accounts Rendered*, p. xxii.

[4] *Privilèges Accordés à la Couronne*, ed. A. Tardif, nos. 121, 171, and see nos. 228, 292.   [5] E.g. *CCR 1247–51*, p. 223.

[6] *Register of Th. of Corbridge*, ed. W. Brown and A. Hamilton Thompson, ii, 92–4.

L

deaneries, but its own pope as well. Despite the ties which bound king and pope, subjection to the papacy was not easily acknowledged. In a guarded way the king let it slip that royal free chapels were exempt from the pope. The claim represents in this particular case more a change in attitude than a change in policy. It is a little reminiscent of the contemporary claim that the French king was 'not only *imperator in regno suo* but pope as well'.[1] Papal reform and the ensuing ecclesiastical reorganisation had set the royal deaneries apart. Skilfully, if dishonestly, Henry III and Edward I had succeeded in creating an aura of papal sanction even for these ecclesiastical anomalies.

Sadly, there is no way of ascertaining how well the royal deaneries were administered. Pecham asserted that the immunities of the chapels endangered the cure of souls,[2] but how far plurality and non-residence—which were completely unchecked in the royal free chapels—affected the administering of the parishes it is impossible to judge. Because the royal free chapels make very infrequent appearances in bishop's registers, and also perhaps because of the freedom of action enjoyed by the royal clerks to whom the deanships were given, there are no records upon which to base a balanced account of their spiritual administration. All the surviving evidence suggests that the canons lacked discipline, but this evidence comes from the twelfth and early thirteenth centuries, and in each case is connected with a scheme to convert the secular college into a monastery. We learn that the canons of Dover ' . . . pour lour franchises devindront trop jolifs; qe nul home ne les poait chasties de lour mesfaitz . . .' and Henry II had no high opinion of the canons in the church of Waltham: ' . . . cum in ea canonici seculares nimis irreligiosa et carnaliter vixisserit.'[3] And Peter of Blois wrote to the pope about Wolverhampton, where he had himself been dean:

The clergy there were completely indisciplined as though they were Welshmen or Scots, and so greatly had their life been overtaken by

---

[1] M. Wilks, *The Problem of Sovereignty in the Later Middle Ages* (Cambridge, 1963), p. 83.

[2] Above, p. 104.   [3] Above, p. 59, and *Monasticon*, vi, 63.

vice that their wickedness passed into contempt of God, peril to souls, infamy to the clergy, a thing to be hissed at and derided by the whole people. And while I was preaching the meaning of the Scriptures they would be singing their disgraceful songs in the highways of Gath and at the cross-roads of Ascalon. . . . Indeed, fornicating publicly and openly they proclaimed like Sodom their own sin, and they took as wives each other's daughters or nieces. . . . With the utmost diligence I tried to cut out the poisonous offspring of their vices, but it would have been easier to change wolves into sheep, and wild beasts into men. . . .

Peter of Blois appealed to the pope: 'Convert this sty of pigs, this whore-house of Satan into a temple of God . . . root out malice and sow innocence, Holy Innocent.'[1] But how typical Wolverhampton was we cannot judge.

To understand medieval kingship we must draw to some extent upon the work of theorist-historians, whose interests lie in philosophy, theology or law. Much has been written on the priest-king, to whom a 'certain spiritual capacity was attributed . . . as an effluence of his consecration and unction'.[2] There came to be no place in papal doctrine for the clerical character of the king; but belief in a Christian polity in which the king played his part kept open the door through which he might exercise direct spiritual power. It is hazardous to cross the shifting sands which stretch out between the concepts, the claims and counter-claims, and the actual exercise of jurisdiction and authority. Occasionally the sand is firm. The claims concerning royal chapels can be seen for what they are worth: more defensive than aggressive. Some aggression there was from Edward I, but it was an aggression which sprang from much more than a belief in his own sacerdotal authority. The story of the royal free chapels appears to substantiate the belief that 'the English monarchy of the thirteenth century had preserved, perhaps more fully than any of its West European contemporaries, the early medieval

---

[1] Based upon the translation of *Patrologia Latina*, ed. J. P. Migne, 207, ep. clii in Styles 1936, pp. 67–8; and see above, pp. 42–3.

[2] E. Kantorowicz, *The King's Two Bodies* (Princeton, 1957), p. 44.

tradition of royal sacrosanctity'.[1] Indeed, among the pleas in the eyre of Stafford of 1292–3 it is noted that a king's chapel 'is so *sacred* that no archbishop or bishop shall have anything to do with it; and if the advowson of a church or land or rent appurtenant to the chapel be recovered against the dean and chapter by judgment of the king's court, he who recovers shall be put in seisin, not by the bishop of the place but by the king's sheriff'.[2] Here is a statement of the sacred nature of kingship. But it would be dangerous to interpret on face value an assertion of this kind, which seems to put the sanctity of the king above that of the clerical order. The statement has legal, even constitutional, rather than socio-religious implications. Its significance is derived more from a study of Roman law than from a tradition of royal sacrosanctity. The jurists showed that the royal *palatium* and the *domus fiscalis* were *sacra*, and that all things *sacra* were the subjects of public law.[3] Much more than protecting his proprietary rights the king in the thirteenth century claimed that he was protecting his dignity and crown.

Many of the areas in dispute between the Church and the State had been resolved, at least in part, by the creation of a dividing line between spiritualities and temporalities. The distinction is often meaningful: the control of advowson disputes and the possession of regalian right could be claimed with some reason as the defence of temporalities. Where the dividing line should be drawn was, of course, open to dispute; but the theory of division was nonetheless widely accepted. As Maitland pointed out,[4] it was recognised by Bracton, who wrote, 'sicut dominus papa in spiritualibus super omnibus habeat ordinarium jurisdictionem ita habet rex in regno suo ordinarium in temporalibus, et pares non habet neque superiores.' The diverging paths of common and

---

[1] J. W. Gray, 'The Church and Magna Carta in the century after Runnymede', *Historical Studies: papers read before the Irish Conference of Historians*, vi (1968), 24.

[2] *Year Books of 20 and 21 Edward I* (RS), ed. A. J. Horwood, pp. 406–8.

[3] G. Post, *Studies in Medieval Legal Thought* (Princeton, 1964), pp. 387–9.

[4] F. W. Maitland, *Roman Canon Law in the Church of England* (London, 1898), p. 106. And see above, p. 21.

canon law accentuated division. But nothing would prompt us to believe that spiritualities and temporalities could in fact be neatly separated. The rights exercised in the royal deaneries, although exercised without sanction from the Church, were no less spiritual rights. Lyndwood fully recognised this, even though he was concerned exclusively with the laws of the church.[1] Can the royal deaneries, he asked himself, be regarded as ecclesiastical benefices? From one point of view it appears that they cannot: they are not under the authority of the bishop and the deans are instituted neither by the bishop nor by any ecclesiastical ordinary; kings, princes or laymen cannot institute clerks to *any* church without consent from the bishop; benefices can be exchanged with each other, but not these deaneries; in the deaneries lapse of time before presentation results in no loss of patronage;[2] and these deaneries could even be visited by the royal chancellor who might be a layman. Yet they look very like ecclesiastical benefices: they have churches, that is, naves and choirs, bell towers and bells, chapters, cloisters and cemeteries, and they have baptisteries and parishioners, and the deans or their deputies administer the sacraments. Only by a papal grant, Lyndwood stressed, could the king exercise these spiritual rights—rights, for example, of institution and induction. Such rights could not be claimed as prescriptive, not even by a king who was no mere layman but a 'persona mixta'. Lyndwood knew, without doubt, that the king had no bulls of privilege. But it is wrong, he concluded, to say that the deaneries are not benefices; rather, episcopal rights are usurped. The deaneries are held illegally. Having devoted a lot of space to royal rights in the deaneries, Lyndwood comes down flatly in denial of any right in canon law.

The royal clerks collated to the king's chapels were quasi-bishops. Leaving aside those deans who were prelates in their own right and leaving aside the dean of St Buryan's, whose rights were established in the fourteenth century, there were at the beginning

---

[1] W. Lyndwood, *Provinciale* (Oxford, 1679), pp. 125–6.

[2] This is, of course, true; but if a dean failed to collate a clerk to a prebend within six months from the date of its vacancy, the king could claim the right of collation by reason of lapse of time (CPR 1334–8, pp. 554, 557).

of the fourteenth century eight royal deans of royal chapels with exempt parishes: the deans of St Martin-le-Grand, Wimborne Minster, Wolverhampton, St Mary's Shrewsbury, St Michael's Shrewsbury,[1] Bridgnorth, Tettenhall and Stafford. The rights which diocesan bishops retained in royal free chapels, however significant, appear small when compared with the *episcopalia* which the king and deans possessed. Royal *dominium* over some large royal churches had survived, and this meant, above all, the right of the king to institute to the deanships as and how he liked and the right of the deans to do likewise to the prebends,[2] with cure of souls or without. The exempt deaneries, taken together, were tantamount to a small diocese. The process whereby the older minsters with their dependent chapels were replaced by parish churches with their single priests[3] was less complete than has been supposed. Likewise, some qualification is called for if we are to conclude that 'before the end of the twelfth century, the old secular idea of lay proprietorship had yielded place to the ecclesiastical idea of patronage',[4] or that 'in the course of the twelfth century the proprietary church gradually disappeared from England, quietly and without any collision between the two powers'.[5] Even in the matter of cure of souls in churches with extensive parishes limits were being placed upon the powers of diocesan, and papal, government.

[1] Above, p. 122.

[2] Except in the case of Bridgnorth: see above, p. 24, n. 2.

[3] M. Chibnall, 'Monks and pastoral work', *Journal of Ecclesiastical History*, xviii (1967), 170.

[4] Cheney 1956, p. 160.

[5] H. G. Richardson and G. O. Sayles, *The Governance of Medieval England*, p. 286.

APPENDIX I

ACT OF BISHOP EUSTACE OF FAUCONBERG CONCERNING THE SUBMISSION OF THE CHURCH OF WITHAM TO THE BISHOP'S JURISDICTION

St Paul's, 1 March 1223

Printed from original: St Paul's Cathedral Cathedral Muniments, A 344 (A Box 29). Two seal tags, with centre part of one seal. Top edge indented, with the word 'CYROGRAPHUM' *through indenture. Endorsed:* 'super ecclesia de Wyham et ordinatione vicarie eiusdem ecclesie'. *The* actum *(residing* 'in domo thesaurarie') *was transcribed by a notary public 6 August 1386, and the notarial instrument was copied, along with other material concerning the chapel of Cressing, which was annexed to the church of Witham, into the register of Bishop Robert Gilbert: London Guildhall Library, MS 9531 vol. 6 (Reg. Gilbert), fo. 210r.*

Abstracts printed in R. Newcourt, Repertorium Ecclesiasticum, *ii. 675.*

[*See above, pp. 35–6*]

Omnibus sancte matris ecclesie filiis presens scriptum audituris Eustachius divina miseratione Lundon' ecclesie minister humilis salutem eternam in domino. Noverit universitas vestra quod cum aliquando mota fuisset contentio inter dominum Galfridum de Boklande decanum Sancti Martini London' et canonicos eiusdem ecclesie super ecclesia de Wiham, quam idem canonici ad communam suam de antiquo iure dicebant pertinere, tandem idem decanus quicquid iuris habebat in predicta ecclesia in manus nostras resignavit. Et tunc tam ipse quam dicti canonici totam predictam ecclesiam spontanea voluntate nostre commiserunt ordinationi. Nos autem neccessitatibus ecclesie Sancti Martini compatientes, ipsius considerato in multis neccessariorum defectu, de assensu capituli nostri ipsam ecclesiam de Wiham cum pertin-

153

entiis suis concessimus ipsis canonicis Sancti Martini in proprios usus ipsorum convertendam, salva perpetua vicaria eiusdem ecclesie ad quam de predictorum decani et canonicorum assensu deputavimus et assignavimus totam terram ad eandem ecclesiam pertinentem cum capitali mesagio et hominibus redditibus serviciis et cum omnibus libertatibus et consuetudinibus suis et omnes oblationes et obventiones eiusdem ecclesie et omnes decimationes totius parrochie ad altelagia pertinentes. Predicte autem vicarie ordinatio et collatio ad episcopos Lundon' absque contradictione in perpetuum pertinebit. Et ipsi canonici Sancti Martini de eadem vicaria percipient in perpetuum singulis annis septem marcas argenti medietatem in festo Sancti Michaelis et medietatem in Pascha donec nos vel successores nostri in loco competenti alias eis assignaverimus aliquod beneficium eiusdem valoris vel amplioris. Habebunt etiam ipsi canonici tantum de terra eiusdem ecclesie in loco competenti ubi grangias suas et alias domos neccessarias commode poterunt collocare. Habebunt etiam apud Kersinges locum illum ubi grangie ecclesie site sunt. Et quicunque per nos vel successores nostros in eadem vicaria vicarius fuerit institutus infra octo dies iurabit eisdem canonicis in capitulo eorum fidelitatem de eorum indempnitate servanda et de predicto redditu statutis terminis persolvendo. Et ipse vicarius omnia onera dicte ecclesie et capelle de Kersinges sustinebit et eam cum capella honeste procurabit in omnibus. Et ut hec nostra provisio et ordinatio perpetuam optineat firmitatem, eam auctoritate pontificali et presenti scripto et sigilli nostri et sigilli capituli nostri appositione confirmavimus. Predicti etiam decanus et capitulum Sancti Martini eandem ordinationem approbantes et ratam et gratam habentes sigillorum suorum appositione corroboraverunt. Hiis testibus Roberto decano Sancti Pauli, W. archidiacono Lund', R. archidiacono Colecestr', P. thesaurario, H. cancellario, J. Witeng', J. de Sancto Laurent', Ph. de Falkoberg' et aliis canonicis Sancti Pauli, magistro W. de Turri, Reginaldo, Hugone, Petro et aliis canonicis Sancti Martini. Act' apud Sanctum Paulum kal. Martii pontificatus nostri anno secundo.

APPENDIX II

AGREEMENT BETWEEN GILES OF ERDINGTON, DEAN OF WOLVERHAMPTON, AND ALEXANDER STAVENSBY, BISHOP OF COVENTRY AND LICHFIELD

Soon after April 1224

Printed from Lichfield Dean and Chapter Muniments, Magnum Registrum Album, fo. 241r, and Oxford, Bodleian Libr., Ashmole 1527, fo. 73r. The reference to the bishop's first visit following his consecration abroad (14 April 1224) provides the only means of dating this composition; it is no surprise that the bishop used the title 'bishop of Coventry and Lichfield' before that title was recognised (see Magnum Registrum Album, *p. 225).*

Translated in Magnum Registrum Album, *no. 587.*

[*See above, pp. 43-4*]

Omnibus Christi fidelibus Egidius decanus de Wolfronhamptone et eiusdem ecclesie canonici salutem in domino. Noverit universitas vestra quod cum venerabilis pater A. dei gratia Coventrensis et Lichfeldensis episcopus nos lege diocesana per litteras domini pape super obedientia sibi impendenda convenisset ita amicabiliter inter nos composuimus, videlicet quod dictus episcopus ista nomine ecclesie sue percipiet canonicam scilicet obedientiam a decano nostro qui liberam in ecclesia sua de Wolfronhamptone more consueto conferendi prebendas retineat potestatem et instituendi et corrigendi excessus clericorum suorum, nisi post canonicam amonitionem ab episcopo factam decessus fuerit repertus ut tunc ad ipsum corrigendi eosdem excessus devolvatur potestas aliter autem non, omni exactione pecuniaria et procuratione exclusa exceptis duobus solidis nomine denariorum beati Petri eidem a dicta ecclesia singulis annis solvendis et exceptis causis matrimonialibus omnibus eiusdem parochie et sacrilegiis

155

et arduis causis que merito sunt ad episcopum referende et exceptis aliis causis de parochia de Wolfronhamptone per appellationem legitimam ad episcopum devolutis. Episcopus autem pro voluntate sua in ecclesia nostra officium celebrandi predicandi confirmandi et publicas penitentias iniungendi cum debita veneratione excercebit, crisma et oleum debito modo nobis impertiendo. Ordinandos ab ecclesia nostra quibus nichil canonicum obstiterit dum modo indempnitati sue et ecclesie sue provideatur cum a nobis fuerit requisitus benigne admittet, processione pentecostali more consueto eidem reservata. Nos autem ipsum in adventu suo primo post consecrationem suam et de partibus transmarinis cum debita veneratione et processione sicut vicine ecclesie admittemus. Ipse autem ecclesiam nostram et eius iura et possessiones pro officii sui debito secundum deum tuebitur, nobis et clericis nostris omni iniuria et rancore remisso. In cuius rei testimonium presentem paginam signis decani nostri et capituli duximus roborandam. Valete.

APPENDIX III

MANDATE OF POPE GREGORY IX

Reate, 20 July 1231

Printed from W.A.M., Book 5, fo. 14r (= A), W.A.M., MS 13167, m. 5v (= B), and P.R.O., C47 (Chancery Miscellanea) 16/8/11, fo. 19r (= C). W.A.M., Book 5, is the fifteenth-century cartulary of St Martin-le-Grand; W.A.M., MS 13167, is a thirteenth-century cartulary roll of the same college, and to the dorse of this roll copies of documents, of which this mandate is one, were added in the fourteenth century; P.R.O., C47 (Chancery Miscellanea) 16/8/11, fo. 19r, is a schedule of bulls concerning royal free chapels transcribed at the king's order in 1346 from originals in the royal treasury.

[See above, pp. 21–2, 28–9]

Gregorius episcopus servus servorum dei venerabili fratri episcopo Eliensi salutem et apostolicam benedictionem. Ex parte karissimi in Christo filii nostri illustris regis Anglie fuit propositum coram nobis quod cum in regum demanio quedam capelle que regie nuncupantur, quarum una decanatus Sancti Martini dicitur, ab antiquo fundate fuerant et dotate et obtentum sit hactenus ut de temporalibus earundem et menbrorum suorum nulli nisi regi Anglie de spiritualibus vero soli Romano pontifici disponere liceat, quidam episcopi regionum illarum in quibusdam capellarum ipsarum menbris disponendi de spiritualibus et temporalibus suis quasi possessionem ecclesiasticam[1] usurparunt, super quo idem rex apostolice sedis providentiam imploravit. Cum igitur non sit clamdestino possessori in preiudicium iuris regii ac Romane ecclesie deferendum, fraternitati tue per apostolica scripta mandamus quatinus vocatis[2] qui fuerint evocandi et inquisita

---

[1] ecclesiasticam A, B; clamdestinam *over erasure* C.
[2] vocatis *omitted* B, *interlined* A.

super premissis solicite veritate[1] quod inveneris ad presentiam nostram transmittas ut per tuam relationem instructi securius[2] in negotio procedere valeamus, constitutione de duabus dietis in generali concilio edita[3] non obstante. Testes autem qui fuerunt nominati si se gratia odio vel timore subtraxerint per censuram ecclesiasticam apellatione cessante compellas veritati testimonium peribere. Dat' Reat' xiii kal. Augusti pontificatus nostri anno quinto.

[1] veritatem C.   [2] securi C.
[3] Canon 37 of the Fourth Lateran Council.

APPENDIX IV

CONFIRMATION OF POPE GREGORY IX

Viterbo, 27 April 1236

Printed from the original (P.R.O., SC7 (Papal Bulls) 46/4), and checked with Registrum Vaticanum 18, fo. 152r, where it is complete only in arenga *and* textus. *Size: approx. 265 mm × 178 mm, plica in addition 26 mm. Holes for string of* bulla. *Pope's name in enlarged minuscules; some ornate capital letters.* Supra plicam: [*extreme right-hand corner*] sal. Endorsed: Regi Angl'. R script' [*script' within loop of* R]; [*new hand*] habeo. examinatur. scribitur in libro; [*new hand; centre, upside down*] E; [? *new hand; centre, below E*] Valtham; erasures; [*new hand; bottom left, upside down*] 8 Gregorius 9us.

Calendared in P.R.O. List and Indexes, *xlix, p. 229,* Les Registres de Grégoire IX, *ed. L. Auvray, no. 3133, and* Calendar of Papal Letters, *i, 153. Not in Bishop Stapledon's calendar of bulls in the king's treasury in 1323 (Palgrave,* Antient Kalendars).

[*See above, pp. 19–21*]

Gregorius episcopus servus servorum dei carissimo in Christo filio . . illustri regi Anglie salutem et apostolicam benedictionem. Suscepti officii cura requirit ut honesta desideria favore benivolo prosequentes, tibi tamquam speciali apostolice sedis filio in hiis libentius et facilius annuamus. Eapropter carissime in Christo fili serenitatis tue precibus inclinati, libertates et immunitates capellis regiis a progenitoribus tuis regibus Anglie obtentu pietatis indultas, prout in eorum litteris dicitur plenius contineri, sicut eas iuste obtinent et quiete, auctoritate ipsis apostolica confirmamus et presentis scripti patrocinio communimus. Nulli ergo omnino hominum liceat hanc paginam nostre confirmationis infringere vel ei ausu temerario contraire. Siquis autem hoc attemptare presumpserit indignationem omnipotentis dei et beatorum Petri et Pauli apostolorum eius se noverit incursurum. Dat' Viterbii v kal. Maii pontificatus nostri anno decimo.

APPENDIX V

SPURIOUS INDULT OF POPE CLEMENT IV

Viterbo, 22 June 1266

Printed from W.A.M., MS 13167, m. 5v, with some minor variants from W.A.M., Book 5, fos. 13v–14r. In the former this indult was copied from a notarial instrument drawn up in 1335.

Ascribed to Pope Clement V in two inaccurate editions: Kempe 1825, p. 190 (from B.M., Lansdowne 170 (fo. 56r), a sixteenth-century copy of W.A.M., Book 5), and Owen and Blakeway 1825, ii, 187–8 (from the untraced 'archives of the Royal Peculiar of Bridgnorth').

[*See above, pp. 100–1*]

Clemens episcopus servus servorum dei carissimo in Christo filio regi Anglie illustri salutem et apostolicam benedictionem. Ex parte tua fuit propositum coram nobis quod clare memorie reges Anglie progenitores tui in regno Anglie, antequam ibidem ordinarentur episcopi, quamplures fundaverunt ecclesias et regia libertate de bonis propriis dotaverunt, que ab ipsarum fundatione a iurisdictione archiepiscoporum, episcoporum et quorumlibet aliorum inferiorum ordinariorum fuerunt prorsus libere et immunes, et usque ad[1] moderna tempora gavise sunt plenaria libertate. Demum autem insurgente in eodem regno turbationis procella, archiepiscopi et episcopi in quorum diocesibus consistunt ecclesie supradicte, que capelle regie wlgariter appellantur, et alii ordinarii earundem diocesium in ecclesiis ipsis sibi iurisdictionem indebitam usurpantes in earum aliquibus visitationis officium impenderunt exercendo censuram ecclesiasticam in eisdem, clericis ipsis propter turbationem huiusmodi non audentibus resistere in hoc archiepiscopis, episcopis et aliis supradictis. Quia vero ex hoc tibi qui ecclesiarum ipsarum patronus existis ac eisdem

---

[1] ad usque.

ecclesiis et clericis posset in posterum preiudicium generari, nos
volentes tam iuri tuo quam indemnitati ecclesiarum et clericorum
predictorum in hac parte paterna diligentia providere, ut premissis
veris existentibus per huiusmodi archiepiscoporum, episcoporum
et aliorum ordinariorum predictorum usurpationem predictorum
iurium, in quorum possessione vel quasi ante turbationem huiusmodi non fuerunt, nullum tibi aut ecclesiis vel clericis vel mem-
bris preiudicium generetur auctoritate presentium indulgemus.
Nulli ergo omnino hominum liceat hanc paginam nostre con-
cessionis infringere vel ei[1] ausu temerario contraire.[2] Si quis autem
hoc attemptare presumpserit indignationem omnipotentis dei et
beatorum Petri et Pauli apostolorum eius se noverit incursurum.
Dat' Viterbie x kal. Julii pontificatus nostri anno secundo.

---

[1] eam.   [2] contra ire.

APPENDIX VI

MANDATE OF POPE CLEMENT IV

Viterbo, 3 August 1267

Printed from Lichfield Dean and Chapter Muniments, Magnum Registrum Album, fos. 232v–235r (= A), and Oxford, Bodleian Libr., Ashmole 1527, fos. 7r–9v (= B).

Abridged and translated in Magnum Registrum Album, *nos. 566–9.*

[*See above, pp. 98n, 99–101*]

Confirmatio apostolica sententie excommunicationis late in decanum Staffordie et capitulum beate Marie eo quod episcopum Lichfeldensem ad visitationem admittere noluerunt.[1]

Clemens episcopus servus servorum dei venerabili fratri episcopo Wigorniensi et dilecto filio priori Sancti Thome iuxta Staffordiam Coventrensis diocesis salutem et apostolicam benedictionem. Exhibita nobis venerabilis fratris nostri Coventrensis et Lichfeldensis episcopi petitio continebat quod cum felicis recordationis Urbanus papa predecessor noster causam, que inter eundem episcopum ex parte una et quondam[2] Simonem decanum et capitulum ecclesie Sancte Marie de Staffordia Coventrensis diocesis, super eo quod episcopus ipse dictam ecclesiam et capellas ad illam spectantes eiusdem diocesis lege diocesana sibi proponit esse subiectas aliisque iuribus episcopalibus exercendis in illis, necnon super excommunicationis in decanum et maiores de prefato capitulo et suspencionis in ipsum capitulum sententiis occasione premissorum ab eodem episcopo auctoritate ordinaria promulgatis, ex altera vertitur, bone memorie predecessori tuo fratri episcopo Wygorniensi et dilectis filiis . . abbati Sancti Edmundi Norwicensis diocesis et . . cantori ecclesie Sancti Pauli

---

[1] *Omit title* B. [2] quondam *changed to* quendam A.

Londoniensis sub ea forma per litteras apostolicas commisisset, ut vocatis qui evocandi forent causam audirent eandem, et ipsam infra unius anni spatium a receptione dictarum litterarum iudicio vel si de partium voluntate procederet in[1] concordia terminarent, facientes quod decernerent per censuram ecclesiasticam firmiter observari, alioquin eam extunc in statu in quo foret remitterent ad apostolice sedis examen, prefixo partibus ipsis certo termino peremptorio quo per ydoneos procuratores sufficienter instructos cum omnibus actis iuribus et munimentis suis se conspectui apostolico presentarent, facture et recepture quod ordo exigeret rationis, iidem iudices causam ipsam, cum eam infra scriptum[2] tempus terminare non possent, ad ipsius sedis remiserunt examen, certumque partibus ipsis prefixerunt terminum quo propter hoc se conspectui apostolico presentarent iuxta dictarum continentiam litterarum. Et licet dictus predecessor noster in causa ipsa dilectum filium nostrum R. Sancti Angeli diaconum cardinalem dedisset partibus auditorem, ac dilectus filius magister Andreas Spiliaci subdiaconus et capellanus noster, cui cardinalis ipse causam commisit eandem, citationes fecerit in audientia publica fieri ut est moris, procuratore tamen supradicti episcopi Coventrensis et Lichfeldensis comparente in huiusmodi termino coram capellano predicto et petente cum instantia in causa ipsa procedi, dicti decanus et capitulum per se non comparuerunt nec per aliquem responsalem, quamquam diutine fuerint expectati. Verum quia dictus capellanus, litteras remissionis et acta remissa ad predictam sedem super causa ipsa per iudices memoratos in contumaciam ipsorum decani et capituli ad instantiam dicti procuratoris aperiens, se tandem transtulit ad remota, dictus cardinalis dilecto filio magistro Nicholao de Sanctis capellano suo commisit audientiam dicte cause, qui premissis citationibus debitis in audientia memorata causam ipsam et actitata in ea discussit et vidit diligenter ac ea fideliter coram cardinale recitavit eodem et ab eo demum mandato habito de sententia proferenda diligenti quoque deliberatione prehabita communicato peritorum consilio et iuris ordine observato, presente procuratore supradicti Coventrensis et Lichfeldensis episcopi, non obstante absentia capituli memorati, sententiando pronuntiavit in scriptis supradictam suspensionis sententiam in idem capitulum promulgatam tam diu fore inviolabiliter observandam et quod dictum capitulum prefato Coventrensi et

---

[1] *Omit* in B. [2] prescriptum B.

Lichfeldensi episcopo tanquam diocesano suo obediat et intendat, donec per se vel procuratores ydoneos ostenderit se exemptum seu liberum a iuribus supradictis. Et quia supradicto Simone decano cedente Bogonem de Clare illi successisse invenit et tempore libelli super hoc dati fore decanum et se gerat [*sic*] pro decano eumque repperit simili contumacia laborantem, ipsum exigente iustitia excommunicavit in scriptis et tam diu noluit sub excommunicatione teneri ac dicto episcopo tanquam diocesano obedire et intendere donec per se vel una cum prefato capitulo personaliter seu per procuratorem ydoneum ostenderit dictam ecclesiam vel se nomine decanatus sui liberum et exemptum ab episcopalibus iuribus antedictis. Eosdem quoque decanum et capitulum prefato Coventrensi et Lichfeldensi episcopo in certa pecunie summa taxatione prehabita et iuramento prestito a procuratore predicto expensarum nomine condempnavit prout in publico instrumento confecto ex inde ac sigillo cardinalis et magistri Nicholai predictorum signato plenius continetur. Nos itaque ipsius episcopi supplicationibus inclinati huiusmodi pronuntiationem et condempnationem provide latas ratas et firmas habentes discretioni vestre per apostolica scripta mandamus quatinus vos vel alter vestrum, pronuntiationem et condempnationem easdem auctoritate nostra per vos vel alium aut alios executioni debite demandantes, dictas suspencionis et excommunicationis sententias faciatis iuxta pronuntiationem huiusmodi observari ac dicto Coventrensi et Lichfeldensi episcopo vel procuratori suo eius nomine de huiusmodi summa pecunie a prefatis decano et capitulo satisfactionem plenariam exhiberi, contradictores per censuram ecclesiasticam appellatione postposita compescendo, non obstante si aliquibus a sede apostolica sit indultum quod suspendi vel interdici aut excommunicari non possint per ipsius sedis litteras non facientes plenam et expressam de indulto huiusmodi mentionem. Tenorem autem ipsius instrumenti de verbo ad verbum presentibus fecimus annotari qui talis est:

In nomine domini amen. Dudum venerabilis pater dominus . . Coventrensis et Lichfeldensis episcopus, asserens quod in ecclesia seu capella Sancte Marie de Staffordia et capellis ad eam spectantibus Coventrensis et Lichfeldensis diocesis utpote lege diocesana sibi subiectis ad ipsum spectabat iura episcopalia exercere necnon cognoscere de causis omnium servitorum ministrorum et parochianorum ecclesie ac capellarum ipsarum que noscuntur ad forum ecclesiasticum pertinere, et quod ipse extitit ac predecessores sui extiterunt ab antiquo in quasi possessione iura ipsa exercendi et de causis huiusmodi cognoscendi et quod decanus et capitulum ipsius ecclesie Sancte Marie quominus idem episcopus iura huiusmodi exercere posset et de causis cognoscere impedire contra iustitiam presumebant in eiusdem episcopi et sui episcopatus preiudicium et gravamen, ad venerabilem patrem Wygorniensem episcopum et discretos viros abbatem Sancti Edmundi Norwicensis diocesis et .. cantorem Sancti Pauli ecclesie Londoniensis felicis recordationis domini Urbani pape quarti sub hac forma litteras inpetravit:

Urbanus episcopus servus servorum dei venerabili fratri episcopo Wigorniensi et dilectis filiis .. abbati Sancti Edmundi Norwicensis diocesis et .. cantori ecclesie Sancti Pauli Londoniensis salutem et apostolicam benedictionem. Ex parte venerabilis fratris nostri Coventrensis et Lichfeldensis episcopi fuit propositum coram nobis quod ad ipsum in ecclesia Sancte Marie de Staffordia et quibusdam capellis ad eam spectantibus sue diocesis utpote sibi lege diocesana subiectis spectat iura episcopalia exercere necnon de causis cognoscere omnium servitorum ministrorum et parochianorum ecclesie ac capellarum ipsarum que noscuntur ad forum ecclesiasticum pertinere, idemque episcopus extitit ac predecessores sui extiterunt ab antiquo in quasi possessione exercendi iura ipsa et de causis huiusmodi cognoscendi. Set dilecti filii decanus et capitulum ipsius ecclesie in eadem ecclesia iura ipsa et huiusmodi causarum cognitionem predicto episcopo subtrahentes indebite non permittunt dictum episcopum in predictis capellis servitoribus et ministris iurisdictionem debitam exercere. Propter quod dictus episcopus in predictum decanum et maiores de prefato capitulo excommunicationis et ipsum capitulum suspencionis sententias auctoritate propria canonica monitione premissa exigente iustitia promulgavit. Quare ex parte ipsius episcopi petebatur a nobis ut dictos decanum et capitulum super hiis compesci et easdem sententias observari faceremus. Pro parte vero dictorum decani et capituli fuit ex adverso propositum quod ecclesia et capelle predicte que sunt karissimi in Christo filii nostri illustris regis Anglie speciales una cum ministris et parochianis eorum a iurisdictione cuiuslibet ordinarii sunt per specialia privilegia apostolice sedis exempte, sicut ecclesie ac capelle cetere dicti regis fueruntque gavise plena et pacifica libertate a tempore quo regnum Anglie ad cultum fidei Christiane pervenit et antequam ibi aliqui episcopi crearentur, tali videlicet libertate quod nullus episcopus vel quivis alius ordinarius ullo unquam tempore aliqua iura episcopalia exercuit in eisdem, ipsis dumtaxat decano et capitulo exercentibus in eisdem capellis a tempore huiusmodi iura ipsa scilicet ea que possunt sine episcopo exerceri ac de causis cognoscentibus supradictis. Verum dictus episcopus super hoc sibi indebitam iurisdictionem usurpans in dictos decanum maiores et capitulum prefatas sententias pro eo quod ipsum ad exercendum prefata in ecclesia et capellis predictis admittere noluerunt sicut nec etiam tenebantur post appellationem propter hoc legittime ad predictam sedem emissam motu proprio promulgavit, eosque tanquam excommunicatos et suspensos facit ab omnibus artius evitari. Propter quod iidem decanus et capitulum nobis humiliter supplicarunt ut ipsum episcopum ab huiusmodi exactione compesci ac denunciari eos non esse vitandos pendente questione huiusmodi tanquam excommunicatos vel suspensos de consueta sedis apostolice providentia faceremus. Quo circa discretioni vestre de procuratorum utriusque partis consensu per apostolica scripta mandamus quatinus vocatis qui fuerint evocandi audiatis causam et eam infra unius anni spatium a receptione presentium iudicio vel si de partium voluntate processerit concordia terminetis, facientes quod decreveritis auctoritate nostra firmiter observari. Testes autem qui fuerint nominati si se gratia odio vel timore subtraxerint per censuram ecclesiasticam cessante appellatione cogatis veritati testimonium perhibere. Alioquin eam extunc in statu in quo fuerit remittatis ad dicte sedis examen prefixo partibus ipsis termino peremptorio trium mensium proximum predictum annum sequentium quo per ydoneos procuratores sufficienter instructos cum omnibus actis iuribus ac munimentis suis compareant coram nobis facture et recepture super hoc quod ordo dictaverit rationis. Diem autem citationis et formam et quicquid inde feceritis nobis per vestras litteras harum seriem continentes fideliter intimare curetis. Quod si non omnes hiis exequendis potueritis interesse tu frater episcope cum eorum altero ea nichilominus exequaris. Dat' Viterbii vi kal. Januarii pontificatus nostri anno primo. [*Viterbo, 27 December 1261*]

Predicti vero iudices causam ipsam, cum eam non possent infra ipsum terminum terminare, remiserunt ad ipsius sedis examen, prefixo eisdem partibus termino trium mensium quo per se vel per procuratores ydoneos cum omnibus actis iuribus et munimentis suis contingentibus ipsam causam apostolico se conspectui presentarent. Sane pendente dilatione huiusmodi ab eodem domino Urbano papa impetratus fuit auditor in dicta causa venerabilis pater dominus Ricardus Sancti Angeli diaconus cardinalis et dominus Andreas Spiliaci domini pape subdiaconus et capellanus ab ipso domino cardinale qui dictos decanum et capitulum citari fecit in audientia publica pluries et peremptorie ut est moris ex parte dicti domini cardinalis. Quia vero iidem decanus et

capitulum per se non comparuerunt nec aliquem responsalem licet post
terminos diutius expectati, procuratore dicti episcopi semper in terminis comparente eorumque contumaciam incusando cum instantia
postulante litteras remissionis et acta remissa ad sedem apostolicam
super dicta causa per dictos iudices delegatos in eorundem decani et
capituli contumaciam aperiri. Idem dominus Andreas, ad instantiam
procuratoris dicti episcopi aperiens dictas litteras atque acta, invenit
inter alia libellum datum ex parte dicti episcopi contra decanum et
capitulum supradictos coram commissariis prefatorum iudicum delegatorum continentie infrascripte:

Coram vobis discreti viri commissarii venerabilis patris Wigorniensis
episcopi et venerabilium virorum . . abbatis Sancti Edmundi et . .
cantoris ecclesie Sancti Pauli Londoniensis iudicum a sede apostolica
delegatorum[1] dicit et proponit procurator venerabilis patris Coventrensis et Lichfeldensis episcopi contra decanum et capitulum ecclesie
seu capelle Sancte Marie Staffordie quod ad ipsum dominum suum
in dicta ecclesia seu capella Sancte Marie de Staffordia et capellis ad
eam spectantibus Coventrensis et Lichfeldensis diocesis utpote lege
diocesana subiectis eidem domino suo spectat iura episcopalia exercere necnon cognoscere de causis omnium servitorum ministrorum
et parochianorum ecclesie ac capellarum ipsarum que noscuntur ad
forum ecclesiasticum pertinere. Idemque dominus suus extitit ac
predecessores sui extiterunt ab antiquo in quasi possessione exercendi
iura ipsa et de causis huiusmodi cognoscendi. Set dicti decanus et
capitulum ipsius ecclesie in eadem ecclesia et capellis prefatis iura
ipsa et huiusmodi causarum cognitionem predicto domino suo
indebite subtrahere molientes, non permittunt ipsum dominum suum
in predictis ecclesia et capellis servitoribus ministris et parochianis
iurisdictionem debitam exercere. Propter quod idem dominus
suus in Simonem quondam decanum dicte ecclesie Sancte Marie
Staffordie, magistrum Adam de Phileby et Philippum Lepere[2]
canonicos eiusdem ecclesie excommunicationis et in ipsum capitulum
suspencionis sententias auctoritate ordinaria canonice promulgavit.
Quare petit idem procurator nomine procuratorio pro domino suo
memorato per vos vel per iudices principales seu alios ipsorum
commissarios iura episcopalia in predictis ecclesia et capellis servitoribus ministris et parochianis ipsorum ad eundem dominum suum
iure episcopali pertinere sententialiter declarari et dictos decanum et
capitulum super predictis compesci et, ut predicto domino suo
tanquam diocesano suo obediant et intendant, condempnari sententialiter et compelli et dictas sententias excommunicationis in
predictos Adam et Philippum et suspencionis in capitulum ratas

[1] legatorum A. [2] lepoer B.

observari. Premissa proponit dictus procurator non artans se vel dominum suum ad probationem omnium premissorum nec in ea forma qua proposita sunt set vel omnium vel aliquorum in ea forma vel alia que sibi vel domino suo sufficere debeant ad victoriam cause sue.

Porro eodem domino Andrea se de curia absentante dictus dominus cardinalis nobis Nicholao de Sanctis capellano suo commisit audientiam dicte cause. Comparente igitur magistro Ricardo de Suham procuratore dicti episcopi coram nobis et procedi contra decanum et capitulum prelibatos in dicta causa instantissime postulante citari fecimus solempniter ex parte dicti domini cardinalis in audientia publica pluries et peremptorie ut est moris decanum et capitulum antedictos ut deberent per se vel procuratores ydoneos comparere facturi et recepturi in dicta causa iustitie complementum. Cumque decanus et capitulum sepefati non curaverint per se nec responsalem aliquem comparere etiam post terminos et terminos diutius expectati prefato magistro Ricardo semper in terminis comparente et procedi contra eos ad condempnationem expensarum et ad alia que iustitia requirebat cum instantia requirente, causam ipsam et in ea actitata discussimus et vidimus diligenter et ea que invenimus in eadem ipsi domino cardinali fideliter retulimus et devote, qui nobis precepit ut ad sententiam procedere deberemus. Unde nos per ea que vidimus et cognovimus Christi nomine invocato deliberatione prehabita diligenti communicato consilio peritorum de speciali mandato dicti domini cardinalis, presente dicto procuratore episcopi et sententiam postulante, non obstante absentia dicti capituli que dei presentia repleatur, sententiando pronuntiamus in scriptis dictam sententiam suspencionis in capitulum dictum latam tam diu inviolabiliter fore servandam et quod predictum capitulum dicto episcopo tanquam diocesano obediat et intendat quam diu per se vel procuratores ydoneos ostenderit se exemptum vel liberum a iuribus supradictis. Et quia dicto Simone decano cedente quendam nomine Bogonem de Clare legittimis documentis invenimus successisse et tempore suprascripti dati libelli fore decanum et se gerere pro decano et reperimus eum simili contumacia laborantem, cum nunquam post remissionem supradictam per se vel per alium curaverit comparere, ne transiret talis contumacia impunita, eum excommunicationis sententia decernimus innodandum. Unde pronuntiantes in scriptis eundem Bogonem excommunicamus et tam diu volumus sub excommunicatione teneri et quod predicto episcopo tanquam diocesano obediat et intendat quam diu per se vel una cum capitulo supradicto personaliter vel per procuratorem ydoneum ostenderit dictam ecclesiam vel se nomine decanatus liberum vel exemptum a iuribus antedictis. Dictum autem decanum et capitulum condempnamus in quinquaginta

libris sterlingorum pro expensis taxatione nostra prehabita et sacra-
mento ipsius magistri Ricardi procuratoris secuto quas per ipsius nobis
constitit sacramentum dictum episcopum per procuratores suos fecisse
in causa predicta postquam negotium ut dictum est ad curiam fuit
remissum, et dicti decanus et capitulum in dicta contumacia perstiter-
unt. In huius autem rei testimonium presens instrumentum scribi et
publicari fecimus per Bonaspem notarium infrascriptum et nostri
sigilli una cum sigillo dicti domini cardinalis munimine roborari.
Lecta et pronuntiata fuit hec sententia in scriptis per dictum dominum
Nicholaum, Viterbii, anno domini millesimo cc°lxvii° indictione
decima mense Julii die viii°, presentibus magistro Benedicto canonico
Adrien', Petro scriniario de Capua, Capuano clerico et Jacobello
familiaribus dicti domini Nicholai et Guillelmo clerico de Kirkeby
testibus vocatis et rogatis. Et ego Bonaspes Guiducii de Perusio apostolice sedis auctoritate notarius lectioni pronuntiationi huius sententie
interfui et ut supra legitur de mandato dicti domini Nicholai auditoris
scripsi et rogatus in publicam formam redegi.

Dat' Viterbii iii non. Augusti pontificatus nostri anno tertio.

APPENDIX VII

AGREEMENT BETWEEN THE BISHOP OF LICHFIELD AND THE DEANS AND CANONS OF THE ROYAL CHAPELS OF HIS DIOCESE

3 June 1281 (agreement with Shrewsbury alone, 27 May 1281)

Printed from Lichfield Dean and Chapter Muniments, Magnum Registrum Album, fos. 223v–224r (= A), Lincoln Dean and Chapter Archives, Carte Decani (A.1.7), fo. 55r–v (no. 159) (= B), and Owen and Blakeway 1825, ii. 307, n. 2 (= C). Most variants are noted. The source used by Owen and Blakeway ('God. Edwards from the exch. Salop.') has not been located. The County Archivist of Shropshire, Mary C. Hill, tells me that the 'Exchequer' was the name given to part of Shrewsbury's guildhall. It was demolished in 1783. The records have had a chequered history, and the manuscripts referred to by Owen and Blakeway are not among the present Shrewsbury borough records.

Translated from A in Magnum Registrum Album, *no. 525.*

[*See above, pp. 108–10*]

Compositio inter episcopum Lichfeldensem et capellas que regias se pretendunt.[1]

Pateat universis presentes litteras visuris vel audituris quod nuper[2] inter venerabilem patrem Rogerum dei gratia Coventrensem et Lichfeldensem episcopum ex una parte et Sancte Marie Staff', Derb',[3] Pencrych', Tetenhal', Wolverhampton', Brugg' et Salop' ecclesiarum decanos et canonicos Coventrensis diocesis[4]

---

[1] Compositio cum Lichfeldensi episcopo super capellis liberis domini regis B; *no heading* C.

[2] *Begin* Nuper A.   [3] Derb' *erased* A; de Stafford' de Derb' B.

[4] Sancte *to* diocesis *substitute* decanum et canonicos ecclesie Sancte Marie

ex altera[1] orta[2] materia questionis super eo videlicet quod
memoratus episcopus predictas ecclesias que capelle regie wlgariter
nuncupantur lege sibi diocesana subiectas esse dicebat quodque
spectabat ad eum in eisdem ecclesiis seu capellis visitationis
officium et spiritualem iurisdictionem omnimodam exercere,
ipsis decanis et canonicis asserentibus ex adverso se et predictas
ecclesias suas seu[3] capellas suas dependentes ab eisdem necnon
clerum et populum earundem ab omni ordinaria iurisdictione
liberos et exemptos, tandem episcopus decani et canonici supradicti, volentes potius per pacis viam[4] incedere quam litigiorum
amfractibus implicari, de voluntate et assensu serenissimi principis
domini Edwardi dei gratia regis Anglie illustris qui earum
ecclesiarum[5] patronus esse dinoscitur in hanc pacis formam
consenserunt, videlicet quod predicte ecclesie decani et canonici
servitores et ministri et parochiani earundem una cum capellis[6]
dependentibus ab eisdem ab omni ordinaria iurisdictione re-
maneant et sint exempti liberi et immunes et sacrosancte Romane
ecclesie immediate subiecti, ita quod nulli episcopo seu ordinario
alteri liceat in ecclesiis predictis aut suis capellis visitare, corrigere,
de causis cognoscere vel aliquid aliud in eisdem facere quod in
aliis exemptis ecclesiis fieri minime consuevit, adiecto[7] tamen
quod predicti decani et canonici concesserunt pro bono pacis
ipsi episcopo quod,[8] cum ipsum[9] ad predictas ecclesias declinare
contigerit, cum processione et honorificentia debita admittatur,
liceatque eidem[10] de gratia eorundem decanorum et canonicorum
duratura perpetuo in predictis ecclesiis verbum dei proponere,
ordines celebrare, oleum et crisma conficere et pueros con-
firmare, ita tamen quod pro concessione[11] huiusmodi exemptioni
libertati immunitati predictis preiudicium minime generetur. Et
cum ipsum episcopum in ecclesiis ipsis vel earum capellis[12] ad

---

Salop' Coventrensis et Lichfeldensis diocesis C. *Throughout in C one dean and
one church.*

1 *Add* parte C.   2 *Add* esset B.
3 seu *substitute* et C; subiectas esse *to* seu *substitute* etiam B.
4 per pacis viam *substitute* vias pacis A.
5 earum ecclesiarum *substitute* earundem B.
6 *Add* ab antiquo C.   7 Adiecta A.
8 *Add* ipse C.   9 *Add* episcopum A; *omit* ipsum C.
10 *Add* episcopo C.   11 per concessionem C.
12 capellis *substitute* aliqua B; vel earum capellis *omit* C.

preces et ad requisitionem[1] dictorum decanorum crisma conficere aut ordines celebrare contigerit, clericos dictarum ecclesiarum examinatos et approbatos per decanos ipsos ad presentationem eorundem decanorum ordinabit et crisma[2] et oleum dabit in ecclesiis antedictis si sibi visum fuerit expedire.[3] Hec autem compositio sacrosancte ecclesie Romane summo pontifici presentetur et[4] confirmetur ab eo[5] si ipsam duxerit confirmandam. Predictus vero episcopus pro se et pro tempore et[6] dominus rex pro se et decani et canonici predictarum capellarum suarum huic instrumento ad modum cirographi confecto alternatim sigilla sua apposuerunt in testimonium premissorum. Act' apud Westmon' London' iii non. Junii anno domini m° cc lxxxi°.[7]

[1] ad precem et requisitiones C.

[2] et crisma *interlined* A.   [3] si *to* expedire *omit* B, *interlined* A.

[4] *Add* ab ipso A.   [5] ab eo *omit* A.

[6] pro tempore et *omit* C, et pro tempore *interlined* A.

[7] C *ends* Dat' apud Westm' London' vi kal. Junii anno domini m° cclxxxi°. B *ends* Memorandum est quod ista composcistio [*sic*] inventa fuit apud Westm' inter alia privilegia domini Edwardi regis Anglie ad festum Pasche anno regni regis Edwardi vicesimo.

APPENDIX VIII

CASE CONCERNING DERBY IN THE COURT OF THE KING'S BENCH
1284-5

Printed from P.R.O. KB27 (Coram Rege Rolls) 95 m. 4 (13 and 14 Edward I).

[*See above, pp. 111–12*]

Rogerus Coventrensis et Lychfeldensis episcopus attachiatus fuit ad respondendum domino regi de placito quare, cum ecclesia Omnium Sanctorum Derb' libera capella domini regis sicut et cetere capelle regis ab omni iurisdictione ordinaria tam iure regio quam per privilegia apostolica regi et predecessoribus regis indulta totaliter sit exempta, et dominus rex eidem inhibuerit ne aliquam iurisdictionem ordinariam in predicta ecclesia seu prebendis aut capellis ipsius per ipsum vel suos exerceret et sicut vellet iura et libertates suas sub favore et protectione regia tutas esse ita iura et libertates regias integra et illesa faceret observari, ac idem episcopus nichilominus ut rex accepit in predicta ecclesia et menbris suis iurisdictionem suam ordinariam exercere presumit in regis et sedis apostolice preiudicium et contemptum manifestum et contra inhibitionem regis predictam. Et unde decanus Lincolniensis qui sequitur pro domino regis queritur quod, cum eidem episcopo ex parte regis inhibitum esset in forma predicta, Robertus de Redeswell', Robertus de Thorpe, et Willelmus de Henovere clerici predicti episcopi nomine suo citarunt et citari fecerunt quosdam ministros de ecclesia predicta videlicet Rogerum capellanum, Thomam capellanum, Robertum diaconum et alios vicarios et ministros ecclesie predicte ad faciendum eidem episcopo obedientiam et cetera. Et episcopus per attornatum suum venit et dicit quod predicta ecclesia est infra episcopatum suum et in iurisdictione sua ordinaria et petit iudicium si debeat in curia domini regis de iurisdictione sua respondere. Et donatum est per

173

iudices quod respondeant. Qui quidem episcopus per attornatum suum petit quod decanus Lincolniensis, qui sequitur pro rege versus ipsum, ostendat ei si quid habeat pro se quod predicta ecclesia Omnium Sanctorum Derb' sit libera capella domini regis et quod quieta sit de omni iurisdictione ordinaria. Et decanus dicit quod predicta ecclesia exstitit soluta et quieta ab omni iurisdictione ordinaria a tempore quo non exstat memoria. Dicit etiam quod si aliqua prebenda in predicta ecclesia vacaret quod [sic] ipse idem decanus alium institueret et in eadem visitaret et correctiones caperet pro voluntate sua, idem [sic] quod predictus episcopus nullam habeat iurisdictionem ordinariam in eadem. Et quia dominus rex ex officio suo super premissis vult certiorari vicecomiti precepit quod venire faciat coram rege a die Pasche in unum mensem ubicunque et cetera xxiiii et cetera per quos et cetera ad recognoscendum in forma predicta et cetera.

Postea a die Sancti Michaelis in unum mensem anno xiiii incipiente xv venerunt iuratores qui dicunt super sacrum iuramentum quod iste episcopus et predecessores sui, similiter episcopus Alexander ut audiunt dicere, semper habuerunt iurisdictionem in ecclesia Omnium Sanctorum Derb' videlicet celebrando ordines in predicta ecclesia, capiendo sinodalia et cetera, et faciendo correctiones de capellanis, clericis et parochianis, set dicunt quod decanus Lincolniensis habet talem iurisdictionem quod cum aliqua prebenda vacari contigerit in predicta ecclesia Omnium Sanctorum idem decanus confert prebendas illas et instituit quemcunque voluerit sine aliqua presentatione facienda predicto episcopo.

INDEX OF MANUSCRIPTS

GENERAL INDEX

In most cases the unnamed abbots, priors and monks of monasteries and the unnamed deans and canons of secular colleges are included under the names of the particular houses and colleges and are not indexed separately.